The Stuff of Bits

The Stuff of Bits

An Essay on the Materialities of Information

Paul Dourish

The MIT Press
Cambridge, Massachusetts
London, England

This book was set in ITC Stone Serif Std by Toppan Best-set Premedia Limited.

Library of Congress Cataloging-in-Publication Data is available.

ISBN: 978-0-262-03620-7 (hardcover), 978-0-262-54652-2 (paperback)

In memory of Beatriz da Costa and Mark Poster,
with much regret that we never got to talk about the contents,
because then this would be a better book

Contents

Acknowledgments

When I read a book, I always read the acknowledgments first; the glimpses they provide of how projects emerged helps me place the work in context, and I appreciate the more personal voice that many authors use there. When I write a book, though, I write the acknowledgments last, partly because the cast of characters grows as the book is written, and partly because recalling and acknowledging my intellectual debts is a pleasure that I like to leave as a treat for myself when the process is (nearly) over.

My students and postdocs, past and present, form the center of my intellectual world. During the period of research and writing represented by this book, that group has included Morgan Ames, Ken Cameron, Marisa Cohn, Garnet Hertz, Leah Horgan, Lilly Irani, Silvia Lindtner, Katherine Lo, Lilly Nguyen, Katie Pine, Noopur Raval, Miya Sylvester, Janet Vertesi, and Chris Wolf. They were subject to various halting presentations and meandering accounts of early versions of these ideas, and their feedback was invaluable. More importantly, though, it is a genuine privilege and unparalleled joy to witness their progress and their successes as researchers and scholars. I continue daily to learn an immense amount from them, and the opportunity to do so makes my job the best in the world.

The work that culminates in this book—and particularly the writing process—has unfolded in many places. Primary among these is my home institution at the University of California, Irvine, with the remarkable collection of colleagues there whose thinking focuses on society, culture, and technology. These have included Tom Boellstorff, Geof Bowker, Simon Cole, Martha Feldman, David Theo Goldberg, Gillian Hayes, Mimi Ito, Peter Krapp, Liz Losh, George Marcus, Bill Maurer, Keith Murphy, Simon Penny, and Kavita Philip. Melissa Mazmanian deserves special mention; my first explorations of many of these topics arose in our collaborations, and her thoughtful influence is felt throughout this book (the good bits, at any rate).

The brief flowering of the Intel Science and Technology Center for Social Computing in the period 2012–2015 provided a rich and engaging context for aspects of this research. Among a list of people too long to mention, and in addition to many of those listed above, I owe much to Jeff Bardzell, Shaowen Bardzell, Ian Bogost, Carl DiSalvo, Tarleton Gillespie, Steve Jackson, Chris LeDantec, Helen Nissenbaum, Winnie Poster, Erica Robles-Anderson, Phoebe Sengers, Eric Stolterman, and Malte Zeiwitz, as well as, of course, partners from Intel, especially Ken Anderson, Genevieve Bell, Melissa Gregg, and Scott Mainwaring.

The text of the book largely came together during my sabbatical year in 2015–2016. Over this time, I was generously hosted by a number of institutions that offered not only peace and quiet to write but also stimulating intellectual settings in which to work and think. For conversation and provocation during my visit to the IT University of Copenhagen, I must thank Pernille Bjørn, Marisa Cohn, Rachel Douglas-Jones, Christopher Gad, Naja Holten Møller, Irina Shklovski, Brit Ross Winthereik, and Laura Watts; I am also grateful for support from the Velux Foundation. For my stay at the University of Melbourne, my home away from home, I am indebted to Kat Franks, Frank Vetere, and Justin Zobel; the Russell and Mab Grimwade Miegunyah Fund helped make this trip possible. During my happy months at Microsoft Research New England, I had the good fortune to be working alongside Andrea Alarcon, Nancy Baym, Sarah Brayne, Jennifer Chayes, Kevin Driscoll, Tarleton Gillespie, Mary Gray, Caroline Jack, Butler Lampson, and Lana Swartz; I'm also deeply grateful to others in the Cambridge area who made us welcome, including Judith Donath, Fox Harrell, and T. L. Taylor.

At workshops, conferences, symposia, and lectures around the world, and in the teeming circuits of social media, I am fortunate to have been able to discuss aspects of my emerging thinking with a stunning array of people for whose insight, kindness, friendship, mentorship, example, critique, inspiration, and provocation I am variously and overwhelmingly grateful. These include Yoko Akama, Morana Alač, Panos Antoniadis, Liam Bannon, Nic Bidwell, Jean-François Blanchette, Susanne Bødker, Sandra Braman, Paul Carlile, Kate Crawford, Jon Crowcroft, Pelle Ehn, Ylva Fernaeus, Matthew Fuller, Bill Gaver, Kim Halskov, Lone Koefoed Hansen, Kia Höök, Heather Horst, Katherine Isbister, David Karger, Rob Kitchin, Ann Light, Paul Luff, Adrian Mackenzie, Lev Manovich, Danny Miller, Wanda Orlikowski, Sarah Pink, Alison Powell, Daniela Rosner, Christine Satchell, Kjeld Schmidt, Jolynna Sinanan, Brian Cantwell Smith, Nicole Starosielski, Jonathan Sterne, Lucy Suchman, Fred Turner, Anna Vallgårda, and Mikael

Wiberg. Many have read parts of the text along the way and offered critiques and correctives that have improved it immensely. None bears responsibility for its remaining failings.

Molly Steenson has been a longtime fellow traveler in materialist hinterlands. She was also an early reader of the draft manuscript—a hardship, dear reader, not to be casually dismissed. I am uncertain whether I value her intellectual brilliance or her friendship more, but I'm glad that I don't have to choose. Janet Vertesi gamely read the entire manuscript in the final months of preparation, and her suggestions for how I might sharpen the argument were characteristically astute, incisive, and generous.

At MIT Press, I continue to benefit from the insight and support of Doug Sery, and the editorial and production support of Susan Buckley, Virginia Crossman, and Margarita Encomienda.

And, saving the best for last, the inspiring Susan Hwang makes my world go around. I am a lucky man indeed to go through life with you. Thank you!

1 Introduction: Information as Material

On November 16, 2015, the United States Air Force announced that it had recently completed the third and final test of a B61-12 nuclear gravity bomb. The B61-12 was designed as part of a program called the Life Extension Program, intended to update the US stockpile of nuclear weapons. The weapon tested in the Nevada desert, though, did not itself contain any enriched nuclear material. The test-ban treaties that the United States and most other nuclear powers have signed since the 1960s do not permit actual nuclear detonations. The cold-hearted Cold War calculus of deterrence, however, demands that weapons continue to be designed and improved, even if they can't be detonated in tests. Alternative regimes for experimentation, testing, and assessment need to be found.

The primary alternative for designing and assessing new nuclear weapon designs is digital simulation (Gusterson 1996, 2001). By turning the mathematical descriptions of nuclear fission and fusion, material deformation, the response of the environment to detonation events, and other relevant factors into executable computer code, one can produce, in the form of a computer model, an account of how a new or imagined weapon would perform.

Historically, technologies of simulation have been deeply tied to military needs. So-called Monte Carlo simulation techniques, which manage the complexities of real-world modeling by employing random numbers to explore the divergent paths of probabilities and assessing statistical likelihoods of different outcomes, were initially developed by John von Neumann and colleagues as part of the Manhattan Project (Aspray 1990). Monte Carlo methods were eagerly taken up by those who saw in them opportunities to explore scenarios as diverse as the movements of molecules in a gas or the likely political responses to military crises (Ghamari-Tabrizi 2005; Winsberg 2010).

An algorithm or a formal procedural framework like the Monte Carlo method is one of the key components for simulation technology, but only part of the solution. One also requires a powerful computer system to run one's simulations. Indeed, the effectiveness of the simulation, by which I mean the degree to which it can be put to use in particular contexts such as weapons design, depends crucially on the capacities of the computer system involved, and their match to the mathematical methods being implemented. Algorithms make results *possible*, but implementations make them *feasible*. Incorporating digital simulations into the process of weapons design, therefore, depends on having sufficiently powerful computers.

At Los Alamos during the Manhattan Project, those building the first weapons were constrained by the material processes of uranium enrichment. For contemporary designers, by contrast, material constraints on design are more likely to be processing capacities of their computers. The development of new computer architectures, from vectorization and array programming in the 1980s to advanced high-speed interconnections for large, distributed architectures today, frames the feasibility and possible extent of digital simulation. Indeed, one could argue that the limits on contemporary weapons design are those imposed by digital materials, not radioactive ones.

It is worth stopping for a moment to contemplate this a little more deeply. Where digital information was once being used to model and anticipate goings-on in the physical world, it is here used to displace the world that it purports to model. Where once nuclear and military strategists might have worried over a "missile gap," they might now look at the list of the world's most powerful supercomputers and worry instead about a simulation gap.[1] Nuclear weapon design has become, in a practical sense, an information science.

Information—most particularly, digital information and the processes by which it is generated, collected, managed, distributed, and used—has come to play such a pivotal role in all aspects of Western life that many theorists have dubbed our contemporary condition an "information society" (or similar terms, such as network society or knowledge society; Castells 1996; Webster 2006; Kline 2015). In many of these accounts, a key feature of information is its dematerialized nature. Indeed, the shift to an information society is often framed as a shift from material objects to

1. Computer scientist Jack Dongarra from the University of Tennessee leads a team that maintains and publishes twice a year a closely watched list of the five hundred fastest supercomputers.

digital equivalents on computer screens (as in online shopping, online movie rentals, digital libraries, electronic newspapers, and digital health records, for example). Technology pundits applaud this "substitution of bits for atoms" associated with digital technologies and suggest that the "future" will be fueled by some vague and ideal sense of digitality. In the words of MIT Media Lab founder and indefatigable tech booster Nicholas Negroponte:

World trade has traditionally consisted of exchanging atoms. ... This is changing rapidly. The methodical movement of recorded music as pieces of plastic, like the slow human handling of most information in the form of books, magazines, newspapers, and videocassettes, is about to become the instantaneous and inexpensive transfer of electronic data that move at the speed of light. ... This change from atoms to bits is irrevocable and unstoppable. (Negroponte 1995, 2)

Gabrielle Hecht (2002) calls this kind of discourse "rupture-talk"; it frames its topic in terms of major historical disjunctions and a radical breaking free from the past. Even in this information-rich environment, however, the physical world persistently makes itself felt. Networks are disrupted when undersea cables are broken, and information is lost when cloud servers fail. The microprocessor engineers whose work fuels the digital revolution find themselves locked in daily struggle with the limits of physical fabrication and the properties of semiconductor materials. More broadly, the information that undergirds the "information society" is encountered only ever in material form, whether that is marks on a page, electrons flowing through wires, or magnetized segments of a spinning disk.

Increasingly, social scientists have begun to recognize these material realities and have turned their attention to the intertwining of social phenomena with the material world. Coming from various disciplinary backgrounds, scholars argue that the social world manifests itself in the configuration and use of physical objects and that the properties of those physical objects and the materials from which they are made—properties like durability, density, bulk, and scarcity—condition the forms of social action that arise around them. Organizational scientists (e.g., Orlikowski and Scott 2008), anthropologists (e.g., Miller 2005), sociologists (e.g., MacKenzie 2009), scholars in science studies (e.g., Suchman 2007), communication scholars (e.g., Ashcraft et al. 2009), information scientists (e.g., Blanchette 2011), political theorists (e.g., Bennett 2010), and feminist scholars (e.g., Barad 2003) have begun to unpack the importance of the specific material configurations of our informed world. Research like this has been matched by an increasing interest in popular discourse in the material manifestations of digital technologies, including the geographies of internet infrastructures (e.g., Blum 2012) and the environmental consequences of information processing (Tomlinson 2010).

It's clear, then, that there are many different ways to interpret and approach the topic of the materialities of information (Dourish and Mazmanian 2013). To start with, one might choose to focus on the *material culture of digital goods*—examinations of the cultural currency of particular digital products such as iPhones, USB sticks, or the Linux operating system kernel. One might instead choose to take up the *transformative materiality of digital networks*, examining the role that information and information technologies play in the encounter with space (e.g., Kitchin and Dodge 2011; Graham and Marvin 2001). Alternatively, a third conception might focus on the *material conditions of information technology production*, proffering perhaps a Marxian account of such topics as the economic conditions favored by the speed, ubiquity, and manipulability of information rendered into digital forms (e.g., Harvey 2006), and the labor, both skilled and unskilled, to build technologies, encode information, maintain infrastructures and facilities, and deal with increasing amounts of toxic e-waste (e.g., Pellow and Park 2002; Irani 2015). A fourth approach is to explore *consequential materiality of information metaphors*, examining the growing significance of the metaphor of information as a keyword for speaking of cultural conditions and its place in public discourse (e.g., Hayles 1999; Day 2008; Kline 2015).

This book is concerned primarily with a fifth construal of the materialities of information—the *materialities of information representation*. This approach examines the material forms in which digital data are represented and how these forms influence interpretations and lines of action—from the formal syntax of XML to the organizational schemes of relational databases and the abstractions of 1 and 0 over a substrate of continual voltage— and their consequences for particular kinds of representational practice. The prevailing mythology of information, as laid out by Claude Shannon (Shannon and Weaver 1947), holds that it is an abstract entity, a property of configurations of matter, so that a signal in a wire, a flag on a pole, or an arrangement of tin cans might convey the same information, but the information remains independent of that matter. In this book, I argue that the material arrangements of information—how it is represented and how that shapes how it can be put to work—matters significantly for our experience of information and information systems.

As an illustrative example, consider the case Paul Edwards (2011) raised in his study of climate science, where he notes the problems faced by the

US National Weather Records Center in storing meteorological data on punch cards in the early 1960s. The center's concern was not that it had more data than it might be able to process, but that it might have more data than the building could physically support. One gigabyte of data on punch cards weighs more than thirty-five tons. The point is not simply that this is a lot, although it certainly is. Instead, note that the specific material instantiations of the data have implications for where it can be stored (and therefore for the kinds of institutions that can afford to house it), for how quickly it can be moved from place to place, for how easily elements can be accessed, and so on. In turn, this shapes our ideas about the kinds of questions that can be asked of data, the sorts of information we have available to us, and what we assume is worth collecting. Transformations in storage media play out as reconsiderations not simply of the availability of information, but also of the institutional auspices under which it can be collected and managed, its lifetime, the temporalities of access, its resistance to change, and even what we think of as being practical as a data set in the first place. JoAnne Yates (1993) makes similar arguments in her account of the emergence of scientific management and related phenomena around the novel technology of vertical (hanging) filing systems in the early twentieth century. The same set of documents, physically arranged in a new way, become available for drastically new forms of manipulation and use.

Materials and their properties play a pivotal role in the production of new objects and experiences. Philosopher and educator Donald Schön characterized design as a reflective conversation with materials (Schön 1984, 1990). This evocative phrase immediately calls to mind some quintessential examples of creative production. One can picture the potter shaping a vase with her hands as it spins on the wheel, molding the clay but also responding to its capacity to hold its form. One can picture the carver finding how best the grain and the shape of the wood can accommodate a desired artistic goal. On a teaching tour in Taiwan a few years ago, my hosts took me to see a prized exhibit in the National Palace Museum. The *Jadeite Cabbage* is a sculpture in jadeite of a piece of bok choy in which the color variation in the mineral has been perfectly matched to the variegation of colors in the cabbage, and the flaws and fissures in the stone have been incorporated into the veins and ribbing of the vegetable (and even to a grasshopper depicted as hiding in the leaves). One can picture the "reflective conversation with materials" through which the sculptor came to match artistic goals and the materials at hand.

What does it mean to adopt Schön's perspective in the realm of the digital? What are the materials with which the designers of information systems find themselves in a reflective conversation? Chip designers need to concern themselves with the layout of logical units on silicon, and hardware designers need to pay attention to the propagation of timing signals from one part of a computer to another: material constraints abound. While it's no surprise that people designing hardware deal with material constraints, I want to draw attention to how even software designers and developers have a sense of a "conversation with materials." Throughout this book, I argue that software and digital information—the ultimate "virtual" objects, the poster children for the triumph of bits over atoms—have a material dimension in the interactional processes of their construction and use. Programmers understand the ways in which digital structures can resist their will, every bit as much as clay, wood, or stone. They recognize that different programs and program designs fit more or less easily on different platforms, just as different sculptures or carvings are more or less easily accommodated or executed in different substrates. Materiality—the nature of the substrates and the properties that constrain and condition the designerly encounter—is at the core of each experience.

The topic of this book is the nature of the material encounter with the digital that Schön's phrase identifies. That said, asserting or demonstrating the materiality of the digital gets one only so far. My concern is with the specific materialities that digital objects exhibit. Accordingly, my topic here is not the *materiality* of information but the *materialities* of information. The materialities of information are those properties of representations and formats that constrain, enable, limit, and shape the ways in which those representations can be created, transmitted, stored, manipulated, and put to use—properties like their heft, size, fragility, and transparency. I maintain that understanding the role of digital information in social and cultural contexts requires that we start from the ground up and attempt to understand the specific ways in which the digital is already material.

Material Consequences of Representational Practices

Students of human–computer interaction or the cognitive science of notations are familiar with an example that illustrates the consequences of representational materialities—doing arithmetic with Roman numerals.

Basic arithmetic is, of course, about numbers; numbers are what we add, subtract, divide, and multiply. But our ways of performing arithmetic are often not so much about numbers as about numerals. That is, we don't simply perform arithmetic on abstract numbers; we manipulate the symbolic representations of those numbers. This becomes very clear when we compare the idea of doing arithmetic with different systems for representing the same numbers. So, say I need to multiply 2,631 by 734. In primary school, children learn a simple procedure for doing this, which works by stepping right to left through the digits of 734, taking each digit and multiplying it with each digit of 2,631, noting the places where they might have to "carry" a number across multiplications, and then adding the results. Moreover, the procedure also has a spatial component, a way of laying out the digits so that numbers will be counted to the right powers (1s, 10s, 100s, and so on). Easy.

But now consider being presented with the numbers as Roman numerals and being asked to multiply MMDCXXXI by DCCXXXIV. The numbers are the same, but the representation is quite different, and no rote procedure enables me to transform the problem posed in these terms into a series of operations on individual numerals. Unlike the Indo-Arabic numerals we are used to, the Roman system is not a positional notation; similarly, the appearance of a particular glyph (e.g., X) does not definitively convey a particular number, because other glyphs that appear before it or after it will change its meaning.

The representation of the numbers, then, is not merely abstract. As particular arrangements of marks on paper, numerical representations allow for specific kinds of manipulation that are meaningful without our system of mathematical practice. The material aspects of how we format numbers turn out to have critical properties for what we might hope to do with them.

Although the representational materialities of the digital constitute relatively new objects of study, a broader history of scholarly inquiry delves into the link between representations, notations, knowledge, and practice, originating particularly in studies of writing systems.

Walter Ong (1988), for example, examines the relationship between orality and literacy and argues that each represents not just different forms of expression but different worldviews. From the perspective of a literate culture, we might marvel at the acts of memory involved in remembering and reciting long poems or stories accurately; however, accuracy in the sense of word-for-word reproduction is not a consideration in oral societies, since there is no written record against which something can be compared. So, while the "same" words might be expressed vocally or in writing, the expectations of what these words mean and the role they are to play in communication and coordination are quite different.

In a series of books, influential Oxford sociolinguist Roy Harris (e.g., Harris 1986, 1996, 2000) has argued that the conventional mythology of writing—which is that it is a derivation from, crystallization of, and substitute for spoken language—is fundamentally flawed. In *Rethinking Writing* (2000), for example, he marshals a host of features of written language that have no analog in speech (from the capitalization of proper nouns to street signage) to argue for writing as a parallel but distinct system of practice from speech. Writing, in this view, does not simply preserve speech but does something altogether new.

If writing is not simply crystallized speech, then writing may influence speech, or our conceptions of it, as much as the other way around. Tim Ingold (2007a) takes up this line of reasoning, arguing that the experience of linguistic linearity is a consequence of written notations for language. The very notion of a stable and linear expression—that one thing comes before another and that processes have a beginning, a middle, and an end—is not inherent. Ingold suggests that our ingrained assumption that historical and natural processes are stable and linear emerges from the technologies of written language. When one word is placed before another in a congealed form (be it on a clay tablet or in paperback book), linearity appears fundamental. More broadly, our experience of these external representations for linguistic utterances shapes our idea of what language can be and, in particular, is critical to the sense that information is an object that can be separated from verbal performance. Mark Poster (1990) thus questions whether the move toward digitized language, with the possibility for hyperlink and cut-and-paste, fundamentally reshapes how we perceive ourselves and reality.

The strongest form of the argument for the influence of writing on speech and knowledge has become known as the *literacy thesis*. As first argued by scholars such as Eric Havelock (1963) and Jack Goody and Ian Watt (1963), and further developed in later writings (e.g., Havelock 1982, 1986; Goody 1986, 1987), the literacy thesis argues for a strong link between forms of thought and literacy, including the contentious claim that logical thought itself is a consequence of the development of writing systems (Halverson 1992). Notwithstanding critiques of the strong form of this hypothesis from John Halverson and others, we can find within the historical analysis presented in these writings some valuable foundation for the current project.

In *The Domestication of the Savage Mind*, Goody (1977), one of the first proponents of the literacy hypothesis, looks beyond the basic properties of the written word. He sets out the entwined history of Western knowledge practices and *representational forms*, arguing that different representational forms provide unique structures for encountering, organizing, and knowing the world. Lists, hierarchies, and tables provide structures and techniques for presenting and manipulating information, and thus, for understanding the world. As such, one can see how their development as representational strategies is harnessed to the development of the different modes of knowledge production associated with them—classification and ordering, generalization and grouping, and relationality and comparison. Besides the linearity of text, Goody argues that what can be set out on the page—with the representational capacities of different lexical devices—shapes what can be known. These lexical devices become information technologies with associated material properties. While lists suggest hierarchies, columns create paths for addition and subtraction; lines and arrows enable categories and groupings. Such devices provide written texts with logics of manipulability and preconceived relations.

Studies in the psychology of computer programming have similarly been concerned with the relationship between cognition and representation. Studies of students learning to write software suggest that the types of problems they encounter are coordinated with the lexical properties of the programming languages they are using. According to T. R. G. Green and M. Petre (1996), programming languages, as textual objects, have "syntactic design features that help slips to occur" (149). Green and Petre show that different programming languages—not just conceptually, but lexically, as words on paper or letters on the screen—have different properties that make them subject to different kinds of problems. So, programming in Python is subject to different kinds of difficulties than writing equivalent programs in languages such as Lisp, Prolog, or Java. Green and Petre argue that we need to analyze what they call the "cognitive dimensions" of programming languages as notations, including dimensions like consistency, progressive evaluation (how easy it is to test a partial solution), and viscosity (a measure of how easily change can be introduced).

Goody, then, points toward ways in which representational forms, their associated material properties, and knowledge practices are coupled. Green and Petre provide a bridge to the domain of digital information by focusing on the notational aspects of computer systems. Their analysis, however, focuses largely on the aspects of notations immediately visible to people in their interaction with computers, not on the "internal" representations of information systems.

Lev Manovich's (2001) analysis of new media provides a stronger connection to the broader world of digital representation. Manovich's goal is quite different from that of an anthropologist like Goody or cognitive scientists like Green and Petre. Manovich wants to contextualize the emerging interest in what was known at the time as *new media art* and place it in a broader cultural and historical context. He notes that the fundamental logic of much new media art—hypertext, games, interactive installations—is the associational nature of the database. Indeed he proposes that the database is the major cultural form of the twenty-first century, in much the same way as the novel was for the nineteenth and film for the twentieth. In particular, he draws attention to the increasing primacy of relationality over narrative sequence. While retaining the visual and temporal aspects of film, the modality of hypertext or of computer games eschews a linear modality for the modality of the database, in which objects are linked, but their assembly into a narrative experience is in the hands of the audience. What Manovich's argument provides for us here is a connection between digital practice and the broader arguments raised by people like Goody in the context of historical knowledge production; that is, Manovich begins to outline how the representational properties associated with digital media affect aspects of the interactional experience and, in turn, how we encounter the world through the computer. Matthew Kirschenbaum (2016) explores similar themes in his literary history of word processing, examining the relationship between forms and tools of literary production. Among his examples are forms of *overwriting*, as in William Gibson and Bruce Sterling's collaborative novel *The Difference Engine*, in which each author's text, as well as found materials lifted from Victorian novels, are each written over again and again by each author until the origin points become unreadable even to them; or, again, in the consequences of different styles of document revision on both the production of texts and the scholarly analysis.

The work of Green, Petre, Manovich, Kirschenbaum, and others suggests that we might be able to find, in information representations, a foundation for Schön's reflective conversation with digital materials, and for the way in which that conversation provides a platform for both technological evolution and social practice. Much of the rest of this chapter is devoted to elaborating a series of related examples to make this case in more detail.

Representational Materialities

In his marvelous book on the history and development of the MP3 standard for music encoding, Jonathan Sterne (2012) explores how the history of acoustics, the conditions of digital multimedia, and the political economy of content production and marketing come together in the definition of a technical standard—what Geert Lovink (2014) describes as "the question of how to make a profit from the insufficiency of the human ear or the distracted state of most listeners." Sterne (with his tongue firmly in his cheek) uses the term *format theory* to describe the approach of attending to digital formats and attempting to understand the conditions under which they come into use.

Although Sterne is not trying to suggest that format theory does or should exist, we might nonetheless pick up on his cue as a way to start thinking about representational materialities in digital systems. We can begin to uncover the materials with which digital design is in conversation by thinking through formats with an eye to their commonalities, their differences, the purposes to which they might be put, and the systems of practice that evolve around them. Sterne does this in the domain of the aural, examining digital encodings of sound in the MP3. For my purposes here, I focus more on the visual and the representation of images.

Representing Images

Contemporary digital systems must represent images of many different kinds for many different reasons. We will explore practices around photographic images, but let's begin our investigation with the much simpler formats that might represent icons or similar small visual objects.

The simplest form, diagrammed in figure 1.1, is what we might simply call a *bit map*. First, we imagine our image as a grid, where each square on the grid is either black or white. Then, we imagine counting off the squares of the grid, from top left to bottom right, and use 1 to represent black squares and 0 to represent white ones. Finally, our file representation consists first of one byte to indicate how many columns are in the grid, a second byte to indicate how many rows, and finally the sequence of 1 and 0 in a standard order, row by row and column by column. We now have a way of turning an image into a file that we could store on a disk or on a server; and one should be able to see how one might then take that file, read its contents, and reconstruct it as an image. (This format is extremely naïve but not radically dissimilar in principle from the format of NetPBM or Windows BMP files.)

Now, what we might say about this format? What are its properties and limitations, and what features of this format might push back at us from time to time?

The first thing that we might note about it is that we used a "byte"—an eight-bit number—to record the width and height of the image. This means that we can have no image that is larger than the largest number that can be represented in a single byte. One eight-bit byte has 256 distinct possible

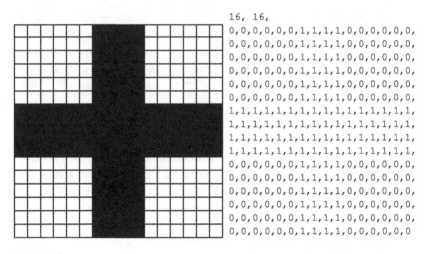

```
16, 16,
0,0,0,0,0,0,1,1,1,1,0,0,0,0,0,0,
0,0,0,0,0,0,1,1,1,1,0,0,0,0,0,0,
0,0,0,0,0,0,1,1,1,1,0,0,0,0,0,0,
0,0,0,0,0,0,1,1,1,1,0,0,0,0,0,0,
0,0,0,0,0,0,1,1,1,1,0,0,0,0,0,0,
0,0,0,0,0,0,1,1,1,1,0,0,0,0,0,0,
1,1,1,1,1,1,1,1,1,1,1,1,1,1,1,1,
1,1,1,1,1,1,1,1,1,1,1,1,1,1,1,1,
1,1,1,1,1,1,1,1,1,1,1,1,1,1,1,1,
1,1,1,1,1,1,1,1,1,1,1,1,1,1,1,1,
0,0,0,0,0,0,1,1,1,1,0,0,0,0,0,0,
0,0,0,0,0,0,1,1,1,1,0,0,0,0,0,0,
0,0,0,0,0,0,1,1,1,1,0,0,0,0,0,0,
0,0,0,0,0,0,1,1,1,1,0,0,0,0,0,0,
0,0,0,0,0,0,1,1,1,1,0,0,0,0,0,0,
0,0,0,0,0,0,1,1,1,1,0,0,0,0,0,0
```

Figure 1.1
Representing the image of a simple cross as a bit map

values, from 0 to 255, which means that the largest image we can represent using this format has 255 columns and 255 rows.

The second thing to note about the format is that we recorded only two values—0 and 1—for the contents of each grid. This means that we can represent images that are made up purely of two colors (most commonly, black and white), but not images with more color tones than that.

The third thing to note, building on this second, is that notions of "black" and "white" are encoded nowhere at all in the format. That is, although we have said "1 will mean black and 0 will mean white," 1 might just as well mean blue, yellow, red, or pink, and 0 might similarly be any color at all. There is no way, in this format, to talk about the difference between a red-and-white image and a green-and-blue image. The idea that the two numbers we have will be mapped onto two specific colors is actually not a property of our image format; it is instead a property of the program that will turn images into files or files into images. Similarly, that the pixels (grid elements) are square, rather than elongated, is not encoded in the image format anywhere but is crucial to how the final image will appear.

Finally, here, our fourth consideration—and perhaps the one that might occur most obviously to a programmer—is that this format is hugely wasteful of storage space. This waste means that our limited storage in a computer's memory or on a disk is not being used efficiently, and it means that the image file will take longer than it must to be transmitted across a network. The waste arises because most images have regularities that can be exploited to reduce the amount of data that we need to store, and more efficient encodings of information can also be exploited to make the images smaller.

Here are two ways that we could change our format to address this fourth problem. The first is to use a mechanism we might call *bit packing*; the second is known as *run-length encoding*.

The bit-packing technique works as follows. We stored a 1 or a 0 in each image data byte in our format. But a byte can store more values than simply 1 or 0; it can store anything up to 255. Technically, we need to use only one *bit* of data (one *binary digit*) to distinguish between 1 and 0, and there are eight bits in each byte. So instead of using a byte of image data to store the content of just one grid cell, we can instead use each byte of image data to store eight grid items, if we use all eight bits in the byte to do so.

The use of binary encodings to store numbers is probably familiar to most readers, but at the risk of boring some, here's how that will work. It's easiest to imagine if we work backward. Any number in the range 0–255 has an eight-bit-long binary representation. For instance, the number 28 is represented as 00011100; the number 104 is 01101000. Any combination of eight 1s and 0s makes up an eight-bit number. So, now imagine that when we go through our image, left to right and top to bottom, we don't examine those grid squares one at a time; we look at them eight at a time and take each eight-square row-segment as a series of 1s and 0s that make up an eight-bit number. Figure 1.2 shows how the same image from figure 1.1 might be interpreted as a series of eight-bit bytes.

In terms of our file format, that's much more efficient; it stores the same amount of information in (almost) just one-eighth of the space. That means we can store almost eight times as many images on a disk, or transmit almost eight times as many images across a network at the same time. (The "almost" is because we have done nothing to shrink the two bits of dimension data at the start of the image file.) There are, however, a couple of wrinkles we might need to pay attention to. The first is that, because we need to take data eight bits at a time, and because most computers can more easily operate on whole bytes, we need to make some design decisions about how to handle images in which each row isn't easily divided into eight-bit chunks. For instance, suppose there were twenty columns in our image grid rather than sixteen. The first chunk of eight bits becomes one data byte, and the second chunk of eight bits becomes a second data byte, but what about the last four? Do we grab the four remaining bits, put them into a single byte, but begin a new byte for the next row? Or do we take four bits from the end of one row, and four bits from the start of the next row,

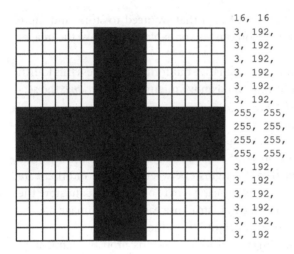

```
16, 16
3, 192,
3, 192,
3, 192,
3, 192,
3, 192,
3, 192,
255, 255,
255, 255,
255, 255,
255, 255,
3, 192,
3, 192,
3, 192,
3, 192,
3, 192,
3, 192
```

Figure 1.2
Bit packing the image

to make a group of eight? The first approach is easier, because it means we always start "fresh" for each row, but it wastes a few bits of storage per line; the second approach maintains the space-efficient storage but potentially complicates the process of encoding and decoding since each row isn't independent anymore.

Here's a second wrinkle. We had two bytes at the start that told us the dimensions of the image—how many rows and how many columns. But what are the units of those dimensions? In our initial format, it didn't matter, because grid squares and data items were the same—one data item for one grid square. But now our data items are clustered. Does that mean that the dimension is given in terms of grid squares (i.e., bits) or data items (i.e., bytes)? If we use data items, we can store larger images, but that creates another confusion, because the eight-to-one ratio applies to only columns, not rows. (In figure 1.2, I chose to leave it in terms of bits.)

So even though we have made only a very small and simple change to the format, all sorts of questions are thrown up—not difficult ones, by any means, but complications nonetheless. What is more, they are complications that show us how thoroughly data formats are enmeshed with the programs that process them, because we can make decisions about these questions, but the choices are not explicit in the data format itself. They are conventions about how the data are processed.

Let's examine a second optimization that we can perform to encode information more efficiently. For simplicity's sake, I will present this in terms of the original encoding.

If we look at how the data from figure 1.1 were originally encoded, we might notice something that is a consequence of the very regular format of the image: the image does not simply consist of a sequence of 1s and 0s at random. It consists of sequences of 1s and sequences of 0s. A 0 is often followed by another and another and another, and similarly for the 1s. Suppose we wanted to exploit this. We might say: in the original format, each data item described one grid square, but in our new format, let's have each data item describe a *sequence* of similar bits. Logically, we might have a format that said "seven 0s, then four 1s, then fourteen 0s," encoding not individual pixels but "runs" of pixels of the same color.

If we look at figure 1.3, we can see how this might work for the same image we have been working with, the image of the cross. Instead of simply marking 0 and 1, we use pairs of numbers as our data items, where the first number in each pair is a count, and the second is a value—so the pair (4, 1) means "four 1s" and the pair (2, 0) means "two 0s."[2]

Is this really an efficient format? Does it save space? The answer depends on the image being encoded. Obviously, we might occasionally be forced to

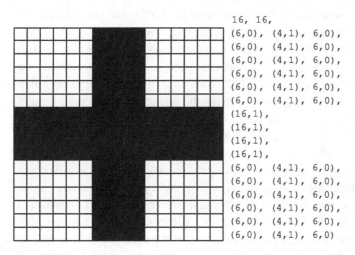

```
16, 16,
(6,0), (4,1), 6,0),
(6,0), (4,1), 6,0),
(6,0), (4,1), 6,0),
(6,0), (4,1), 6,0),
(6,0), (4,1), 6,0),
(6,0), (4,1), 6,0),
(16,1),
(16,1),
(16,1),
(16,1),
(6,0), (4,1), 6,0),
(6,0), (4,1), 6,0),
(6,0), (4,1), 6,0),
(6,0), (4,1), 6,0),
(6,0), (4,1), 6,0),
(6,0), (4,1), 6,0)
```

Figure 1.3
Run-length encoding the image

2. One can also instantly see some potential efficiency improvements—if we could encode run-lengths in two dimensions, for example, or allow a "run" to span rows. In this particular case, and for illustrative purposes, I chose not to include these optimizations, which just highlights further the significance of particular, apparently small, design decisions.

encode a single character as a pair of digits—say (1, 1)—which is less efficient than just saying 1. But if this happens only occasionally, and more often we get to say things like (4, 0)—encoding four grid squares in two numbers—or better yet (24, 1), which encodes twenty-four grid squares in just two numbers—then we will have saved so much space that some occasional redundancy won't matter. Some sorts of images suit this approach better than others. It's not good for encoding things that are like photographs, which have frequent changes of color, but it would be good for encoding flags, since they are made up of uniform blocks. (Or course, to encode flags or photographs, we would need a format that went beyond simply black and white.)

This so-called run-length encoding can produce very efficient storage for images—but there are other costs. For a start, as we just saw, it is an unpredictable format—its efficiency will vary from image to image. Sometimes, in fact, it will be *less* efficient than the more naïve format we began with—and there is no good way to tell in advance whether that will be true. Also, it means that each line of the image might take a different amount of storage—we can't easily jump around in the file.

But there is another issue, one that is crucial for any analysis of formats. When we use run-length encoding, some data bits essentially become more important or more significant than others. We can see this most easily by looking at what happens when an error is introduced into the data—perhaps because of a bad block on a disk, or a glitch on a network connection. In the naïve format—the format in which each item of data describes just one grid square—a single error in the file could affect no more than one grid square. If a 1 turned into a 0 by mistake, or a 0 turned into a 1, then we might barely be able to tell when the image was reconstructed. Even in the more efficient bit-packed format, an error to a single data item would affect no more than eight grid squares, and probably fewer. In a run-length encoded file, however, the results of transient errors are quite different. If a random glitch turns a 4 into a 64, then that might have much bigger consequences. If the pair so affected originally said (4, 1) and became (64, 1), then suddenly a few pixels would have turned into a much longer line—with all sorts of knock-on effects too, since the effects of run-length encoding may not be restricted to a single line. So now, some data units have potentially become more significant than others.

This highlights three tremendously important ideas—ones that, I hope, are important enough to justify the long, laborious, and labyrinthine explanations over the last few pages.

The first is that all digital data might be simply 1s and 0s, but those 1s and 0s are *not all equivalent or equally important.* Some have greater significance than others. Some affect the others, some play more central roles in the representation, and some are more critical. Choices about different representational strategies create patterns of difference and selective significance among the bits that make up a representation. Some single-bit errors will be glitches that might not be noticed or do significant harm; others may affect larger parts of the represented object. Different bits have different import.

The second concerns robustness. The whole point of digital transmission is that it can survive the kind of problems that affect analog representations. Since a 1 is always a 1, if the signal has degraded a little after being stored or transmitted, it can be restored easily because we know that it should be exactly a 1. By contrast, in the analog world, if a signal of 3.6V has been degraded over transmission and turned into a signal of 3.4V, we don't know what to restore it to. This is what makes digital representations robust; it is why I can copy a digital file again and again and again, confident that it will remain the same, but if I try to photocopy a document, and then copy the copy, and then copy *that* copy, it will eventually degrade and become unreadable. As we have started to see from this example, however, while digitality is meant to convey robustness against degradation, it's more accurate to say that digital forms are *robust against certain forms of degradation or damage but also susceptible to others.* What robustness digitality offers comes at a cost. Where errors do creep in—and they always might—their effects are of a different sort. The possibility of error at the point of storage or transmission might have been mitigated, but errors of interpretation can still creep in. We have gained some forms of robustness, but our representations are brittle in new ways: robustness is relational.

The third is the very idea that even such a simple domain has *quite so many alternative representations* (and we have hardly scratched the surface here). Each representation exhibits different material properties and different trade-offs that will affect processing, storage, transmission, error detection, malleability, and the range of characteristics that might matter in different applications or uses. Representational choices match, as best can be anticipated, material constraints to implementations and applications, although since those are themselves often in flux, well-intentioned choices at one moment can become major obstacles later.

Representing Images as Programs

At the risk of taking this discussion from the laborious to the tedious, let's consider for a moment a very different way of representing images, one that moves us a step closer to Schön's reflective conversation.

Whatever the details of the coding, the examples above all do the same thing: they represent an image as a series of dots on a grid. Here is a radically different way of representing the same image. Imagine a file made of textual characters that spell out the following:

```
set pen 0.25in
set color black
set dash solid
move 0, 1in
lineto 2in, 1in
stroke
move 1in, 0
lineto 1in, 2in
stroke
```

Figure 1.4
Representing an image as a program

How is this a representation of an image? Indirectly and algorithmically. Rather than encoding a picture, it contains instructions on how to draw it. Essentially, it constitutes a short computer program that draws the same image of the cross that I used as an example above.[3] Now, it's a computer program in a language that I just made up, although in its principles, it is not entirely dissimilar to Adobe's PostScript language, or its later derivative, Portable Document Format (PDF). PostScript is what is known as a *page description language*. Rather than capturing an image of what a printed page (or a viewed image) should look like, as our earlier formats did, PostScript instead describes the page by providing a program that, when executed by a printer or a screen viewer, will result in the correct image being formed.

The fact that this is not just a page description but also a computer program is important. PostScript and similar systems are full-featured programming languages, with all the facilities one might expect—variables, data structures, conditional operators for branching, looping operators,

3. An approximate translation into natural language would be: with a line 0.25 inches wide, a default color of black, and a nondashed style, and measuring from the top lefthand corner of the page, draw a line from coordinates (0, 1 inch) to coordinates (2 inches, 1 inch), and another from coordinate (1 inch, 0) to coordinate (1 inch, 2 inches).

mechanisms for defining procedures, and so on. Consequently, one might encounter a program (again, in my own invented version of the language) that said something like this:

```
for angle = 0 to 359 by 30 {
   move centerx, centery
   curveto centerx + 100*cos(angle), centery + 100*sin(angle),
30
   stroke
   curveto centerx, centery, 30
   stroke
}
```

Figure 1.5
An image defined by iteration

Here, rather than a simple series of instructions to execute, there is a loop—a sequence of instructions that will be executed multiple times—notated by the "for" expression.[4] Here, it indicates that two curved lines should be drawn at each of a series of rotations around a midpoint. The result of running this is to produce a simple flower-like pattern with twelve "petals" (figure 1.6). If the cross had become indistinct and diffuse in our

Figure 1.6
The image produced by the program from figure 1.5

4. "For" loops are a common feature of many programming languages.

first program, however, then the flower is even more indistinct and diffuse in this, since the petals aren't marked out individually in the program; rather, a loop repeatedly draws petals at different angles. Even one of the most salient features of the visual image—the number of petals to be drawn—is not directly notated in the program; instead, the fact that there are twelve petals is a consequence of stepping through a full 360 degrees 30 degrees at a time. The number 12 never appears.

One might want to represent images in this way for several reasons. Generally, the most important is that the images are resolution independent. The resolution of a display device is how densely packed its many separately addressable picture elements (pixels) are. A medium-sized 4K computer monitor displays around 120 pixels per inch; a contemporary smartphone might have a display with a density of 250–300 pixels per inch; a home printer might print between 300 and 600 pixels per inch; and commercial printing is generally 1,200 pixels per inch and up. Image formats that encode the raster scan of an image—like the formats we discussed to begin with—are generally encoded in terms of pixels, but obviously displays with different resolutions and pixel densities will have pixels of different size. Page description languages generally describe lines, shades, and characters, but not pixels; the imaging engine (the system that executes the "program" of the page description) can render the image at an appropriate pixel density for the screen, printer, or output device so that it makes best use of the technology available. Consequently, lines are always smooth (or as smooth as they can be) rather than potentially jagged, and text is always as crisp as the display device will allow.

A second reason to favor representations of this sort is that they can be much more concise. Being able to say "draw a line from here to there" is both faster and clearer than laboriously detailing every dot to be marked along the way. This allows the files to be smaller (usually) and, as a result, easier to store and faster to transmit.

So much for the benefits. The most obvious cost is that the process of decoding the image becomes much more involved. Instead of simply turning pixels on and off, we must now execute a computer program written in the specialized page description language, in all its generality. This can be computationally quite expensive, but more important, it's unpredictable. A simple raster format can be read and processed in a predictable amount of time; more time for larger images, less time for smaller images, but always predictable because the operations to be performed are the same for any image. In a page description language, however, the result emerges only from running a program, and the execution time of a program has nothing to do with its length. Indeed, a program might have a bug in it that causes an infinite loop, which means that it will never finish executing, and there is simply no way to know this in advance. (That no definite procedure can tell us in advance whether a given program will terminate—known as the *halting problem*—is one of the classic results of Alan Turing's [1936] famous mathematical analysis, the one that arguably gave rise to computer science in the first place.) Even if the program does terminate, the production of the image requires a computational capacity sufficient to execute a program rather than simply decode an image. Printers needed to become considerably more sophisticated when page description languages appeared on the scene, and the adoption of similar technologies for screen layout (in NeXT's Display PostScript, Sun's NeWS, or Apple's Quartz) only became possible when both CPUs (computers' processors) and GPUs (graphics coprocessors) had become sufficiently powerful.

A second cost is editability. Because the relationship between the image and the format in raster formats is quite straightforward, it's easy to build a program that will allow a user to edit the image—to add portions, remove them, or otherwise change them. Doing the same in a page description language, on the other hand, is difficult because the program does not "contain" the image in quite the same way. If we wanted to change the number of "petals" in the flower from figure 1.6, for instance, we couldn't simply go in to cut one out or paste in something new; the number and size of the petals suffuses many lines of the program in complicated ways. We can edit the program, for sure, with a text editor; but we can't directly edit the image with a tool like Photoshop. The contents of the file and the contents of the image do not live in a simple or direct correspondence.

What are we to take away from all this? First, we can see that there are many different ways of encoding "the same" result, each of which has different properties. Some encodings are direct; some are very indirect. Different encodings might produce the same visual result (a cross on the screen or a flower) but have disparate results for other aspects of the computer system (such as processing time, storage space, or transmission speed). In some cases, there is a direct correspondence between something on the screen and something in the representation; in other cases, there is not. Various parts of the representation may have different significance regarding the eventual output, and some bits may be have a bigger influence on the result than others, with significant consequences for errors and other unexpected situations (like disk corruption or a memory problem). Some encodings might be more amenable than others to transformations like compression; some might similarly be reversible in ways that others are not. These properties—reversibility, robustness, directness, correspondence, and so forth—are essentially properties of specific digital materials.

Programs as Representations

The flower example showed how certain systems, like Adobe's PostScript and PDF technologies, represent images as programs. Programs, in other words, are representations themselves—indeed, the fact that data and programs are essentially the same thing is the fundamental insight that John von Neumann contributed to computing in the 1940s and that is the basis of the so-called von Neumann architecture that computers have followed ever since. That programs are representations suggests that we can expand our thinking about digital materialities by thinking of what a programming language notates as a format itself.

Consider the simple program in figure 1.7. Written in the Python programming language, the program reads a file from the network and counts word frequencies.[5] Computer programs are often thought of as painfully detailed sets of instructions for carrying out a procedure, so simple and detailed that a computer can implement them. And so it is with this program—every addition, every movement from one step to another, every

```
import urllib2
from collections import defaultdict
from sys import argv

d = defaultdict(int)

data = urllib2.urlopen(argv[1]).read()
data = data.split()

for word in data:
   d[word] += 1

for word in d:
   print d[word], word;
```

Figure 1.7
A simple Python program

5. An approximate natural language translation: "Using procedures taken from some standard libraries, create a dictionary storage structure. Read data from a URL specified on the command line, and split it into individual words. Now go through each of those words one at a time, adding one to the count for that word stored in the dictionary. Once that has been finished, go through each entry in the dictionary, printing out the word and its count."

data structure access, and so on is specified. The sequence of operations—now do this, now do that—is reduced in the programming system to the absolutely simplest set of operations that the computer can perform. Without a program, as we know, the computer can do nothing at all; everything it does, then, must be given to it in the form of a program.

The program, then, dictates everything that the computer will do. But it does not *notate* everything that the computer will do. This seems a little odd at first. A programming language is a notation, after all, a way of writing; the program is a notation for a set of operations that the computer is to carry out, and the computer does only what the program says. And yet, while the computer does "only" what the program says, there is more to what the computer does than what the program directly describes. There are ways of carrying out the tasks specified in the program that are not part of the program's text; and the computational platform has properties that affect the program's execution but that are also not described in the program itself.

It's instructive to examine what is *not* notated in the program text. The type and characteristics of the network to which the computer is connected are not notated, although perhaps that is more than we would expect, even if they have an important influence on the operation of the program. But other, more detailed questions remain. The speed with which the computer proceeds from one instruction to the next is not notated, for example. Nor are the different speeds at which different instructions might be executed, depending on the particular features of the computer and processor on which the program is running. The size of the computer's memory conditions circumstances under which the program will eventually fail, but this is not notated; similarly, the size of the maximum representable number in the computer is not notated but can also cause the program to fail at some indefinite moment. The size of the program itself is not notated, nor the memory capacity needed to run it, nor the performance characteristics of its interpreter.

The materialities of digital systems lie not least, then, in this gap between what is denoted and what is expressed, or between the specification and the execution. A computer program may be a precise series of instructions, and yet the experience that results from the program's execution is radically underspecified by that program.

In this radical underspecification, and in the slippage between notation and enaction, we find the lie of virtuality. The denial of materiality that is at the center of virtuality rhetoric could be maintained only if the specification were complete: if a program really were an adequate account of what will happen in execution, if an MP3 file really were a complete explanation of how music will be produced, or if a digital 3D model really specified what you'll see through a display. Yet, none of these are, in fact, the case. The mechanics of devirtualization—of the production of actual effects based on digital specifications, be that the running of a program or the rendering of an image file—inherently exceed the reach of the specification itself.

Working with Images

One last critical introductory point needs to be made, which concerns the braiding of representational materialities and human practice. To keep for the moment to the example of digital images, we can look at a number of cases from research literature that show how the constraints and demands of digital images make themselves manifest in the practices of those who produce, analyze, compare, manipulate, and view them.

Janet Vertesi (2014a, 2015) discusses image processing and manipulation by planetary scientists working on the Mars Exploration Rover mission. Her ethnographic work highlights the embeddedness of forms of image representation within larger systems of capture, transmission, manipulation, and analysis. Different kinds of encodings allow for easier or more difficult forms of image transformation—extracting components, recoloring, removing artifacts, combining multiple images, and other techniques that form part of the analysts' arsenal as they attempt to glean as much scientific insight from each precious image as they can. Further, they must "read" the images not as proxies for human vision, but as statistical representations of reflected light being sensed by specific scientific instruments, the array of filters and cameras mounted on the rovers (which are themselves subject to accumulated dust and wear). Vertesi situates her analysis of how scientists engage in acts of drawing-as and seeing-as within a broader history of what Charles Goodwin (1994) has called "professional vision"—the exercise of professional expertise through the collective production of visual experience. Her analysis highlights how image practices are organized around image mechanisms, many of which are designed in relation to representations as objects.

Morana Alač (2011) highlights a different form of scientific image work in her study of fMRI (functional magnetic resonance imaging) researchers working with images of the human brain. Like Vertesi, her broader concern is the interfunctioning of digital image manipulation with configurations of bodies, as well as the interleaving of speech and gesture as researchers sit together at screens on which brain images are displayed and explored. The format of digital representations is not directly her topic. Nonetheless, in the careful interplay of speech and image manipulation on-screen, characteristics such as the responsiveness of digital images to different sorts of manipulation, the way in which two-dimensional images are combined to create a three-dimensional model, and the limits of resolution all play a significant part. The image is not merely a view onto or a proxy for an otherwise inaccessible brain; it is a material object arising out of and deeply embedded within skilled, embodied practices.

An example of a quite different sort is provided by Rebecca Grinter (2005), who studied the struggles of amateur photography clubs coming to terms with the arrival of digital photography. Clubs that ran competitions found themselves engaged in complicated processes of boundary work around acceptable and unacceptable practices in photographic production in the analog and digital domains. For example, members felt that to manipulate and retouch a digital image with a tool like Photoshop— perhaps to remove a drooping telephone cable from a shot, or to move elements around to improve composition—went against the spirit of photographic production that they had developed in the world of film photography. On the other hand, they were already committed to the idea that the darkroom is itself an important site of artistic creativity in the production of prints. Finding ways to delimit the different kinds of postproduction image manipulation that could be deemed acceptable, in the face of radically different kinds of material expression made possible by different approaches to taking and making photographs, tested the boundaries of their practice, as artists and as members of social collectives.

What is especially relevant to my argument here is that the representational forms associated with these visual practices are not directly substitutable in terms of the sorts of practice they enable. While a digital print may be nearly indistinguishable from a traditional film print, at least to the untrained eye, as records or outcomes of a history of practice, they are quite different sorts of objects. Their material natures carry different potentialities and different constraints. In all three of these cases of digital image manipulation and use, the materialities of representation are inescapably present.

It is precisely this complex and evolving relationship between the forms and possibilities of digital materials and the shape of human practices that create and respond to them that is hinted at by Schön and that will concern us throughout the chapters to come.

Examining Materialities

This, then, is the project of the book and its focus on the materialities of information. As defined above, the materialities of information are those properties of representations and formats that constrain, enable, limit, and shape the ways in which those representations can be created, transmitted, stored, manipulated, and put to use—properties like robustness, consistency, compressibility, malleability, and others that we encountered above. As this definition suggests (and as illustrated by the case of the amateur photographers), I take it as a premise that social and material are entwined, and that the materiality of the digital shapes the cultural experience we can have of it and the purposes to which we put it.

To many readers, the language of affordance might seem more natural or familiar than that of materialities. The concept of affordances has its origins in J. J. Gibson's (1979) studies of visual perception. Gibson argues against a disembodied account of perception couched in terms of the cognitive analysis of visual stimuli. He argues that visual perception is performed by animals and humans who are situated within and moving around in the world, and that this embodiment is fundamental to their visual experience. For Gibson, the key element of perception is not the visual feature nor the object in the world but the affordance, which he defines as a property of the world that affords actions to appropriately equipped individuals. A chair affords sitting to full-grown humans because of the alignment of its surfaces to our legs and lower bodies; but so too does a low wall or a small boulder. A door affords passage to us because of the alignment of its size and its aspect ratio to our own body shape and patterns of movement, but it does not afford passage to an elephant (most likely). The affordance is a relational property—it relates the environment, the perceiver, and action.

Gibson's pioneering work gave rise to an entire discipline of ecological psychology (Heft 2001), but the concept of affordance has had a broader impact. Cognitive scientist and human–computer interaction (HCI) pioneer Don Norman (1988) employed it in his massively influential book *The Psychology of Everyday Things* (later republished as *The Design of Everyday Things*), although he changed the concept somewhat in his adaptation (Norman 2008); William Gaver later adopted a version closer to Gibson's intent (Gaver 1991), and the concept has been widely influential in user interface design and analysis (cf. Karat et al. 2000; McGrenere and Ho 2000). The term has also been widely used in communication studies, although, as in HCI, it has often been used generically to refer to the ways in which objects and media offer opportunities, ways that lose critical aspects of Gibson's intent. This has lately led researchers in the area to suggest some rehabilitation and reconsideration of how the concept might offer value (e.g., McVeigh-Schultz and Baym 2015; Nagy and Neff 2015).

Although the concept has proved to be both illuminating and productive, I am loath to contribute to this history of adapting affordance to fit a slightly different content. I recognize that the language of materialities shares with that of affordance the intent to strike a middle ground between the logics of social constructionism and technological determinism, as McVeigh-Shultz and Baym (2015) point out. For my purposes, however, using the language of affordance might actually be counterproductive. It seems to me that the relationality of affordance is critical to its effectiveness, and I turn to materiality explicitly to discharge this relational component. Notwithstanding Brian Cantwell Smith's (1994) unavoidable observation that digitality is a thoroughly human achievement, I nonetheless want to turn our attention to those aspects of digital information that lie within its own structures. This is not a relational opportunity for action in the sense of Gibson's analysis. No more is it a property of perception, not least because the materialities of digital information often lie hidden multiple levels from view.

I want further to place this reflection on digital information explicitly into conversation with other ongoing investigations of materials and materiality, as I lay out in chapter 2. This is not to say that one could not adopt the frame of affordance to have something useful to say in this domain, particularly in those studies that turn more directly on user experience, and certainly as I have presented aspects of this work in different settings, some in the audiences have seen affordances lurking (affordances are units of perception, after all). Nonetheless, I have chosen to adopt a different frame, that of materialities, in order to structure the conversation differently.

We might ask overarching questions of such an enterprise. To start, what does the project involve? First, it involves thinking of digital media and digital technologies as, themselves, a collection of historically specific forms, and so as objects that are continually evolving. Second, it involves reformulating our notion of digital media as assemblages of hardware, software, data representations, diagrams, algebras, business needs, spatial practices, principles, computer languages, and related elements, linked by conventions of use and rules of thumb. Third, it requires formulating an analysis on multiple scales, multiple levels of abstraction, and multiple domains of practice simultaneously. Fourth, it demands that we understand the contemporary digital media comparatively as elements within a framework of possibilities that reflect competing needs, interests, and accounts of both the present and the future.

The second overarching question is, what might such a project deliver? This is a question to which I return repeatedly, but the most significant consideration might be how this contributes to an opening up of the different layers of analysis to which software systems and digital systems might be subjected. One might consider Kirschenbaum's (2008) examination of digital storage media, Mackenzie's (2012) examination of the mathematical philosophy underlying databases, and Montfort and Bogost's (2009) detailed tracing of the operation of a particular machine as each offering a way to slice through the complex whole of digital systems. My focus here complements these by examining algorithms and implementations particularly at the nexus of representation, encoding, and digital manifestation. The hope is that such a project can speak to the historically situated practices of information processing and provide a perspective from which some of the mutual influences of evolving technical practice and evolving material forms become visible.

I begin, in chapter 2, by more fully situating this project within the many related but distinct scholarly discussions about materials and materiality that have arisen in different disciplines. Many disciplines, including science studies, anthropology, and media studies, have exhibited some sort of "turn to materials" over the last ten to twenty years, although of course the specific considerations of a material turn in each depends crucially on the broader intellectual and conceptual context within which the turn was motivated. My goal here is certainly not to develop some Grand Unified Theory of materiality that will subsume and incorporate all others. Yet, by looking at how notions of materials and materiality have been fruitfully (or not so fruitfully) incorporated into different areas of scholarly inquiry, we might better be able to determine what related concepts have to offer studies of digital technology and its systems of practice.

Following that discussion, I introduce a series of cases that illustrate how a materialist perspective can be brought to bear on contemporary information technologies. The cases are organized roughly by scale or scope, and at each level of scale, a somewhat different set of concerns arises.

Chapter 3 explores the relationship between notions of materiality and virtuality. The notion of the virtual is, perhaps, the key animating force in contemporary discussions of digitality and its consequences; if the digital is associated with any kind of transformation, it is the transformation wrought by how virtual objects or practices displace those that are physical or spatially grounded—the triumph, as Nicholas Negroponte would have had us believe, of bits over atoms (1995). Investigations into the chemical pollution associated with technology manufacture (e.g., Pellow and Park 2002), the spatiality of transnational networks (e.g., Starosielski 2015), the environmental impact of cloud computing infrastructures (e.g., Hogan 2015), and the labor economics of online platforms (e.g., Chen 2014) make clear that no such separation between a world of bits and a world of atoms can be sustained. Nonetheless, the logic of "the virtual" persists on a smaller scale inside the world of a single computer. This chapter takes the case of emulation—the creation of a virtual computer inside another—to explore the material configurations that support the creation of the virtual. Of particular concern are those things, such as temporal patterns, that are left outside the conventional inscriptions of digital forms like data models, software architectures, and programming languages.

Moving out of the computer itself and into the social world within which it is embedded, chapter 4 centers on the organizational and professional practices that surround particular digital objects. The focus here is specifically on digital spreadsheets as a representational form and more broadly on the ways in the which the form structures how people come together to organize working activities. By analogy with Hubert Knoblauch's (2013) "PowerPoint events" (meetings organized around the presentation of digital slideshows), I look at how "spreadsheet events" are organized and the role played by the particular material constraints of the spreadsheet form. Thinking through the spreadsheet as an interplay between two representational elements, the grid and the formula, we begin to see particular material properties—such as granularity, convolution, dynamism, and persistence—as features of representational forms that provide the substrate for social engagement with and around them.

In chapter 5 I pursue similar themes, but in a different focus area—that of relational databases. If the spreadsheet is a representational form that has consequences for the organization of particular working practices, the representational form of the database has even broader significance, given how thoroughly databases are embedded in the institutional fabric of settings like banking, commerce, healthcare, policing, and civic regulation. Databases are collections, and frequently what they collect are records and archives of human activity; but databases also have particular shapes, and the shape of the database determines how effectively different kinds of records can be maintained. Objects, activities, or people who cannot easily be represented in a database become, to some extent, invisible to the institutional processes that databases represent. A simple example—conceptually simple, but politically complex—concerns how databases record gender, and the consequences for any case in which a simple, fixed, lifelong male/ female binary is insufficient (e.g., Haimson et al. 2016). More generally, though, we can examine not just databases but practices of "databasing" and the categories of "the databaseable." Tracing the history of the most widely adopted database form, the relational database, shows how the emergence of this form is entwined with, on the one hand, the hardware and software architectures of the systems on which those databases run and, on the other, the applications those databases themselves support. One reason to take up this particular example is that recent and ongoing shifts in the architecture of large-scale data-processing infrastructures have produced an interesting experimental moment in which alternatives to the relational form have come to a new prominence, again with implications that reach both downward into technological platforms and upward into applications and uses of large-scale data stores. Here, then, we see the emergence of a particular set of representational materialities as carrying significance not only in themselves, but also in their entanglements with technological and social aspects of infrastructure and institutions.

Broadening my scope still further, chapters 6 and 7 take as their case the contemporary internet. Again, a case has been made by others for under-standing the materiality of digital networking in general, in terms of both the physical architecture that grounds "the cloud" of contemporary digital services (e.g., Mosco 2014; Hu 2015) and the tangle of wires, cables, and connections that stitch the internet together (e.g., Blum 2012; Starosielski 2015). Taking up the focus on representational materialities from earlier chapters, my goal here is to understand not just the physical infrastructures of digital networking or client-server computing read broadly, but the spe-cific materialities of "the Internet"—one particular network among many.[6] Understanding the Internet as a specific network, one that has been designed around particular protocols and particular technological and ideo-logical commitments, is sometimes difficult given how universal it has become, so that talk of "the Internet" and of "digital networking" is some-times hard to distinguish. It is necessary, however, if we are to be able to historicize the Internet, to understand its material shifts and reconfigura-tions, and thus recover a sense of its current specificities and potential futures. By following the evolution of digital networking in general and

6. Following contemporary convention, I do not generally capitalize "the Internet" but use the lowercase form as generic. However, I do sometimes need to distinguish one particular worldwide network from other networks-of-networks and related technologies; in those cases, I occasionally use the capitalized form to make the meaning clear.

hence contextualizing the Internet in particular, and then by looking at particular protocols and their representational entailments, these chapters illustrate how a materialist account can provide a entry point to much broader concerns than simply infrastructures and their configurations, opening up questions of power, policy, and polity in the realm of the digital.

One aspect of these cases is that, given their different scales, they respond to and evoke materialist understandings that arise in different disciplinary sites. The discussion of spreadsheets, for instance, is perhaps most closely in dialog with research in organizational studies, while the discussions of Internet protocols speak most directly to scholarship in media studies and information policy; others might find different cases speaking more to their own background and interests. Questions relevant to science studies and software studies run through all of them. This strategy is (at least somewhat) intentional on my part, since all these disciplines are relevant. My hope is that each case might serve as an effective entry point for different groups, but that the set of them will draw various disciplines into dialog.

Having stepped through the cases of chapters 3–7 and seen how a materialist reading can be undertaken at different scales, it will be time, in chapter 8, to return to the conceptual project. What does materiality mean in the context of the digital; how are the various materialities that the book has examined related to each other; and how does this draw on, reframe, or extend discussions about materialities in other domains? What relationships are at work between a materialist account of the digital and current discussions in HCI about new interactive materials? How does a materialist account provide new purchase on discussions of the virtual in digital culture? We will see here that questions of the phenomena being studied, including issues like scale, character, and abstraction, cannot be easily teased apart from questions of method and discipline.

2 The Landscape of Materialities

An old joke in computer networking holds that the nice thing about standards is that there are so many to choose from. Something similar might be said about materiality, a term that seems to have come to mean many things to many people in different disciplines. Several distinct areas of scholarly inquiry have taken a "material turn," following, in many cases, semiotic turns, linguistic turns, and cultural turns. Taking a sequence of turns in quick succession might lead one through a maze, but it might also leave one dizzy and disoriented.

At the same time, one must be careful not to allow a term like *materiality* to simply expand without end. As a colleague of mine likes to remark, if everything becomes material, then nothing is material; the term ceases to do any useful work. So, when using any term as freighted as *materiality* (or worse, *materialities*), particularly when using it near words like *digital* and *virtual*, one has some explaining to do. What, if anything, justifies my use of the term here? Is this the same meaning of materiality that others have examined? If not, what can be learned from those other uses, and what justifies the elaboration of another conception of the term?

The goal of this chapter is to review and learn from material turns in a range of disciplines and scholarly areas that surround and touch on the central topic of information and digitality. "Learning from," in this context, means first understanding what has, in each area, spurred a conversation about materials and materiality, and then attempting to take from the conversation that has arisen some lessons for the materialities of information. In particular, I want to use prior thinking about the nature of materialist analysis to develop four themes that will shape the larger project of the book: (1) how investigations of materiality in multiple disciplines might provide us with the grounds for the sort of investigation of digital representations that we saw in the previous chapter; (2) how the material might operate as a site for analysis that is simultaneously technical and cultural;

(3) the need to collapse the boundaries between traditionally distinct areas of inquiry and intervention; and (4) the importance of historical thinking in understanding the coevolution of representational forms and social practice.

As Jonathan Sterne (2014) notes in a volume that itself bridges science studies, communication, and media studies, it seems to be impossible to set out on a project like this one without rehearsing, to some extent, the long history of debates around constructionism and technological determinism, even though there has been nothing particularly new to say on the topic for a couple of decades. I share his dismay at finding myself in that same fatiguing spot. What I want to try to do is maintain a focus on what materiality has meant to these different domains, and what drove them there to begin with, first to understand the material turn as a tactical move, and second to upset some of the presuppositions that haunt discussions of the digital.

Encountering Materials in Human–Computer Interaction

Human–Computer Interaction (HCI) is, as a discipline, primarily focused on the relationship between interactive technologies and human experience. Accordingly, it seems like a reasonable place to begin looking at the ways in which people might have examined how experience and practice arise in conversation with material forms. Indeed, beginning roughly in the 1990s, and associated, among other things, with growing interest in mobile devices and so-called ubiquitous computing, which envisioned an everyday world augmented with digital sensors and computational devices (Weiser 1991; Dourish and Bell 2011), researchers in HCI showed increasing interest in blending digital and material in interaction (e.g., Ishii and Ullmer 1997). For some, this meant envisioning new kinds of devices and experiences that left behind the traditional "desktop" as both a metaphor and a physical site; for others, it meant an increasing interest in interactive experiences distributed across multiple objects, devices, or interfaces rather than locked within the "personal" computer (and its "one person, one computer" approach).

The possibilities opened up by this new direction—and the concomitant interest in sensors and embedded computational technologies in interaction design—have sparked, in turn, a significant discussion about the role of materials and materiality in HCI and in interaction design. The boundaries of this discussion are expansive. Mikael Wiberg and Erica Robles (2010) present materials drawn from the annual creation of the Icehotel in northern Sweden, a temporary but large-scale habitation created afresh each year from snow and ice, advocating a hybrid digital-material aesthetic practice based on texture, substrates, and scales. Meantime, projects like Leah Buechley's LilyPad Arduino (Buechley et al. 2008) provide platforms for building user experiences around materials radically different from those of conventional computational devices.

Daniela Rosner, for example, has demonstrated the potential of alternative materials for interaction, working with materials such as yarn (Rosner and Ryokai 2008) and ceramics (Rosner et al. 2015). These projects build on the idea that the materials from which user experiences are created are intrinsic to our interpretation and experience of them. Not only are different tactile, tangible, and embodied skills activated in the encounter with these objects, but they also evoke different ideas, memories, and forms of reflection and engagement. Projects like these, then, have also been vehicles for exploring the relationship between craft practice and traditional narratives of engineering innovation and the opportunities for alternative form (e.g., Rosner and Ryokai 2009).

At the IT University of Copenhagen, Anna Vallgårda and her colleagues have been developing a comprehensive program of investigation into computational materials, in an attempt to combine interaction design and the creative practices of material form giving that are the foundation of many craft practices (e.g., Bergström et al. 2010; Vallgårda and Sokoler 2010). They work with materials like wood, color-changing concrete, shape wire, and textiles to enhance the expressive qualities of computational and interactive objects (e.g., Dumitrescu et al. 2011; Winther and Vallgårda 2016; Vallgårda 2008). Central to this investigation is the idea of understanding the properties of different kinds of materials and how they can be deployed in different sorts of combinations. That is, rather than just designing an experience and offering it up as a case, they are attempting to understand the different properties that different potential design materials embody, recognizing that what is being built are "computational composites" (Vallgårda and Redström 2007).

Inspiring as these projects are, they are built on an ontology that sees the digital as a priori and problematically distinct from the material and then proceeds to ask how these two quite different things might be brought into new alignments. Much of the relevant scholarship in HCI, I argue, eschews an interest in materiality for an interest in materials and their possibilities. Design-oriented research in HCI is concerned with how new materials and new ways of incorporating them into interaction might extend the range of ways in which people can encounter computation and digital media, potentially producing experiences that are richer, more effective, or more meaningful. This approach does not oppose digitality to materiality, given that it seeks new experiences that are both digital and material, but it does equate materiality with physicality, and suggests that it is only in the encounter with new materials and new kinds of physical externalities— with yarn and putty, bricks and sand—that a material form of digitality can be expressed. The digital, from this view, is inherently immaterial and must be *made* material through creative design. Similarly, the materiality that can be produced is material only ever in the manifestations of interactive experiences in the world—in the form of the things that can be touched, sensed, pushed, squeezed, and manipulated. Indeed, Wiberg (forthcoming) suggests that a turn toward materiality in HCI is in fact a turn *away* from a practice focused on representation.

What this leaves unexamined is how digital systems and their representations might already be material, and the consequences of the particular materialities at work. This concern reaches beyond the interface and, as we will see, might encompass network protocols, digital document formats, and software architecture. Materiality may not be about the interface, but it is clearly about interaction and the factors that shape it—central concerns for a discipline that musters under the banner of human–computer interaction, even if it lacks HCI's traditional and somewhat overweening preoccupation with the design of new objects (Dourish 2006). The sort of representational materiality that drove the examples of image formats in the previous chapter remains somewhat out of scope, even though, as we could see there, representational constraints and possibilities worked their way in to any number of ways in which digital image processing, as a human activity, can take place. HCI's broad interests in the relationship between technical arrangements and human experience make it central to the broad argument that materialities have a role to play in our understandings of the digital as a cultural form, but adopting materialities as a topic might also require us to push past the idea of design as destination.

Increasingly, though, HCI finds itself in dialog with other intellectual arenas where questions of materiality and human experience come to the fore. This dialog opens up the possibility for considering what alternative programs for HCI might be. Science and technology studies is one of these, offering several potential resources for investigating the materialities of information.

Practices, Networks, and Vital Materials

One could make a strong case that materiality, in the sense of a recognition and an examination of the material conditions of social practice, is one of the cornerstones of research in science and technology studies (STS). Although STS is concerned with the social processes that make up the development, movement, and mobilization of scientific knowledge, the discipline has from its beginnings been concerned with science as a practice of grappling with the material world in various ways. Indeed, it is just this focus on the materiality of practice that undercuts the misguided criticism of the relativism of social constructionist analyses in science studies—the point of STS studies is not that "scientific truth is simply whatever you can get everyone to agree to" but that the development of scientific facts requires the acquiescence both of social groups and of the physical world, each of which are obstreperous and difficult in their own ways.

One prominent line of work in this direction, particularly in the early days of STS as a discipline, comprises studies of laboratory practice. Studies of the daily working life of bench scientists (Latour and Woolgar 1986; Lynch 1997), or of the emergence of so-called big science in the latter part of the twentieth century (Traweek 1988; Galison and Hevly 1992), reveal the complicated assemblies of materials—from particle accelerators, telescopes, and chemical reagents on the one hand, to whiteboards, marks on paper, and coffee cups on the other—that undergird the actual conduct of scientific work. Studies of experiments and reproduction (e.g., Collins 1974, 1985) have shown how even concerns as fundamental to science's self-conception as the reproducibility of scientific results can be based on uncountable physical and material details going well beyond what scientific reports and publications can include. This is not a consequence of the specific complexity of contemporary science; Steven Shapin and Simon Schaffer's (1986) influential historical account of the work of Robert Boyle and his disputes with Thomas Hobbes makes clear not only that the difficulties of managing and manipulating material arrangements are as old as science itself, but that the modern conception of science as a mode of inquiry deliberately placed materials at the center. Boyle's development of what Shapin and Schaffer call "the experimental life," and the form of collective witnessing that was produced through the centrality of experimentation and empirical demonstration, made science a thoroughly material enterprise.

Beyond these empirical and historical accounts, some of STS's theoretical and conceptual developments have similarly sought to understand how materiality matters in the social world. One of the more prominent manifestations of this interest is actor-network theory, particularly its treatment of agency. Actor-network theory (ANT) seeks to understand social affairs in terms of the complex comings together of people, objects, artifacts, ideas, and environments that make them up. In doing so, it displaces simple accounts of agency—the ability to act—as a uniquely human attribute, noting that, in practice, human "acting" is frequently shaped, provoked, constrained, and demanded by a universe of others (and not just other people, either). ANT argues for a more distributed notion of agency, one in which we recognize the ways in which agency can be delegated to material objects that intervene in the world and play a role in shaping the emergence of human action. For ANT, the fact that material things might perform the sorts of actions that in other circumstances a human might (e.g., automatic door closers), or might configure our environment in such a way as to make certain actions comfortable or necessary but others difficult or impossible (e.g., speed bumps to regulate traffic), suggests a delegation of agency from the human to the nonhuman sphere that warrants a more even-handed analysis of agency than traditional human-centered approaches allow.

Contemporary STS research is strongly influenced by ANT as a broad perspective, if not as a formal theoretical framework, a position with which ANT's originators are generally quite comfortable. After all, ANT pioneer Bruno Latour famously commented that there were only four things wrong with actor-network theory: the word *actor*, the word *network*, the word *theory*, and the hyphen (Latour 1999). Even when ANT is not in the theoretical foreground, its influence is strongly felt in STS approaches that attempt to place human action within a broader frame of material contingency. To an extent, this reflects the significance of ANT as an early analytic framework in science studies, although, as Wendy Chun (2016) explores, it also speaks to the centrality of "networks" and network thinking to contemporary culture. Networks operate in terms of relatedness—that is, their primary analytic strategy is to draw connections—but at the same time, they commit to the separateness of those elements that they relate. If ANT seeks to open up the broader context or environment for technoscientific practice, in recent years a somewhat different concern with materiality in STS has arisen in relation to questions of environment, broadly construed. Many of the elements of this program have come up in conversation with scholars of posthumanism and nonhuman-centered anthropology. As is so often the case, Bruno Latour has played a central role in this, in various ways. One is through his call (Latour 2004b) for a reorientation of science studies from "matters of fact" (broadly, the examination of the social construction of scientific facts) to "matters of concern" (sites where science butts up against topics of contemporary political interest). A second is via his own demonstration of this reorientation in a book (Latour 2004a) that directly engages with questions of society's relationship to what, for want of a better term, we might call "the natural world." Both aspects of this program can be seen in work such as Laura Watts's studies of energy and materiality in Orkney (Watts 2014), Max Liboiron's studies of pollution and plastics (Liboiron 2013), and examinations of hydraulic fracking by Anna Willow and Sara Wylie (Willow and Wylie 2014).

Whereas the first examinations of materiality in anthropology typically grew out of an interest, as we have seen, to develop "an anthropology of consumption," in the words of Mary Douglas and Baron Isherwood (1979), more recent work has sought more generally to develop a form of anthropological theorizing that discharges anthropology's traditional humanism. Here, in efforts to understand how human cultures emerge in conversation with and alongside nonhuman actors of many sorts, and to think past the dualism of culture and nature (e.g., Kohn 2013; Tsing 2015), anthropologists find themselves engaged with others in the social sciences and humanities who have been similarly engaged in what Richard Grusin has called "the nonhuman turn" (e.g., Grusin 2015; Haraway 2007), and others, "posthumanism" (e.g., Hayles 1999). One element of this is what is sometimes known as the *new materialism*—a reexamination of the nature of the relations between human and nonhuman in philosophy that is often driven from physics and ecology (Barad 2007; Bennett 2010; Coole and Frost 2010; Dolphijn and van der Tuin 2012).

To take Jane Bennett's work on "vital materialism" as a key example, it's helpful first to review the different motivations at work. One is the contemporary context of climate change and mounting environmental pressures across the world, changes sufficiently significant to have caused some to claim that we have entered a new geological age, the Anthropocene, in which human activities have become the single most significant determining factors in planetary ecology (e.g., Angus 2016; Purdy 2015). A second, as suggested above, is made up by the various currents in contemporary intellectual thought that seek to displace the human-centeredness of philosophical investigation—one that postulates humans as the sole actors and relegates matter, material, and other species to purely passive roles—with some alternative formulation that both recognizes our own material being and simultaneously distributes agency, causation, and activity more evenly throughout the world. For Bennett, this is both an ontological project and

an ethical one. She argues that our own material foundations and our con-
joined embodiment alongside various elements of the world render traditional accounts of the separateness of the human and nonhuman no longer
viable. Detailing the action of "more-than-human assemblages"—in the
case of a large power failure, for example, these include "coal, sweat, electromagnetic fields, computer programs, electron streams, profit motives,
heat, lifestyles, nuclear fuel, plastic, fantasies of mastery, static, legislation,
water, economic theory, wire, and wood"—she calls for a new theory of
agency based on "vitality."

By 'vitality' I mean the capacity of things—edibles, commodities, storms, metals—
not only to impede or block the will and designs of humans, but also to act as quasi-
agents or forces with trajectories, propensities, or tendencies of their own. My aspi-
ration is to articulate a vibrant materiality that runs alongside and inside humans
to see how analyses of political events might change if we gave the force of things
more due. (2010, viii)

By contrast, Karen Barad's (2007) materialist philosophy is grounded in the
writing and thinking of Niels Bohr—physicist of quantum theory but also a
philosopher of its implications for our understandings of reality. Ideas from
quantum theory—or, at least, some of its rhetorical furniture, terms like
superposition and *uncertainty principle*—have often been adopted as a metaphorical structure to suggest that social theories of limits of knowledge or
identity arise somehow in a macroscopic analog to quantum effects, but
Barad is engaged in a quite different project. Rather than simply draw metaphorical relations between social theory and quantum mechanics, Barad
explores the implications that quantum mechanics hold for the nature of
the material world and human experience. She anchors much of her discussion in a distinction between the two theorists whose work gave rise to
what's called the Copenhagen interpretation of quantum theory, Niels
Bohr and Werner Heisenberg. While both subscribed to the importance of
the mathematical model that enshrines what came to be known as Heisenberg's uncertainty principle, which concerns the nature of our ability to
measure different aspects of a quantum system, they interpreted that principle quite differently. Heisenberg read it as an epistemological argument,
that is, as an argument about what we could know or measure. In the epistemological reading, the quantum system has a state, but we cannot know
for sure what it is. Barad argues that Bohr, by contrast, read the principle
ontologically; from this reading, the uncertainty does not arise from a difficulty of measuring the state of the system, but rather from the fact that
the system does not have any state without measurement. Measurement

produces the condition that it purports to measure. From this—and from her close reading of Bohr's extensive papers on the philosophical aspects of what was revealed through quantum theory[1]—Barad develops a theory of agential realism, one that challenges conventional notions of causation, identifies the constitutive roles of interaction (or *intra-action*) among elements of a system, and examines the "agential cuts" that produce distinctions between objects in material configurations.

There are several lessons we might want to draw from scholarship and research in this area. Two are worth noting quickly here. The first is that taking a materialist perspective does not imply that we must take materials or objects as given. There is no concession to technological determinism here, although we most certainly are concerned with the ways in which elements of the technical world may resist our will. Nonetheless, following Barad's injunction to think intra-actively, we must recognize how technical "objects," from databases to network congestion, are produced in and through our engagements with those things that we take as informational or treat as digital.

The second related implication is that we might approach a materialist study of information as an inquiry into the functioning of digital assemblages (to borrow a term from French philosopher Gilles Deleuze, whose writings inspired much work in the new materialism). Deleuze's notion of assemblage implies more than simply a coming together of different pieces. As new materialist philosopher Manuel DeLanda elucidates in his book *A New Philosophy of Society*, Deleuze's goal was not only to undercut traditional accounts of individualism in political philosophy but also to open up new ways to think about scale and about relationships of dependence and identity (DeLanda 2006). For our purposes here, the materialist perspective warrants both an inquiry into the heterogeneous collections of elements that make up technological objects and an examination of how those elements acquire or maintain individual identity as they are assembled, disassembled, and reassembled as sociotechnical settings develop, evolve, and reconfigure.

In comparison to HCI or to laboratory studies in STS, these perspectives enable us to take the questions of the relationships among materiality, objects, experience, and practice much deeper, particularly showing how materialities shape how objects emerge out of and participate in dynamic and ever-shifting regimes of practice. They provide a less sure foundation,

1. Barad uses the term *physics-philosophy* to highlight the idea that Bohr saw these "two" aspects of his work as one and the same.

however, for the sorts of empirical investigations that might allow us to step outside our own experience to see the dynamics and the detail of these practices in action. So, while holding onto the insights that we have drawn from these areas, we must look elsewhere to find how they can be incorporated into a fundamentally ethnographic approach.

Empirical Encounters

When seeking a warrant for ethnographic investigations of materiality in practice, one might naturally turn toward anthropology, where ethnography is a primary means of investigation. This doubly makes sense since cultural anthropology was one of the earliest areas in which a thoroughgoing interest in the material world developed, and where a subdiscipline known as *material culture* emerged during the 1980s. Many working in the area of material culture trace the emergence of the field to early work by Mary Douglas on the anthropology of consumption, particularly in her book with Baron Isherwood, *The World of Goods* (Douglas and Isherwood 1979), in which they examine such topics as how the movement of goods reflects patterns of kinship and social inclusion, how consumption signals status, and how solidarity is marked when British men in the pub all drink their beer at approximately the same rate.

The turn toward material questions seems unusual—or perhaps inevitable—given cultural anthropology's traditionally dominant concern with symbols and symbolism. To cultural anthropologists, culture comprises a "web of signification," in Geertz's (1973) terms; that is, it concerns itself with the systems of meaning that, as participants in different cultures, we ascribe to acts, artifacts, and experiences. Culture is a set of ways to make sense of the world, a prism through which we see it and experience it as meaningful. So, anthropologists such as Claude Levi-Strauss, working within the structuralist tradition, set about unpacking the structure of myths in order to reveal systems of meaning that people carried with them and used to make sense of everyday life. Symbols and symbology are paramount concerns within this broad tradition, and to the extent that artifacts appear as objects of attention (as they most certainly do), what matters about them is how they come to have meaning within the symbolic system.

Studies in material culture represent an attempt to give artifacts, objects, and materials a more central role in studies of culture—not as carriers of symbols but as things in themselves. Here, specific properties of objects—as durable, as heavy, as expensive, as portable, as fragile—begin to play a role themselves in the ways in which they participate in or are incorporated into cultural practices. Similarly, the patterns in the traffic or movement of objects—as elements in commercial exchange, as commodities found everywhere, as artisanal products, as objects traded in common, as neglected elements of social scenes, and so on—began to come into focus. The inversion here is significant. As Daniel Miller (2005, 1) notes, "Wisdom has [in most religions] been attributed to those who claim that materiality represents the merely apparent, behind which lies that which is real." Much the same has been true in many aspects of academic inquiry, including in traditional cultural anthropology, which Miller and others felt had traditionally brushed objects to one side in order to find the "real" standing behind them—the sort of move that, in a different context, Harold Garfinkel (1967) described as getting the walls out of the way so that we can see what's holding the roof up.

Take, for example, the case of denim jeans (Miller and Woodward 2007, 2010). Daniel Miller and Sophie Woodward open their "Manifesto for the Study of Denim" with the delightfully provocative statement, "This paper considers the challenge to anthropology represented by a topic such as global denim. Using the phrase 'blindingly obvious' it considers the problems posed by objects that have become ubiquitous" (Miller and Woodward 2007, 335). As we trace the movements of denim, both historically (from working garb to counterculture icon to daily wear) and geographically (from an American item of dress to a worldwide one, and in terms of the sites of production, consumption, and capital accumulation), it becomes clear that denim is an object through which much of contemporary life can be read. However, this is importantly not simply a case of the symbolism of a fashion item. It is also connected, for example, to questions of durability and fragility (durability in terms of the connections to the Western frontier lifestyle and to the very possibility of maintaining jeans years old but still serviceable, and fragility in terms the expected lifetimes of fabrics and fashions). It has to do with the specific dyes, their availability, and their patterns of fading. It has to do with the nature of durable, rollable, foldable fabric, as something that can move around the world more easily than, say, automobiles and can therefore play the global role that denim has come to play. It is, in other words, a thoroughly material story even as it is a semiotic one. One key idea, then, is to move past a simple duality of material and symbolic concerns to recognize the nature of their entanglements. This is an approach that, in step with Barad and Bennett (although arising from a quite different line of investigation), recognizes the intra-actional and the mutual constitution of materials and meanings. Further, as in our examples of image formats in chapter 1, it focuses on the ways in which specific properties of material objects are interwoven (pardon the pun) with the forms of practice in which they are embedded. Most usefully, in terms of the problems we were left with before, it sets this up as something that can be studied empirically.

One area of lively—and for my purposes here, highly relevant—debate within anthropological circles that grows out of this work is a concern with the relationship of materials and materiality. I have already alluded to Miller as a significant figure in contemporary material culture studies, and someone whose explorations in the area have manifested themselves in studies of, inter alia, Coca-Cola (Miller 1998), kitchen cabinets (Miller 1988), and rubber ducks (Miller 2008). However, Miller was also the editor of a 2005 edited collection entitled *Materiality*—a shift of attention from things to thingness. In making this shift, the anthropologists represented in that collection (and others) were to some extent enacting in their own discipline a broader intellectual turn toward the nature of materials and their neglected significance in different domains. Nonetheless, others— perhaps most notably Tim Ingold, whose own work on material objects and material practice forms a distinctive and influential corpus (Ingold 2000, 2011, 2013)—have expressed concern about the notion of materiality as a topic of inquiry, suggesting that it engages in exactly the move that material culture studies set out to counter, that is, a move away from objects in themselves and toward some more abstraction theorization. In labeling an article "Materials against Materiality," Ingold (2007b) seeks to shift the conversation away from the discussion of the materiality of objects and toward the properties of materials themselves.

Within the specific context of anthropological discussion, these are each important moves—from symbols to objects, to materiality, to materials, and onward. Within the context of the investigation that this book is undertaking, though, the discussion takes a different form. Ingold's defense of materials, and his critique of discussions of materiality, arises in the context of things—denim jeans, cars, stones, reeds, houses, gold, sand— that are indubitably material themselves. In the case of the digital, more groundwork needs to be laid. For all that I have already used and will continue to use the term *digital material* to describe the object of our attention, more work needs to be done to uncover the specific ways in which the digital is material—its material properties, or what I refer to as its materialities. So we might find ourselves allied with Ingold for materials against materiality but wanting to move beyond materials to materialities.

While these anthropological framings open up materiality to empirical inquiry, they tend to have had little to say about the digital in particular (although this is changing—see Horst and Miller [2012] and Pink et al. [2016]). By contrast, a substantive body of work has arisen within the domain of organizational sociology, where the label *sociomateriality* is often used to examine how the digital plays a role in organizational practice.

In many ways, the contemporary interest in materiality in organizational sociology emerges out of a pendulum swing between different explanatory accounts of organizational practice. Historical studies of the emergence of contemporary organizations have emphasized the entwining of organizational practice with the forms of technology and associated arrangements around which organizations are designed and that allow them to operate at scale. Technologies of communication, large-scale transportation, and information processing are foremost among these. JoAnne Yates, for example, has detailed the way in which key organizational communication genres, such as the memo, arose in symbiosis with contemporary forms of organizing (Yates 1993). Systematic models of management require, for example, information about past and current practice, which depends not only on particular forms of documentation and recordkeeping, but in turn on particular kinds of recordkeeping technologies, such as vertical files (which, in contrast with press books and horizontal document storage, allow for quick and easy "random access" to records).

In the early stages of information technology adoption in organizations, analysts and scholars less careful than Yates had a tendency to talk too casually of the effects technology would have. Technologically determinist analyses placed the locus of change firmly on the technology, which might be seen to speed up, transform, or reorganize organizational practice and organizational work. The idea that technology has social effects is a powerful one, but it all too easily led to taking technology very much for granted and ascribing to technology per se the causal force at work in organizational evolution and change. Critiquing this position, others argued for a social constructionist view that could counter the technological determinism of early accounts. Scholars working from this perspective highlighted how technical artifacts and the problems to which they are applied are products of social systems. Social constructionism examines the social settings within which technologies are developed, such as the contests for resources and legitimacy between different technological paradigms, social and organizational controversies about the limits and effects of technological intervention, or the systems of measurement and account-ability within which alternatives, including technological alternatives, are evaluated and assessed. From this perspective, technology must be seen itself as a social product, and the effects of social processes appear prior to, not simply as a result of, technological developments.

Sociomateriality emerges in organizational science not least as a way to recognize the significance of material arrangements while resisting an excessive technological determinism (Leonardi and Barley 2008, 2010). Yates's colleague Wanda Orlikowski has been perhaps the most prominent exponent of a sociomaterial analytic sensibility in organizational studies, particularly in a series of writings with her colleague Susan Scott (Orlikowski 2007; Orlikowski and Scott 2008, 2014; Scott and Orlikowski 2012). Observ-ing that organizational studies either downplayed the material conditions of organizational life or tended to treat them as exceptional circumstances, Orlikowski sought a new position:

Moving beyond these conceptual difficulties and conventional approaches requires a way of engaging with the everyday materiality of organizational life that does not ignore it, take it for granted, or treat it as a special case, and neither does it focus solely on technology effects or primarily on technology use. Such an alternative view asserts that materiality is integral to organizing, positing that the social and the material are constitutively entangled in everyday life. A position of constitutive entanglement does not privilege either humans or technology (in one-way interac-tions), nor does it link them through a form of mutual reciprocation (in two-way interactions). Instead, the social and the material are considered to be inextricably related—there is no social that is not also material, and no material that is not also social. (Orlikowski 2007, 1437)

One can see that Orlikowski was strongly influenced in this thinking by some of the other strands of work described here, including the work of Barad and other STS scholars such as Latour, Suchman, and Mol (e.g., Mol 2002; Suchman 2007).

Orlikowski is particularly known for research that examines the relation-ship between information technology and organizational life, and indeed, the need to account for information technology in organizations prompted Orlikowski's first writings on sociomateriality. Subsequently, she has used the sociomaterialist framework to examine the ways in which social and organizational practice arise around, and in "constitutive entanglement" with, information technologies, looking, for instance, at the role that Tri-pAdvisor and other online review sites have come to play in the hospitality industry (Orlikowski and Scott 2014). It is perhaps not surprising, then, that others who have heeded the call to focus attention on the interfunctioning of the social and material in organizational studies have been particularly drawn to questions of information systems and perhaps especially the topic of virtuality. For instance, Paul Leonardi's (2012) book *Car Crashes Without Cars* provides an ethnographic account of the work of automotive engineers as they participate in an industry-wide move toward computer-based simulation environments for crash testing. Studying how the engineers move back and forth between physical crash samples and simulation data, how they learn how to map features of different packages of simulation software onto the needs of their design processes, and how technical changes and organizational changes are intertwined, Leonardi unpicks the twin materialities at work—the materialities of physical automotive testing (which live in tension with the putative virtuality of computer-based simulation) and the materialities of technology as an aspect of organizational practice.

The focus on information technology and digital practice in organizational studies of sociomateriality makes sense, given the significance of digital technologies for organizational life in a world of Skype, smartphones, online teams, and distributed work. It is also, though, something of a risk. In light of the dominant rhetoric of virtuality and displacement in cultural discourse—that of Negroponte from the previous chapter, for example—it is all too easy to oppose the material and the virtual, to conceptualize online practice as a form of dematerialization. Bailey et al. (2012) caution against the "lure of the virtual," warning researchers against the dangers of treating "the virtual" as a domain apart, and as a homogeneous space. By the same token, there is the danger of conflating "the material" with "the tangible." In collections such as those by Carlile et al. (2013) and Leonardi et al. (2013), a wide range of positions on the nature of the material as a topic for organizational inquiry are on display.

Materiality functions, across these different disciplines, as a way to reassess the relationship between the social and the technical and to reconfigure both conceptual and empirical inquiry that erodes traditional separations between disciplinary spheres of attention and practice. In each context— that of cultural anthropology, say, or of organizational sociology—the specific concerns that are addressed are different and are couched in terms of evolving disciplinary concerns. *Materiality* as a term ends up referring to different things in different places, but the turn to the material represents a common tactical move, one that attempts to open up a space to examine how objects and object properties frame cultural practice.

When taking this same move specifically within the arena of digital media, we need finally to turn to media studies, broadly construed, to see how questions of materiality have been taken up there, and with what consequences for this book's project.

Materiality in Communication and Media Studies

Early work in cultural and media studies was concerned primarily with media effects. While Marshall McLuhan's iconic pronouncement that "the medium is the message" suggests an attentiveness toward the particularities of media forms and the kinds of communication they achieved, many found in this statement a deeply problematic technological determinism. As Raymond Williams dismissively comments in *Television*, "the medium is the message" seems to suggest that any given medium can transmit only one message, and the uses of television in capitalist and communist societies would seem to offer a telling counterexample (Williams 1974). Media scholars addressed themselves more to the struggle for meaning and expression, whether they saw "the culture industry" as an oppressive tool of indoctrination, like Theodor Adorno (1991) and his colleagues in the Frankfurt school, or whether, like Williams or Stuart Hall (1980), they saw mass media as a site of appropriation and meaning making on the part of people otherwise framed as consumers. These accounts of media and ideology, however, rarely directly addressed media as material.

During the 1980s, though, a number of writers addressed themselves to questions of the political economy of media, and the materialities of media begin to appear as questions of ownership, reach, control, and centralization came to be of interest (e.g., Webster and Robins 1986; Schiller 1986, 1989.) For theorists like Manuel Castells, the shift from analog to digital means a new salience for media ownership and control, a power that is exercised through access to and control over information (Castells 2009).

At the same time as these scholars have focused on media corporations, media ownership, and corporate conglomerates, many in media studies have turned their attention to the infrastructures of distribution for digital media. Rachel O'Dwyer and Linda Doyle (2012) draw on contemporary revisions of theories of rent and capital to examine the relationships between different actors in the fields of telecommunication provision, with a particular focus on the kinds of infrastructure ownership associated with the substrate network on which the contemporary internet is built. Nicole Starosielski (2015) uses the worldwide network of undersea fiber-optic cables to highlight the continued relevance of colonial settlement as well as the reach of different forms of sovereignty governing the location of cables and the movement of data (which are always, of course, located in one jurisdiction or another). Lisa Parks (2005) has similarly examined the materialist foundations of satellite television broadcasting, where, again, technological and geographical considerations may not match well with the geopolitical; satellite signal "footprints" are no respecters of national boundaries.

One of the most significant and influential strands of materialist thinking within media studies is associated with Friedrich Kittler. Kittler's writings—provocative, wide ranging, idiosyncratic, gnomic, frequently infuriating, but unquestionably groundbreaking—are as likely to draw their inspiration from Pink Floyd as Goethe and have had such an impact that "Kittler studies" is now sometimes figured as a subfield of media studies in its own right (e.g., Sale and Salisbury 2015), although more commonly the term "German media studies" is used to refer to the work of Kittler, Wolfgang Ernst, and others operating in that tradition (whether German or not).

Drawing on Michel Foucault, Kittler argues that the nature of communication and discourse (and indeed the history of knowing and being) is subject to periodic discontinuities and disruptions. His early work focuses on *discourse networks*—"the network of technologies and institutions that allow a given culture to select, store, and process relevant data" (Kittler 1990, 369). Although inspired by Foucault's writings, this work nonetheless embodies a significant critique of the limits of Foucault's thinking. Geoffrey Winthrop-Young argues that, from Kittler's perspective,

hunting down documents in libraries in Paris, Warsaw, or Uppsala, Foucault "simply forgot" that "[e]ven writing itself, before it ends up in libraries, is a communication medium" (Kittler 1999: 5). Throughout his career Foucault remained a thinker of archives and libraries rather than of technologies; for all his admirable inspections of discursive regimes and effects, he shied away from analyzing what happens when the processing of discourse networks is entrusted to modern storage and recording devices. (Winthrop-Young 2011, 58–59)

For Kittler, the media and media production technologies themselves are crucial. On the other hand, this shouldn't be taken as pure technological determinism. Kittler doesn't see technologies as utterly determining the discursive arrangements but as producing a rupture that requires a reconfiguration *within which they will be themselves incorporated*. Kittler's approach—at least in some of his writing—is to read various texts as "discourse on discourse channel conditions"—that is, as commentaries on the technological conditions of their own production. He applies this analysis to texts as disparate as Pink Floyd's "Brain Damage" (as an allegory on the evolution of recording technologies) and Bram Stoker's *Dracula* (with the frequent intrusion of gramophones and their structural relationship to the Freudian "talking cure").

As signaled by the "Kittler studies" banner, the impact of Kittler's thinking has been so singular and so wide ranging that it would be impossible to elucidate it in its entirety. Kittler's writings and those of others working in the same tradition, such as Wolfgang Ernst (2012, 2015), have most directly impinged on the topics of interest here through their influence on the program of work labeled *media archaeology*.

Media Archaeology
The starting point for media archaeology, as Erkki Huhtamo and Jussi Parikka (2011) express it, is the frustration that studies of "new" media (digital forms, video games, networked media, and so on) are often so thoroughly invested in the idea of their own novelty that they "often share a disregard for the past." The goal of media archaeology is to place contemporary media conditions in context by uncovering their embeddedness in experimental forms that came before.

As both a theoretical and an empirical project, this draws on the work of a number of significant figures. From Foucault, media archaeology draws an attentiveness to the history of systems of thought and the ways in which discursive regimes operate. From Kittler, it draws a concern with the technologies of media production as objects of academic investigation as both conditions and topics of discourse. From Walter Benjamin, it draws an understanding of the interweaving of culture, material form, and sensation explored through a historical reconstruction of aesthetic experience. Bringing these elements together, media archaeologists "have begun to construct alternate histories of suppressed, neglected, and forgotten media that do not point teleologically to the present media-cultural condition as their 'perfection.' Dead ends, losers, and inventions [that] have never made it into a media product have important stories to tell" (Huhtamo and Parikka 2011, 3).

And so they do. As befits their critique of technological Whiggishness, media archaeologists have spent much time uncovering the stories of such "dead ends" and producing careful and illuminating examinations of media such as the camera obscura (Zielinski 2006), the mercury delay line (Chun 2011a), and the pneumatic postal system (Steenson 2011). Indeed, media archaeology has largely become specifically an analysis of dead or dead-end media. What place might we find within it for a study more directly of contemporary media?

Let's step back a moment to identify different elements of the program that Huhtamo and Parikka set out in their quotation above. We can begin with the idea of media that "do not point teleologically to the present ... as their 'perfection.'" Here, two important ideas are encapsulated. The first is the acknowledgment that technological development proceeds by fits and starts, without any master plan or guidance, and with no natural progress toward imagined points of completion. The second is that we need to see current conditions similarly, not as complete or perfected but as happenstance waystations along the multiple developmental paths of the disparate elements of the media landscape.

We can then look toward the attention to be given to "inventions [that] have never made it into a media product." Here, again, several different ideas need to be identified. The first is the call to recognize unsuccessful, as well as successful, media products as embodiments of the hopes and expectations of designers, producers, and consumers of media of all sorts. The second is that both "dead" and "dead-end" media, every bit as much as successful products, have shaped our understandings and interpretations of what media are and might do.

Here, Jay Bolter and Richard Grusin's (1999) concept of "remediation" is tremendously useful, alerting us to the ways in which media shape each other—media from the past frame our understandings of new media that come along (e.g., electronic mail messages operate like letters, with addresses, sign-offs, and signatures), but new media also cause us to understand old media in new ways (e.g., in the pervasive presence of e-mail, a handwritten letter comes to have new significance). So, in terms of the media archaeology program, the analog computer may have been displaced and consigned largely to history, but it plays a key role in the process by which we come to think about what digital computers might be, for example.

I take both the historical argument and the quest for nonteleological readings seriously, but the overwhelming focus of much media archaeology writing on "dead-end" media, from automated semaphore systems to the zoetrope, seems to me somewhat misplaced. One can agree that obscure Victorian mechanisms for projecting moving images has something to tell us about cinema—but so do contemporary digital projection systems. One can heed the call to attend to the neglected and forgotten stories without distancing oneself entirely from current technologies, and one can investigate current technologies without engaging in Whiggish history.

Lest it seem as though I am accusing media archaeology of some sort of steampunk sentimentality, I should make it clear that there are reasonable methodological warrants for the focus on the dead ends. Some of these are made clear in Thomas Apperley and Jussi Parikka's (2016) exploration of the relationship between media archaeology and platform studies (which we will explore in more detail shortly). Much of the critique concerns the extent to which platform studies' examinations of recent or even contemporary digital platforms risk being, purely by dint of historical proximity, too much in thrall to the narratives of their commercial developers or their most eager enthusiasts. Noting media archaeology's antipathy toward Silicon Valley hype and self-promoting narratives of "creativity," Apperley and Parikka point out the dangers inherent in adopting a historical study of platforms that are essentially still in (cultural) formation. Nonetheless, they do not suggest that this cannot be done; rather, they criticize the proponents of platform studies for selecting topics and titles that are insufficiently obscure.

To the extent that media archaeology sets out to recontextualize contemporary technologies by recovering the alternate histories embodied by dead media, it is worth bearing in mind one critical consideration when thinking about digital systems—dead-end technologies are often not so much abandoned as buried within contemporary systems. When William Faulkner (1951) famously wrote "The past is never dead. It's not even past," it turns out that he could have been identifying the outlines of a media archaeology of digital technologies. The latest iPhone, sitting beside me on my desk as I write these words, is not just influenced by older technologies— it embeds them. Its operating system, for instance, includes an implementation of the FAT file system, originally developed as part of Microsoft's floppy-disk BASIC programming language implementation in 1977; though an evolutionary dead-end, it is still the way we read data from memory cards. The iPhone's network operations are typically wireless, but it includes, too, vestigial support for wired networks originally designed in the 1980s. As Faulkner recognized, the past remains present.

Software and Representation

Media studies largely place contemporary digital media within the broad historical and political frame of other large-scale public media infrastructures that came before them, to good effect; indeed, as will be more of a focus in chapters 6 and 7, key insights are lost when we overlook the politics of the digital. That said, though, a materialist perspective requires too that we find a framework that deals with the particularities of software and digital representations, in terms of their cultural effects but also in terms of the specific (historically given) ways in which we encounter them. When looking particularly at questions of software and digital representations, the body of work with which this volume is perhaps most closely aligned is the loose collection of related perspectives that go (sometimes) by the label of "software studies."

The first full-throated call for the humanistic and cultural study of software systems came from Lev Manovich in *The Language of New Media*:

New media calls for a new stage in media theory whose beginnings can be traced back to the revolutionary works of Robert Innis and Marshall McLuhan of the 1950s. To understand the logic of new media we need to turn to computer science. It is there that we may expect to find the new terms, categories and operations that characterize media that became programmable. *From media studies, we move to something that can be called software studies—from media theory to software theory.* (2001, 48, emphasis in original)

Manovich argues that procedural and data-driven systems need to be recognized as a new cultural form—not just a new medium, but a medium in which creative work of cultural significance is being done. He likens the arrival of digital media on the cultural scene to the earlier arrival of cinema and visual media alongside print. Just as, during the twentieth century, scholars came to recognize the cultural significance of visual media and develop a scholarly practice around the analysis, interpretation, and academic critique of visual media, broadly under the umbrella of "film studies," Manovich argues that a "software studies" is now (or rather, was then) needed.

Many heeded Manovich's call, yet his own work exemplified what software studies *could* be without setting out or defining what software studies *should* be. Consequently, as others took up Manovich's challenge and applied similar cultural analytic lenses to the various digital objects and phenomena of their own interest, some jostling over nomenclature followed, with various people proclaiming their work to be most accurately defined as software studies, new media studies, critical code studies, platform studies, infrastructure studies, media archaeology, or just plain old cultural studies. Certainly, one can draw useful and meaningful distinctions here between different programs, although if a cynical reader were to conclude that the corporate university context in which scholarly work is done these days places too great a store on the kinds of self-branding efforts that these labels represent, I would be unlikely to disagree. For the purposes of this book, I am going to generally gloss the effort to bring the techniques of textual analysis and critical inquiry to software objects as "software studies," except where other more specific terms are warranted.

A particularly rich vein of research in this area has been conducted by scholars working from a sociological and cultural studies perspective in the United Kingdom, including Matthew Fuller, David Berry, and Adrian Mackenzie. Fuller's edited lexicon of software studies is an early expression of the range of interests that fall under the "software studies" banner and brings together many key thinkers in the area (Fuller 2008). In his own writings, he places digital systems in broader cultural context by, for example, examining the ways in which artists, activists, and cultural entrepreneurs have navigated their way through complex ecologies of different media, online and off (Fuller 2005). Berry's (2011) *The Philosophy of Software* is perhaps most particularly connected to a program within software studies that Mark C. Marino (2006, 2014) has dubbed "critical code studies," taking up specific artifacts of program code and inquiring into code and coding as textual practices embedded in cultural contexts. Adrian Mackenzie, both a prolific contributor and a generative thinker in these areas, has contributed a remarkable range of studies that encompass investigations of programmers, programming languages, code, algorithms, and the technological imagination while maintaining the critical distinctiveness of each (e.g., Mackenzie 2003, 2005a, 2005b, 2006a, 2006b; Mackenzie and Vurdubakis 2011). Mackenzie's ethnographic approach provides a detailed view of not just software but software practice.

As an alternative demonstration of the potential of the critical code studies approach, Nick Montfort and colleagues (2012) take a single line of code written in BASIC for the Commodore 64 microcomputer and related devices as a launching-off point for a wide-ranging exploration of algorithmic art, graphical representations, digital representation, sequentiality, and randomness, among other topics. The program itself generates an infinite maze-like pattern, and even within a single line (which also serves as the title for the book), the authors (writing with a collective voice) find resources for examinations of mazes and their history, character encodings both visual and digital, looping and iteration, randomness and predictability, textual production, textural production, and numerology. The goal, in the spirit of critical theory generally, is to unpick and lay out the historical, cultural, and discursive backdrop that makes the program "make sense" in context, and which is indexed and cited by the program's own artifactual status—what the authors refer to as the "fundamental relationship between the formal working of code and the cultural implications and reception of that code" (6).

In parallel to these code-focused studies, Nick Montfort and Ian Bogost (2009) have called for a corpus of what they term "platform studies"—detailed examinations of the specific materialities of particular digital platforms, with a concomitant explanation of how platforms can realize particular digital experiences. Their volume, the first in a formal series on platform studies published by MIT Press, provides a compelling example of the mutual entwining of platform and interactive experience in their analysis of the Atari 2600 Video Computer System (VCS). The VCS was a home game console that played a significant role in the development and spread of video games as a medium. The technical constraints of the hardware platform, including video display timing and memory considerations, significantly shaped the sorts of games that could be played on it, while in turn, the success of the console gave it a particularly significant role in shaping the emerging genre of games and game-based interaction techniques in that period. Montfort and Bogost provide an extremely detailed account of the VCS hardware, its capacities and its constraints (arguably a more detailed guide to the operation of the Atari VCS than Atari ever provided its developers), illustrating how visual, auditory, and interactional features of VCS games arise in response to particular platform considerations. In doing so, they argue for an approach to software studies that starts from, and is grounded in, the specific technical nature of different technology platforms. The book series has continued with similar examinations of platforms like the Commodore Amiga (Maher 2012) and the BBC Micro (Gazzard 2016).

As noted by Apperley and Parikka in their critique of the platform studies program (2016), platform studies was articulated (to the extent that it was ever articulated at all) in relation to other contributions in critical humanities, particularly the writings of Alexander Galloway (2004) and Matthew Kirschenbaum (2008). Galloway, whose thinking is discussed in more detail in later chapters, has focused especially on networking and digital communications, in work that goes beyond simply linking the technical with the economic, drawing connections with the political, cultural, and ideological as well. He takes the notion of *protocol* as it is deployed in networking standards (to maintain control in decentralized systems) as a launching-off point for a broader examination of the cultural contexts within which network design operates and to which it speaks back. Galloway writes from the perspective of media studies and communication; Kirschenbaum, by contrast, is a professor of English whose particular interest is in technologies of inscription and what it means to read and write through technological artifacts. He attempts to reinvest digital media with a sense of their material foundations through a *forensic* examination of the media objects themselves, such as the patterns of both digital and analog information encoded on disks. He suggests that the disk has been curiously absent from analyses of digital media, given its critical enabling role, and his turn to the disk as an object of examination undermines conventional accounts of the digital as inherently ephemeral and fleeting in comparison with the traditional inscriptions of literary analysis. The work of another influential scholar in this space, Wendy Chun, stands somewhere between Galloway and Kirschenbaum (e.g., Chun 2011b). Like Galloway, her work dwells in the space between technological arrangements and cultural tropes; like Kirschenbaum, her disciplinary affiliation is with English and her concern is to recover the practices of reading and writing with, through, and around technological objects.

The critique that Apperley and Parikka offer turns largely on the implicit (they assert) heuristic device by which platform studies attempts to distinguish itself as a new domain of inquiry, leaving behind methods and concepts of value in prior academic discourse—what they term an "epistemic threshold." As one would perhaps expect of scholars in media archaeology, they find that an archaeological perspective may have more to offer, particularly by making clear what sorts of bracketings of technological and cultural evolution are at play. Notwithstanding their conceptual critiques, it may be too early to determine quite what "platform studies," as a domain within software studies, holds—as they note, proponents have "primarily performed platform studies rather than explicate its methods" (2016, 2).

The torrent of definitional work in this area—around software studies, platform studies, media archaeology, critical code studies, and more—certainly signals some disarray but signals too an area of considerable intellectual interest and multifold disciplinary implications. From English, game studies, art and cultural criticism, media studies, and critical humanities come a host of scholars whose work centers on different aspects of the digital, working through a series of topics that are themselves in flux. To some, this is a cacophonous confusion; personally, I rather enjoy the productive ambiguity.

A Context for Inquiry

This exploration was not intended to be exhaustive, and it certainly has not been. Neither was it my intent that it be exhausting, although I may have missed the mark on that one. Apologies. The goals instead have been twofold—to find, within prior and ongoing programs of work around materiality and digitality, a set of conceptual and methodological resources that might be of value in the chapters to come, and to identify those scholarly conversations to which this work might contribute.

While the topics and scope of materialist analysis differ across disciplinary areas, what is perhaps more common is the tactical move that materialist analysis represents. It opens up a new space for examining social and cultural life in a world of technical objects, a space in which we can (indeed, must) recognize the intractable configurations of those objects and their consequences without placing those objects outside social processes of design, interpretation, distribution, and appropriation. It is a space, too, where we can do more than simply assert the brute materiality of things and start to examine the particular materialities that come to matter in different settings. This tactic has not only conceptual significance but also disciplinary significance, in that it demands we dissolve the traditional boundaries that separate domains of analysis and intervention—technical, political, social, cultural, spatial, artistic, historical, academic, activist—to find new configurations that reflect the complexity and dimensionality of actual experience, recognizing that all these different considerations are simultaneously relevant at each and every point. Talking of a "materialist analysis" sounds as though one seeks to place the political, the cultural, and the historical to one side, but that would be quite wrong; rather, a materialist analysis seeks to understand the specific sites at which the political, the cultural, and the historical (inter alia) are brought into particular and temporary alignment.

Of the various bodies of work surveyed over the last several pages, that on software studies sets the primary context for my own. Of course, given that software studies scarcely comes together as a homogenous or definitive enterprise, that may not be saying much. From software studies, however, we can take a warrant for investigations that are simultaneously technical, social, and cultural, and that seek to find, with the particular configurations of code and digital objects, manifestations of and provocations for the cultural settings in which they are developed and deployed. My concern is with technologies as both representational artifacts and practical tools; for that reason, my interests lie less in the more metaphorical examinations of the textual practice of code. I am content to leave to others the examination of poetry written in the Perl programming language. To the extent that the expressiveness of code is of importance here, it is in how that expressiveness comes to stand between human understanding on one side and machine processing on the other, and how the temporalities, spatialities, and specificities of its expressiveness play a role in how settings of human affairs are organized in parallel with digital ones.

Certainly, the work to follow is inspired by and influenced by aspects of the media archaeology program, even if I generally do not apply that label to it. From media archaeology, I take a historical orientation that examines the multifold paths that technical devices have followed over time, and the reading of contemporary settings in terms of layers of historical evolution and accretion. So too will nonteleological perspectives be important, and a recognition—in line with the so-called strong program in science studies— that accounts of technological success and failure need to be symmetric. That said, the technologies examined in the chapters that follow are very much active in our current digital landscape, even if, as I suggested earlier in discussing the FAT file system, they cannot be read as homogeneously "new." As one might expect from readings in the new materialism, we can take neither the identity conditions for digital systems nor their mani- festations as particular collections of objects for granted—within historical patterns of technological development, deployment, and reevaluation, we continually let go of and then re-create boundaries, identities, and entities in our practical encounters with Bennett's "more-than-human assemblies."

Such readings are never neutral, of course; to the extent that the entities we "find" within databases or identify in big data are human, social, and cultural objects, the politics of digital materiality are key. Representational practices in the kinds of systems that undergird human communication, civic accountability, and the operations of states could scarcely be less consequential. Where Latour recommends an orientation toward and an engagement with "matters of concern," he speaks to both the possibility and the duty that technoscientific studies deal with matters of public import. So to the extent that digital materialities are bound up with profes- sional practices and activist interventions at sites of what Carl DiSalvo (2012) has termed "adversarial design," or where the rhetorics of virtuality and frictionless connection are at odds with the practical experience of, say, the "smart city" (Greenfield 2014), then reading these digital objects as simultaneously technical, cultural, and political brings Latourian matters of concern into focus.

Again, this comes about not simply through the identification of digital things as material objects, but through an examination of their specific materialities. As Pierre Lemonnier (2012) writes:

"Materiality," as we have shown, explains nothing unless one can show which prop- erty, elements, and mechanical aspect of the artefacts and of their making or physi- cal manipulation can be associated with some aspect of the local social practices and imaginary world, and why. (128)

The material properties that shape our engagements and uptake of digital objects, that contribute to their fleeting ephemerality, their delicate fragility, or their obdurate presence must be central to the examination. These are properties of code, to be sure, but also of data, of systems, of protocols, of configurations, of standards, and of structures. Most importantly, they are properties not of abstract things but of instances and implementations. Even when abstractions come into view, they will generally do so as material things themselves, with their own host of material properties.

I take it too that this focus on specific material properties warrants an approach that is grounded in detailed, empirical examination of particular cases, whether those be cases of social practice or of technical objects (and most commonly, of course, both). Indeed, the focus is not so much on the virtual but on how the virtual comes about (or fails to) and how it can be sustained—which is the particular topic of the next chapter and the first of the major cases.

3 Finding the Material in the Virtual: The Case of Emulation

In 2003, Pittsburgh's Andy Warhol Museum revealed a series of artworks by Warhol that had been lost for many years (Heddaya 2014). In collaboration with artist Cory Arcangel and computer scientists from Carnegie Mellon University, the museum had recovered a number of digital images that Warhol had created on an early Commodore Amiga personal computer. The Amiga, something of a cult device among aficionados of 1980s microcomputers, was introduced in 1985 and was marketed largely on its advanced graphics and media capabilities (Maher 2012). To draw attention to these functions, publicists overseeing the product launch developed relationships with several prominent artists, including Warhol, to use the Amiga to produce original works of art. The images recovered in 2003 were among these. Archived on floppy disks and held in the museum's collection, the images had been unnoticed and unseen for many years.

The process of recovering the images from the floppy disks was a complicated one, though. The Amiga line of computers was discontinued in 1995, and functional devices are rare. Worse yet, Warhol had used one of the earliest computers, running software that was never ported to another platform. Computer systems decay over time, and the evolution of a product line tends to make more recent systems incompatible with older software. So, there was no handy Amiga that the museum could simply boot up to load and display the images that Warhol had produced. In fact, as it turns out, even though they had been produced on an Amiga and were in principle accessible only through that platform, no Amiga computers were involved in the recovery of the files. Instead, the images were retrieved using a version of the original software running on an Amiga emulator—a software program running on a contemporary personal computer that reproduces the behavior of the Amiga so faithfully that original Amiga software can be executed without modification. In 2003, the only Amiga that could load Warhol's art was a virtual one.

The use of an emulator speaks to an interesting conundrum. On one hand, digitization and digital information are often associated with preservation and archival practices; think, for example, of efforts to digitize ancient manuscripts to make them available even as the material on which they are written crumbles, or, on a more mundane level, of the services that promise to "preserve" your family members by digitizing old photographs, film, and videotape. Yet the digital devices on which these digital materials are dependent are not themselves eternal or even particularly long-lived. Computer systems from even just a few years ago are already obsolete and aging. Moreover, a considerable leap of faith is required to imagine digital media as long standing; given that the very earliest general-purpose computer systems became operational only in the 1940s, there could literally be no digital storage format that has ever lasted more than seventy years.

One solution to this mismatch, as we see in the case of Warhol's Amiga art, has been a turn to emulation—the use of contemporary digital devices to create emulators or software simulators of older devices. For example, the computer on which I first learned to program—the Commodore Pet 2001— has long been a museum piece, but I can recapture something of the experience of using it through the availability of software programs like VICE, which emulates the instruction set, software configuration, and hardware architecture of the Commodore Pet and related microcomputers, but runs on contemporary platforms such as PCs and Macs running Windows and macOS. Similarly, emulators are available for any number of venerable older computer systems, from high-end mainframes and minicomputers like the DECSYSTEM-20 to cheap 1980s microcomputers like the ZX81, and the app stores of many mobile phones contain emulators for much-loved but long-gone 1980s arcade game machines.

When I load the VICE emulator on my Mac and use it to run an old program for the Commodore Pet, what computer is running that program? The Mac is providing the computational resources, but the old Pet program is essentially invisible to it. Contemporary discourse would insist that emulation has produced a virtual computer running on my laptop. Virtuality here is a form of absent presence, one that makes it seem as though an absent object is available to us. The logic of virtuality in general means that our world is populated by "virtual" objects of all sorts: virtual books, virtual organizations, virtual realities, virtual memory and more, all marked by this condition. Even when the moniker "virtual" is not attached, there is a sense that virtualization attends other aspects of life, such as communication with friends and loved ones mediated by digital technology, such that even mourning and grieving for loved ones becomes an online pursuit (Brubaker et al. 2013). In this world, at least as it is imagined, online shopping replaces the high street or shopping mall; books, CDs, and DVDs are replaced with digital downloads; massive online courses replace traditional classroom teaching; paper bills and coins disappear in favor of online transactions. As a site of design, the virtual is compelling precisely for the ways in which it both reproduces and offers the opportunity to reconfigure aspects of the world that might otherwise be beyond our reach as designers (cf. R. Smith 1986).

Just what does it mean for something to be "virtual"? How should we think about virtuality, virtualism, and virtualization in light of a thorough-going materialist stance on the digital? In this chapter, I want to explore these questions through the lens of computer emulation as one site at which we see these questions played out. From the perspective of the dominant rhetoric, this is a case that is twice virtual, involving virtual objects produced through a virtual computer; however, in practice, it is a site where the problems of virtuality become particularly visible, and where perhaps it is more instructive to think of the doubly material rather than the doubly virtual.

Emulation and Computation

While *retrocomputing*—using emulators to re-create the computers of yesteryear—is a somewhat arcane practice, the notion of emulation runs right to the heart and the origins of computer science as a discipline.

One of the foundational results that made computer science possible was published in Alan Turing's (1936) paper "On Computable Numbers, with an Application to the Entscheidungsproblem." In this paper, Turing made significant contributions to an open mathematical question first posed by David Hilbert in 1928, which essentially asked whether a mathematical language could be defined in which a definitive answer could be given to the question of whether any statement in that language was valid. Turing showed that the answer to this question was "no." In his paper, he identified a class of problems that were not algorithmically decidable: that is, problems for which one could not, through examination, determine whether they could be definitely answered. It's ironic, perhaps, that although the primary message of Turing's paper is negative—that no, not everything could be computed algorithmically—its influence has been positive. In the course of identifying a set of problems that could not be decided, Turing demonstrated that another very large class of problems *could* be solved mechanically. Every computer program ever written falls into this class.

Turing's approach was to imagine two types of machines. Although called "machines," these are not mechanical contrivances but mathematical formalisms, albeit with distinctly machinelike properties and imagined components like tape and optical scanners.[1] The first type of machine is one whose configuration is equivalent to a mathematical function, so that when the machine operates, its actions produce mathematical results according to that function—perhaps the digits of pi, or the shortest path through a network, or the fixed points of a numeric function. The second type of machine that Turing imagines is one that can behave like any of the first class of machines according to a configuration that it processes in the form of a set of rules. This is what Turing called a "universal machine," and which is conventionally known now as a Turing machine, and the mathematical analysis of this sort of machine that Turing provides in his paper laid the foundation for contemporary computing. The set of rules for Turing's universal machine is like the software for a modern computer; it encodes a series of instructions that allow a general-purpose device (a computer) to act like a wide range of more specific devices (a word processor, a game, a music player, and so on). Turing's analysis highlights an oft-overlooked aspect of what it means to "run software"; it means, in the terms of his paper, to configure a general-purpose machine to act like another, more specialized one.

In this sense, all software is some form of emulator, but the term *emulation* has a narrower use in conventional technical discourse. An emulator is a piece of software that specifically uses one computer (often called the *host*) to mimic the operation of another computer (the *guest*). One might want to do such a thing for a number of reasons, but three are the most common, and are distinguished, interestingly, by their different temporal relations.

The first is a projection into the past. In these cases, one might want, as in the Warhol example, to emulate a computer that is no longer available, to be able to gain access to functions, information, and software that has been lost. As we have seen, one might do this purely for the sake of nostalgia; but for librarians and archivists for whom the preservation of digital materials is an important concern, this form of emulation also keeps old documents and old software alive. As more and more materials are "born digital," perhaps never being committed to paper, this is likely to become

---

1. As historian Thomas Haigh (2014) wryly notes, Turing's 1936 paper was no more directed to the construction of real machines than Erwin Schrödinger's research was directed toward advances in feline euthanasia.

ever more important; and if we think of software programs as artifacts that might need to enter the historical record alongside documents, memos, and similar traces of human action, emulation may provide the only effective means of doing so (Satyanarayanan et al. 2015).

The second is a condition of contemporaneous reference. In these cases, one might want to emulate a different type of computer that one could possess but doesn't, perhaps to run some software that is only available for that computer. For example, most software for mobile phones is written on desktop computers and tested and debugged first by being run on an emulator for the phone, which runs on that same computer, for convenience. Similarly, many people who use one computer might run an emulator for another in order to run a specific piece of software without having to maintain two computers at the same time. Indeed, these facilities might be incorporated directly into the operating system. For instance, in 2006, when Apple began a design transition from computers based on the PowerPC processor to the x86 Intel architecture, they also modified their operating system to include a facility called Rosetta, an emulator for the PowerPC processor, so that users with new computers that used Intel processors could nonetheless still run software they owned that had been designed and compiled for the PowerPC and not yet ported to the new processor.

The third is marked by conditions of anticipation. Here, one might emulate a computer system that does not yet exist. This is most commonly done during the development of new computer systems; emulating a new computer's hardware allows software to be developed before the hardware is entirely debugged and available. Similar mechanisms allow software developers to create new applications for computers that are still in development.

As well as the temporal dimension, there is a spatial one. With a single device, many other devices can be emulated. On my Mac laptop, I can run VICE, that emulator of the first computer I ever used; BeebEm, an emulator of the first computer I ever owned; or SIMH, to emulate the minicomputer I supported for a research group as my first job. I can run SALTO, an emulator of the Alto (Thacker et al. 1979), Xerox's pioneering workstation, the first device with a modern graphical user interface, a computer I have never used or even seen operating.[2] If I want to reproduce the experience of running an early Macintosh, I can visit a web page with a Mac emulator

2. SALTO is available for download from Bitsavers' Software Archive, downloaded August 18, 2014, http://bitsavers.informatik.uni-stuttgart.de/bits/Xerox/Alto/simulator/salto/salto-0.4.2.

running in JavaScript.[3] The technical enthusiast website *Ars Technica* recently carried a review of a computer game, *Karateka*, which had been released before the reviewer was born, re-created for a new generation through emulation (Johnston 2013); and as I was completing the first draft this chapter, a posting was distributed online describing the procedure by which an enthusiast had booted Windows 3.1 on a virtual MS-DOS PC emulated in JavaScript within a web browser.[4]

Varieties of Virtualization

Emulators have their roots in a system development approach known as the *virtual machine*. Virtual machines were pioneered by software designers and researchers working in programming language implementation who were concerned with the development of new notations and systems for creating software programs. Programming languages are traditionally translated into machine instructions for execution, a process known as *compilation*. Programming language developers, then, find themselves faced with the problem of the very many different kinds of computers for which their system must work, often with quite different instruction sets and machine languages. The x86 instruction set that powers most personal computers and laptops, for instance, is quite different from the instruction set of the ARM processors that are found in most mobile phones, or that of the MIPS processors in many network devices and game consoles. Developers are faced with a difficult choice between picking just one or two machine languages to support (and hence making their system unavailable on other platforms) or laboriously reimplementing their system many times over for different machine languages. Neither is an attractive option.

One solution is to imagine an idealized computer that is specialized to execute programs written in the new programming language. The programmer compiles programs to the instructions for this imaginary computer, and then writes a series of smaller programs that will execute or translate the instructions of that imaginary computer on different platforms. These smaller programs are much easier to write and allow most of the system to be reused with different instruction sets. The idealized processor is known as a virtual machine—it plays the role of a regular computer for some part of the system, but it does not in fact exist. Virtual machine approaches

3. PCE.js Mac Plus emulator running Mac OS System 7, accessed August 18, 2014, http://jamesfriend.com.au/pce-js.

4. Jason Scott, "The Emularity," ASCII by Jason Scott, accessed January 27, 2015, http://ascii.textfiles.com/archives/4546.

were pioneered by early interactive programming systems, such as the Smalltalk-80 system at Xerox's Palo Alto Research Center (PARC) and the p-System Pascal implementation at UC San Diego (Goldberg and Robson 1983; Overgaard 1980), while the SECD virtual machine was developed to aid in the development of functional programming languages (Landin 1964). More recently, the Java language brought the virtual machine concept to wider prominence (Lindholm and Yellin 1996).

The difference between a virtual machine and an emulated machine is that the virtual machine is an imaginary construct, while an emulated machine is absent but real (or anticipated); there is a real computer whose behavior is being simulated and to which the emulation can be compared. Virtual machines tend to be simple, consistent, well understood, and designed to fit naturally with the anticipated behavior of the software; the machines that are being emulated, though, can be complicated, messy, poorly documented, and designed with other purposes in mind. Worse yet, it is rarely enough for an emulator to simulate the behavior of only a computer processor; the emulator needs also to capture the behavior of memory, storage devices, input devices, networks, speakers, microphones, and other peripherals.

In recent years, the term *virtualization* has come to be used for a related but somewhat different technological arrangement, in which a single computer makes its hardware and resources available to one or more "virtual" computer instances. Two primary differences separate contemporary virtualization from emulation as I describe it here. The first is that emulation generally involves two dissimilar processor types—that is, it involves hosting, say, an Apple II on a Macintosh. By contrast, virtualization is an attempt to produce "like on like"—that is, to take a single Intel x86 processor but it make it seem like several Intel x86 processors. The second, related difference is that since emulation involves dissimilar processors, it requires an active process of producing the virtual computer, step by step, as a program is executed. In virtualization, though, the goal is typically to maximize performance by having the host system "get out of the way" of programs running on a virtual instance; as far as possible, virtualization has the virtual instance run software directly on the host processor. Virtualization then is an attempt not so much to create an emulated processor instance but to multiplex multiple virtual processors on a single processor platform. Virtualization is frequently used for large-scale, high-performance, and cloud-based systems; Amazon's Elastic Compute Cloud, for example, is a virtualization service with which users can dynamically configure and deploy virtual processor instances across the internet. Virtualization in this sense is not directly a concern of this chapter, and so where I use the term *virtualization*, I use it more traditionally to mean the production of virtuality, including in the case of emulators.

Rematerialization

Placing emulation in this context, though, makes clear that it speaks to a broad cultural logic, the logic of the virtual. Invocation of the virtual is the central discursive move of digitality. To the extent that digital phenomena are rhetorically opposed to nondigital equivalents, and that they further are connected through a notion of displacement, virtual objects—virtual books, worlds, organizations, spaces, meetings, communities, and on—are the stock-in-trade of the digerati. The notion of virtuality marks an absence—the designation of *virtual* marks something that seems to be there but isn't. A virtual book allows us to read without a real book being present; a virtual musical instrument allows us to produce music in the absence of the instrument itself.

One would imagine that the case of emulation is the perfect demonstration of the power of virtuality. If software is already thoroughly virtual, then what could be more appropriate than to "run" that computer on "hardware" that is *itself* constructed from the virtual medium of software— that is, an emulator. This rhetoric of absence, though, draws our attention away from the very specific presence of technologies that manifest the emulator and the emulated device. The emulator, after all, does not simply conjure up a virtual computer—a virtual Commodore Amiga or whatever. Rather, it makes that virtual computer manifest within a host platform—a PC running the UAE emulator, a Mac running the Bochs PC emulator, a Raspberry Pi running MAME, and so on. I want here to use the case of emulators to examine virtualization as *rematerialization*—not as a move away from the material to create a domain of the virtual, but rather a new material foundation for digital experience.

Shifting from a language of virtualization to a language of rematerialization turns our attention from questions of absence to questions of presence. It depends on the idea that we have encountered throughout the preceding chapters that software and digital information have their own materialities that manifest themselves in our encounters with them. What material properties does an emulator exhibit? What constrains its own actions? How do we navigate the relationships between the material domain of the emulation and the material domain of the host platform?

In the next section, I examine a series of problems that occur in the production of an effective emulation. By doing so, I hope to show how virtuality in practice is perhaps better seen as rematerialization and how we might answer some of these questions. With that in hand, we can take a step back to consider the notion of the virtual as an aspect of the digital landscape.

Problems of Materiality in Virtual Computers

In what ways do the material manifestations of digital objects challenge the idea of a virtual computer in the world of emulation? I discuss four considerations here—instructions, timing, input/output, and the limits of fidelity.

Instructions and Representations

The essence of emulation is the creation of an environment that can run specific pieces of software. Essentially, it does just what a computer should— it reads a program, and then it executes it. To understand the difficulty, we need to think for a moment about what a program actually *is*.

A computer program, as stored on a disk or downloaded from the internet, is a series of instructions. These instructions are themselves simply numbers; each number corresponds to a function that the computer's processor can perform, or a data item to which that function should be applied, or a memory address where data to be processed can be found or where execution should shift. Why then is there any need for emulation to make some software run? It is needed because different processors and different processor architectures (such as the x86 processors in most desktop computers and the ARM processors in most mobile phones) execute different instructions. It is not simply that they encode the same instructions with different numerical codes (although that is sometimes true); it is rather that they use different so-called instruction sets—sets of functions that make up the processor's catalog of operations. These differ because processors might provide different kinds of functions in hardware (e.g., one processor might have an instruction for multiplying two numbers directly, while another might support only addition and require that multiplication be performed through repeated addition or through bit shifting). Recall again the distinction between representation and notation in the small program example from chapter one; the program describes a sequence of action but many gaps are left unspecified about what will actually take place and how.

The instructions that make up a program are not simply mathematical functions or descriptions. They can be thought of that way, but they can also be thought of as objects that manipulate how a computational mechanism works. Just as a key, inserted into a lock, will reconfigure the tumblers in the lock (hopefully, to open the door), so an instruction being executed by a processor activates different parts of the processor to produce its effect; the key doesn't simply *represent* the configuration of tumblers, and similarly the instruction doesn't simply represent the sequence of action to be taken. The instruction, then, is something that has meaning only relative to the processor in question. There are two important considerations here for the problem of emulation. The first is that, since different types of processors have different kinds of capacities, as described above, an instruction that makes sense on one processor may not make any sense on another. You can't simply follow an instruction to add together the values of two registers if your processor doesn't have two registers. In this way, the problem of emulation is more than simply "finding the equivalent instruction"—there is no logic of equivalences, and local facilities cannot simply "stand in for" the facilities being emulated. The emulator makes up for these deficiencies—it explicitly stands between the original software and the new processor, reading each instruction and directing the processor to act in a manner that is somehow equivalent.

A second way in which instructions are tied to particular manifestations—and arguably, the more complicated one—lies in the fact that processors may have bugs, errors, or limits to their use, which are part of their implementation but not part of the mathematical formulation. Therefore, to produce an accurate emulation, an emulator needs to pay attention not just to what the instruction *ought* to do, but to what it *actually does* in the computer being emulated. A sterling example is documented in Michael Hiltzik's (1999) account of the history of Xerox PARC, concerning the development of a "clone" (not quite an emulation) of the DEC PDP-10 mainframe computer. The PARC researchers wanted to purchase a DEC PDP-10 computer, so that they could run software developed by academic researchers elsewhere who had made extensive use of this computer. However, the PDP-10 was a competitor to Xerox's own recent entry into the minicomputer market, so corporate management refused to authorize the purchase. In response, the researchers decided that rather than buy a PDP-10, they could build their own version, one that would be sufficiently compatible with the original that they could run software developed for the PDP-10 at other research sites. The task of reproducing various elements of the PDP-10 system was divided up among lab members, and researcher Ed Fiala was assigned to build support for floating-point mathematical functions. In the course of his work, he discovered some small bugs in the PDP-10 implementations of the functions and fixed them for the clone machine so that it would behave correctly. When the machine was nearing completion, however, and people began bringing up software that had been developed for original PDP-10s, they found that some of it failed mysteriously. Investigation revealed that some software was failing because it depended on the very bugs that Fiala had corrected. With software compatibility as a key requirement for the new computer, only one solution was possible; Fiala was asked to program the bugs back into his implementation, so that it would be wrong again, but wrong in the same way as the real PDP-10 was.

The object of attention in an emulation, then, is not simply the sequence of instructions that need to be transformed into some different sequence that suits the host processor; rather, the emulation needs to reproduce and reenact the entire mechanism into which those instructions fit when they are taken not as representations of computational action but as components of the mechanism.

Timing

As we discussed earlier, the conventional wisdom about computer programming is that computers must be given complete and detailed descriptions of what to do, and that these descriptions are what constitute a computer program, with no detail left unspecified. This is quite true as far as it goes, but as we saw in chapter 1, computer instructions leave much unsaid, and what is unsaid must nonetheless be recaptured in emulation. The time taken by computer operations is an important case in point. On a MOS 6502 processor—the type of processor that powered the original Apple II computer, among others—the machine instruction sequence A1 44 00 means "fetch the contents of memory address $4400, add to it the value of the X register to produce a new memory address, and load the value stored at that computer address into the accumulator." However, it doesn't specify, for example, how long that operation will take. Producing an accurate emulation means not just performing the same or equivalent instructions but doing it in such a way as to produce the same effect. Why does the timing matter? Well, it might matter if the computer program relies on the delay produced by issuing a series of instructions to make sure that on-screen activities happen with appropriate synchronization, or that a value will be read from a disk at the right moment, or that an interrupt will be handled before an operation times out.

There are two problems here. One is a problem of scale, and the other a problem of imbalance.

The problem of scale is most visible when there are drastic mismatches between the host system and the guest system. One of the major uses of emulation is in the retrospective mode highlighted earlier—reproducing the experience of using older, perhaps unavailable computer hardware in software on modern hardware. In any emulation, performing the same operations in software as one might in hardware is a good deal slower, and so when one performs an emulation of contemporary hardware in software, there is a significant performance reduction. Modern hardware is, of course, generally much faster than older computer hardware, which means that the situation is different when emulating older hardware. It is quite possible that a contemporary software emulator will operate more quickly, perhaps much more quickly, than the older hardware that is being emulated. There are times when this is an advantage. For instance, in my first research position, I wrote software on workstations, from Sun Microsystems, that ran an emulator for the custom "Wildflower" architecture of prototype research computers that was developed at Xerox PARC in the 1970s. The modern emulation was much faster than the original hardware had ever been, representing a significant performance enhancement. In other cases, though, this speed "advantage" might be significantly problematic. If an emulated game runs one hundred times faster in a modern emulation than on the original hardware, it may be too fast to play.

The difference between the performance of contemporary computer systems and that of what is sometimes called *legacy hardware* may be large, but the issue for emulators is not simply the scale of the difference, but also the fact that different aspects of computer systems develop at different rates. Processors, for instance, have generally become faster over time at a rate higher than that of storage systems—so while contemporary storage systems are generally faster than older storage systems, they are not faster by the same factor that characterizes changes in processor performance. To account for this, computer system designers have, over the years, developed new computer architectures, or arrangements of system elements, to compensate for the different rates of change in the components that make up a system. These shifts in relative performance may challenge the kinds of trade-offs we saw at work in our survey of image formats in chapter 1, since those may explicitly involve the anticipated relationships between storage speed and processor speed, for example.

Modern computer processors, then, are not simply faster than old ones—they also have larger caches, are more heavily pipelined,[5] and might have

5. Pipelining is a technique for taking the various steps that a processor has to go through to execute an instruction and breaking them down into separate units so that the processor can essentially be executing multiple instructions "at the same time," all at different stages of completion. A more heavily pipelined processor architecture breaks instruction execution down into more steps—creating more parallelism but also requiring more complicated synchronization.

multiple cores operating simultaneously, as ways of making more efficient use of their "excess" capacity relative to the data storage system. Similarly, modern graphics processors do more advanced processing on their own, without involving the central processor of the computer, introducing another source of parallelism and hence another architectural difference with implications for performance. The architectural changes mean not only that, as systems advance, different aspects of their operation become faster or slower at different rates; they also mean that performance characteristics become more variable, relying not on one instruction after another, but on sequences of instructions and on sequences of memory access. To further complicate the problems of timing in emulation, we should remember one other important thing—computers consist of more than processors. Those other things—peripheral devices, subsidiary electronics, and non-digital components—all have their own timing considerations that software might need to account for.

As an example, remember that, before the days of LCD screens, most computer displays were cathode ray tubes (CRTs). A CRT operates by sweeping an electron beam rapidly over a phosphor-lined screen, from side to side and top to bottom, switching the beam rapidly on and off to cause spots of phosphor either to glow or not. These spots of glowing phosphor become the pixels that make up the display; and since they rapidly decay in brightness, they must be "repainted" again and again by the scanning electron beam. This constant need to repaint the screen, and to do it within the timeframe demanded by the electron beam and the phosphor, and to supply the data to drive the display, became a significant demand on the design of early personal computers—Xerox's original Alto computer spent fully 66 percent of its time managing the display. (Butler Lampson, the principal software designer for the Alto, recounted in a 2014 oral history that one of his most important contributions to the project was to reduce the time taken by the code supplying the display driver with data from seven micro-instruction cycles to six, so that it consumed only 65 percent of the computer's time rather than 75 percent.[6])

One especially important aspect of this arrangement for many micro-computers and game systems was the existence of what was called the *vertical blanking interval*, which is the period when the CRT's electron beam would be turned off and would reposition itself from the bottom right to the top left of the screen, to begin a new painting cycle. Many pieces

6. Butler Lampson interview by Jeffrey R. Yost, December 11, 2014, http://conservancy.umn.edu/bitstream/handle/11299/169983/oh452bl.pdf.

of software—especially programs like graphical games—would pay a lot of attention to the vertical blanking interval, for two reasons. The first is that a period when the screen is not being painted might suddenly be a period when more processing time is available—a good time to do more complicated calculations. The second is that a period when the screen is not being repainted is a good time to make updates to on-screen objects so that there won't be any of the flickering that might result if the objects were updated at the same time as they were being painted onto the screen. As Montfort and Bogost (2009) document in their book *Racing the Beam*, discussed in chapter 2, programmers on the early Atari VCS game system needed essentially to organize their entire programs around the timing of instructions relative to the horizontal and vertical sweeps of the electron beam.

The timing that needs to be reproduced in an emulator, then, is not simply the timing of the processor but the timing of analog elements such as the CRT beam, not to mention such features as the characteristic operating speed of disks or the temporal performance of memory. In other words, the production of the virtual guest computer means the reproduction not only of the digital elements of the original machine, but also of the thoroughly nondigital components—a further intrusion of the obstreperously nonvirtual. Here we see the limits of the virtuality argument, which suggests that an operation can be performed as easily by one computer as another—what is in focus here is the whole computational assembly, and the measures of its effectiveness reach well beyond the behavior specified by its program. Further, the production of an emulation depends as much on the material constraints of the host platform as on those of the emulated guest machine. What matters is not simply the production of an effective simulation, but the appropriate matching of materialities across the two.

Input and Output

Perhaps one of the most complicated areas of challenge that emulation throws up is the problem of input and output—recreating and emulating aspects of how graphics and perhaps especially sound work. The problems here reflect and intensify some that we have already discussed. Part of the difficulty is that input and output operations go beyond the traditional mathematical descriptions that are the foundation of how we reason about computers.

As I have outlined, the mathematical theory on which computer science is founded—the Church-Turing theorem—describes a class of computable functions (basically, a class of solvable mathematical problems) and a computational mechanism that can solve them. So called Turing-equivalent machines are machines or mechanisms that can solve any of that class of functions.

In practice, however, it turns out that actual computers—the ones we all use—are both *more than* and *less than* Turing-equivalent machines. They are less than Turing-equivalent in that the abstract description of the Turing machine postulates infinite storage. In comparison to the extremely simple operation of a Turing machine, a modern computer might have so much storage that it is *essentially* infinite—but it is (obviously) not *in fact* infinite. In other words, there can be functions that are solvable by a Turing machine but not necessarily solvable by specific actual computers that we might use, not because the problems make unresolvable computational demands but because they make unresolvable storage demands. So in this way, contemporary computers are less than formal mathematical Turing machines. At the same time, though, they are also *more* than formal mathematical Turing machines in that they have capacities that Turing machines lack, especially in their connection to the world. For instance, we expect that any computer we buy today will be capable of playing music; and yet, the functions needed to play music—that is, to be able to control the voltage on a connection to speakers or headphones so that music can be heard—is unavailable to the formal mathematical Turing machine. The theory of Turing equivalence is the theory of what can be calculated, but it stops where calculation ends. So we might be able to show how a Turing-equivalent machine can decode a description of music that has been encoded in the MP3 format that Sterne examines, but there is no way to describe the actual playing of the music.

The case of input/output—of playing music, for instance—highlights the way in which computer systems, as physical objects and as cultural objects—escape the mathematical accounts of computation. A real Turing machine wouldn't sell very well in the marketplace, because those functions that we demand of our computers—the ability to print documents, to communicate on networks, or to video conference with friends—are entirely outside its capacities. This means that, while we might imagine that Turing's theorem—which after all, describes a machine that can emulate another machine—should be a guarantee that emulation is straightforward, the truth is rather more complicated. To make things even more difficult for someone writing an emulator, these functions, like network communication and processing audio and video, are generally not performed by the central processing unit of the computer, but rather delegated to dedicated signal processing hardware that can be controlled by the processor. Input/output operations, indeed, are often handled in parallel with the operation of the processor—especially in modern machines, whose separate graphical processor units—themselves highly parallel—are often more capable computational devices (within a limited sphere) than the central processor itself.

As in other cases we have seen, then, there is no simple one-to-one equivalence between one context and another. Emulation is not simply a question of looking at each instruction and issuing the local equivalent; rather, the behavior of the original system must be reproduced, in all its material specificity.

Fidelity and Boundaries

Fidelity is clearly a significant concern for emulation—accurately and correctly reproducing the behavior of the emulated system. This fidelity is of a practical sort, delimited by the tasks at hand—resurrecting old software, recovering old data, anticipating new behaviors, and so on. Within this process of delimitation, however, we find an interesting phenomenon, which is the way in which we draw boundaries around definitional aspects of computational experience. What is deemed as being within the range of "reproducing computational behavior" is clearly provisional. For example, before speakers were built in, some of the earliest efforts in computer music were achieved by indirect means, by placing a transistor radio close to a computer and "listening in" to the electromagnetic leakage from the computer's circuitry (Doornbusch 2005). Reproducing the radio-frequency emissions of an old computer might be interesting but is unquestionably beyond the capacities of most emulators, or even of what we imagine it means to be an emulation. Reproducing other iconic, often sensory, aspects of old computers' behavior—the feel or sound of their keyboards, the rattle of cases, or the flicker of screens—are seen as outside the domain of emulation, but other aesthetic considerations, such as the reproduction of native fonts, might well be included.

What this prompts is a reflection on the boundaries of the computer, or perhaps more interestingly, on what happens at those boundaries—on how computers fit into and are encountered within a broader ecology of both materials and practices. As we learned in chapter 2 from perspectives such as those offered by science studies and vital materialism, this is not just about placing technology in a social context; it's about recognizing that the boundaries of these categories are themselves unstable. The encounter with digital technologies is sensory and affective as much as, if not more than, it is utilitarian and cognitive. To the extent that retrocomputing efforts at emulation are frequently driven by nostalgia, those sensory elements play an important role. And some of those elements are within the domain of emulation for sure—color palettes, sound, and so forth. Nonetheless, even at the same time as I want to use it to undercut accounts of virtualization, emulation is grounded in an essentialization of the computer—the reduction of the computer to just one set of functions and processes, with a boundary that doesn't match the limits of the computer's case, its interface, its architecture, or its ports, causing us to question quite what it *does* match.

In part, the question arises precisely because these other elements of the computer's operation *can* be simulated or emulated to some degree. Digital simulation can anticipate radio frequency emissions. Retrocomputing efforts do, occasionally, involve the resurrection of old hardware, cases, and keyboards.[7] These are outside the mainstream, though, and I do not believe it is enough to simply declare that the details are irrelevant to practice. More productively, perhaps, we might observe that particular kinds of materialization suit our image of what computers are and do, even in the domain of the virtual. That is a view, it would seem, that is rooted primarily in software performance rather than in human experience, but the very flexibility or indeterminacy of those boundaries in particular cases draws attention to the practices by which some material expressions are deemed significant while others are discarded.

Virtualization and Rematerialization

I have focused here on the example of emulation because it provides us with a particularly fruitful perspective on the questions of virtuality. Software is already a thoroughly virtual good, in the terms of the traditional rhetoric—born digital, it lives entirely in digital media, operates entirely within the computer, transmitted wholesale from place to place; it can be duplicated digitally, protected cryptographically, and processed algorithmically. Emulation, then, is by that same logic doubly virtual—by using one piece of software to produce the actions of another, it constitutes an even more radical separation of software from hardware, creating a thoroughly virtual environment for the operation of an already virtual object.

In practice, though, this realm of pure virtuality is hard to find. The practice of emulation seems to be not so much an exercise in virtuality as one in overwhelming materiality—an engagement with all the specific material constraints of both platforms, those elements that lie outside what

7. See, for example, the Retrochallenge on the Retrocosm blog, accessed August 28, 2016, https://retrocosm.net/2013/07/26/retrochallenge-its-a-wrap.

is notated by software systems but that are critical to the manifested expression of running software.

If software is apparently virtual, then software running on a virtual computer seems doubly so. Rather than being doubly virtual, though, emulation is instead doubly material. First, the software being executed as the guest system cannot be regarded purely as a virtual description of desired behavior; it is instead a tool for configuring a material arrangement of the delicately entwined digital and analog components that made up the original computer system—complete with flaws, mistakes, problems, undocumented features, and unexpected idiosyncrasies. Second, the challenge is not to dissolve away these material considerations, but rather to reenact them in the context of a new materiality—the materiality of the host system. Not only, then, does someone developing emulation software need to pay attention to, for example, the timing arrangements between processor, memory, and tertiary storage on the original computer, but these need to be configured so as to operate effectively in light of the timing arrangements among processor, memory, and tertiary storage on the current one. Emulation is perhaps, then, less a case of producing a "virtual" computer to run the original software, than a matter of "rematerializing" that computer in the context of a new one.

As hinted earlier in the discussion of emulation, virtualization, and virtual machines, the production of virtuality that emulation involves is in practice quite thoroughgoing. Emulation in the sense in which I have described it here is a relatively unusual phenomenon. In other forms, though, it is more than commonplace. For instance, microprogramming is a technique whereby the instruction set of a computer processor is not directly realized in the processor, but in fact produced by the execution of lower-level, intraprocessor instructions that then produce and enact the instruction set of the computer. In other words, it is a level of programming even more fundamental than the "raw" machine language and makes even the hardware description of the processor itself a virtual entity of a sort. Microprogramming simplifies processor design, speeds the development of new technologies, and helps to produce compatible designs on different platforms, by making the processor itself a virtual entity.

Most importantly, these things may all be going on at once. When running an emulator (or any other piece of software), one might be running on a virtual instance in a virtualization cluster, doing real-time instruction-set translation, all supported by a microprogrammed processor. In this hall of digital mirrors, one might begin to question what reality the apparently fixed points of instruction-set architecture have. One thinks of software programs as being compiled down into the specific machine language for a given processor, only to discover that this is potentially just another way-point in the materialization of specific computational behaviors. The question in some ways becomes what is the relevance or practical utility of the machine language as a level of description—merely a convention? An institutional convenience? The fulcrum on which a division of labor turns? One lesson that we can draw from this dive into a world of the practical production of virtuality is to be suspicious of where the boundaries of the virtual and the material might fall and for what purposes.

A second lesson that we might take from this chapter concerns the notion of digital representation. Digital systems are representational though and through; at every level, digital objects represent, point toward, or stand for something else. Of course, we are familiar with the representational nature of the objects of user interaction, from avatars in a video game to files and folders on a desktop or icons on a phone screen. But the representations continue throughout the software *stack*, or layers of abstracted functionality. Metadata in the file system are representations; data structures in computer memory are representations; and the instructions themselves that make up the program are representations. At this point, then, it is useful to cast our minds back to the simple computer program that appeared in the first chapter and the idea that it illustrated, which is that much of what makes a computer system operate effectively *escapes these representations*. The representation is not, itself, notated. When we read programs "between the lines," we find limits of materialization, conventions of practice, and expectations of implementation that need to be maintained for programs to work effectively.

What is dissolved here is the illusion of layered abstractions—the idea that software systems can be effectively built up, layer by layer, with each layer adding new functionality that depends on the layer below. The notion of layering is most widely deployed when we talk about networks—so, we talk about a cloud service being defined "on top of" HTTP, which itself is implemented "on top of" TCP, which is "on top of" IP, which runs "over" the underlying hardware communication mechanisms of the connective media. The idea is that at each layer, the lower layer is both augmented (with new functions) and hidden (so that upper "layers" of the system need not worry about the details lower down). This idea is not limited to networking but is fundamental to computer science instruction and interoperation—a processor instruction set that abstracts over actual architectural details, providing a hardware "layer" on top of which an operating system provides new functions, that operating system itself creating a new abstract interface that can be offered to application programs. These questions will come back into focus in chapters 6 and 7.

Thinking about emulation and about the need to read between the lines of representations forces us to adopt a vertical, rather than a horizontal, view—one that "cuts through" the layers and understandings the complete instantiation of mechanism that makes a system operate. Understanding the way in which constraints at one "level" shape experience at another—to the extent that a distinction between levels is worth retaining—is a recurring feature of the analysis offered in chapters to follow.

We should similarly take this stance toward other productions of virtuality. Although this chapter has concerned itself primarily with the virtual computers produced through emulators, the context of inquiry in the opening pages included other virtual entities—the virtual books that we download onto document readers, the virtual spaces in which digital games are played, the virtual presence that we project into remote spaces when collaborating over a distance. These too stack digital materialities and platform materialities, endure reconfigurations of timing, and demonstrate the practical disappearance of layers of abstraction in ways that demand new analytic stances. The fact that one cannot rip a page out of a virtual book is not simply a discounting of its book-ness; it speaks to the material relations between elements that make up the different objects.

So, it is important not to read this argument as an attempt to undermine the virtual as an experience or to dismiss it as a concept. *Virtual* means something as a term in contemporary discourse; the concept has value in the distinctions that it enables us to draw and in the relationships it builds between online and offline experience. An argument that frames the experience in terms of rematerialization is not meant to displace a notion of the virtual but rather to draw attention to how it comes about. If virtuality is an achievement, partial and provisional, and if it is an outcome of a series not only of technical moves but also of conceptual, perceptual, and discursive ones, then the goal is to be able to see those moves taking place, in order to be able to inquire into their conditions and effects.

Emulation turns our attention toward the manifestations of the material on a microlevel. Our attention here has been directed toward the timing of digital circuits, the rematerialization of platforms, and the compatibilities of machine language representations. The chapters to come gradually shift in their scope, from one person sitting in front of a computer, to groups and organizations engaging around data, to the nature of large-scale data processing and the institutional arrangements of networking. The same fundamental set of questions, concerning the material nature of our engagements with the digital, remain on the table, even as the virtual slips out of sight.

4 Spreadsheets and Spreadsheet Events in Organizational Life

In the previous chapter, looking at virtuality and emulation provided us with an opportunity to find the material within the virtual. By looking at how virtuality is produced and enacted—what Mackenzie calls "practical virtuality" (Mackenzie 2006b) in the encounter with code—we saw that a strong conceptual distinction between the virtual and the material cannot be supported. The virtual is also material. This is not to say that the term *virtual* has no value or significance, but rather that an examination of its manifestations must recognize the ways in which the material also intrudes.

In this chapter, we begin to look at the specific materialities of different kinds of digital information objects as they are put to use in everyday settings. In particular, I take the case of spreadsheets as digital forms whose materialities manifest themselves as practical concerns for people in the business of generating, examining, manipulating, talking about, and working with data.[1]

Spreadsheet Events

The scene is a familiar one. Around tables gathered to form a U, a group of coworkers are meeting. They face the front of the room, where a document is presented on a large screen; close by, someone stands or sits at the computer projecting the image. What it projects is a spreadsheet, faint lines on the screen marking a grid that records both work already resolved and that yet to be discussed. Copies sit on the tables in front of participants, on paper and on open laptops. The meeting has been convened to evaluate alternatives and make decisions; the spreadsheet is both agenda and record. As the meeting progresses, the grid of the spreadsheet is gradually filled in;

1. This chapter is based on unpublished material originally drafted in collaboration with Melissa Mazmanian and Janet Vertesi.

tentative proposals become documented decisions, and the colors, formats, and markings of the spreadsheet indicate the progress that has been made. At the end of the meeting, this same coordinative artifact becomes an archive of the event, emailed around the organization or stored on a networked file server.

As an occasion, the details are varied. Perhaps the group is gathered to evaluate the reviews of papers and to assemble a program for a workshop or professional meeting. Perhaps the group is made up of members of an academic department, reviewing their graduate students or planning next year's teaching schedule. Perhaps it is a group of scientists debating recent observations and planning their next round of experiments. Perhaps it is a city council balancing budget requests. In general, whatever the details, we know roughly what to expect when we sit down to find the familiar grid projected onto a wall.

A spreadsheet is a form of digital document. It is also an organizational tool, not just in the way it is incorporated into organizational processes such as financial planning, but also in the way in it is incorporated into the practice and routines of organizational life, such as meetings. It is this

Figure 4.1
A spreadsheet event in progress (photo by Janet Vertesi)

latter, performative aspect of the spreadsheet—and more broadly, of digital media—that I investigate in this chapter. I am interested in exploring here the ways in which the materialities of the spreadsheet as an artifact are thoroughly enmeshed with the organizational practice of the meeting.

Studies of the impact of various technologies on organizational life are legion; contemporary organizations are so deeply entangled with their information infrastructures that studies of organizations and studies of technology are almost indistinguishable. Databases have replaced paper-based and earlier forms of recordkeeping; e-mail and social media have become customary routes by which information is shared between organizational members; workflow systems encode organizational rules and procedures (e.g., Bowers et al. 1995; Orlikowski 1993). Yet, information technologies do not merely augment or supplant prior forms; they also create new ways of working. One such, the PowerPoint presentation, has been examined by a number of researchers. In their paper, "The PowerPoint Presentation and Its Corollaries: How Genres Shape Communicative Action in Organizations," organizational scholars JoAnne Yates and Wanda Orlikowski (2007) show how PowerPoint software as a genre "shapes the ongoing work of organizational actors" (68). They approach the software package as a genre of communicative action, an organizing structure that shapes and constrains organizational work. Sarah Kaplan demonstrates, too, how the material-discursive work of working with PowerPoint is an essential part of developing a business strategy. That is, PowerPoint as both a tool to think and present with, and a tool to work with, is "part of the machinery that produces knowledge" (Kaplan 2001, 321). But this software "machinery" is not limited to PowerPoint: other commercial software and visual modes also participate in the production of knowledge and social order in the collaborative laboratory. Further, I argue, discussing these software packages as "genre" risks obscuring the performative and practical work they accomplish for the team as they are deployed in practice, a focus that Herbert Knoblauch (2013) has taken as central to his examinations of what he calls "powerpoint events"—meetings and presentations structured around the presentation of digital slideshows.[2]

Presentation software tends to be packaged alongside other so-called productivity applications (a term that tends to produce wry smiles) in packages like Microsoft's Office or Apple's iWork. Spreadsheet applications are

---

2. I largely follow Knoblauch's convention of using the term *powerpoint* to refer generically to presentation software, reserving the capitalized PowerPoint for the Microsoft software package.

key parts of these packages. In ethnographic work in a range of settings, it has been impossible to ignore the central and repeated appearance of spreadsheets—and "spreadsheet events," to mirror Knoblauch's term. Spreadsheet events are different from powerpoint events, and differently shaped and constrained in relation to the materiality of the software and its content.

In this chapter, I use the spreadsheet as an example through which to examine the tangled relationships between digital materiality and social practice. The questions at the center of this examination are, how do the materialities of spreadsheets—as both interactive tools and representational systems—shape, constrain, and enable aspects of how people can work with them? How do we project our work into the form of the spreadsheet, or read off from that form a set of rules, limits, capacities, and opportunities? How do material and social come together in the spreadsheet form? This analysis is informed by much insightful work on sociomateriality in organizational studies (e.g., Orlikowski and Scott 2008; Kaplan 2011; Yates and Orlikowski 2007; Bailey et al. 2012), but in the context of this book, my interest is in the specific representational materialities at work in the spreadsheet as a digital form. I draw too on empirical observation of spreadsheet use in team science, work that was conducted in collaboration with a number of colleagues, although my use of this material here is more inspirational than ethnographic. As artifacts, spreadsheets are ubiquitous within the practice of this group; more particularly, they frequently recur as the central coordinative artifacts of face-to-face decision making, drawing our attention to their performative materialities. In this chapter, my focus is on the Excel spreadsheet as it manifests itself within this organization: a commercial software and visual organizational technology that accompanies and performs work on a large distributed spacecraft mission to the outer planets. Such software is essential to mission operations not because of its secret code or robotic extensions, but rather because it enables and produces the coordination and continued orderings of each mission team. That is, the software and associated visual interfaces used for planning by each team are part and parcel of producing their organizational orientations. In this domain, the software does not so much represent the spacecraft or its capabilities, but instead presents opportunities for the science team to perform their organizational commitments and reproduce their sociotechnical orientation.

Software Practices in Organizations

Despite the centrality of spreadsheets to many aspects of organizational life and their status as one of the core elements of working software on personal computers, spreadsheets and their use are remarkably underexamined. An early ethnographic study of spreadsheet creation as an example of end-user programming was conducted by Bonnie Nardi and James Miller (1991), who anticipated the importance of spreadsheets as ways of creating active content and identified the collective aspects of apparently individual programming tasks, enabled by how the spreadsheet's form encourages tinkering and appropriation. This casual flexibility has caused others to be concerned about the risks of spreadsheet errors, particularly given how many organizations depend on them for analysis, and several papers have analyzed these errors and proposed potential solutions and mechanisms for detection (e.g., Panko and Halverson 1996). The significance of these errors has been made glaringly visible lately, in the hotly disputed case over an economic analysis with profound implications. The analysis in question was an economic report that constituted the academic evidence supporting so-called austerity policies in Europe, in response to the global financial crisis of 2007–2008, policies that have had transformative social effects and toppled governments—and which may, if critics are correct, have been based on a simple programming error in a spreadsheet, which skewed the analysis and suggested that these policies had been much more effective in the past than they had in fact been (Reinhart and Rogoff 2010; Herndon et al. 2014).

Presentation software, in contrast, has received more scholarly attention, especially PowerPoint. Erica Robles-Anderson and Patrik Svensson (2016) discuss the viruslike spread of powerpoint presentations from corporate meetings to settings as disparate as the White House situation room and California mega-churches, and place them in a broader historical context of charts and other information-dissemination devices. In some cases, encounters with powerpoint arise in passing; for example, the rhetorical style of powerpoint-driven presentations was cited by a NASA board of study (Tufte 2006) as contributing to the "normalization of deviance" (Vaughan 1996) in project reviews in the run-up to the Columbia space shuttle disaster. More direct studies of powerpoint such as those of Yates and Orlikowski or of Kaplan are instructive here because they help define the parameters of our particular interest in this chapter. Knoblauch (2013) distinguishes three levels of analysis in his study of what he terms "powerpoint events" (that is, powerpoint-driven presentation occasions rather than the electronic documents). The *internal* level concerns the organization of material on a slide and the production of speech around it. The *intermediate* level concerns the grosser orchestration of the presentation, including gesture, the use of the body, and the arrangements of the triad of speaker, projected material, and audience. The *external* level concerns the broader institutional aspects of the settings within which powerpoint events occur, addressing questions such as those of formality, space, the organization of meetings, and the role of presentations within them.

Across such studies, scholars have drawn attention to the work of the software *in practice*, embedded within an organizational regime but also in local logics of accounting, public performance, and participation. Despite its use of templates and formal program aspects, powerpoint does not dictate how it should always be used: different organizations have different expectations of and interactions with powerpoint presentations that satisfy (or otherwise slot into or fit in with) organizational concerns. Examining Excel as a comparison case exposes the role of the structural aspects of the software in concert with its practical application in an organizational context of use: in this chapter's case, in the management of a large, distributed, multi-institutional technoscientific team. I first discuss the history of the spreadsheet and its implementation into code as commercial software, and then outline three aspects of spreadsheets that are enrolled in practice in an organizational context.

The Spreadsheet's Organizational Devices

The origins of the spreadsheet are, by now, a reasonably familiar part of computer lore (e.g., Isaacson 2014). The first spreadsheet program was Visi-Calc, developed by Dan Bricklin and Bob Frankston for the Apple II computer; it subsequently became the "killer app" to which much of the success of that computer, and by extension of the personal computer as a business tool, was attributed. The term *spreadsheet* was already in use, referring to the physically large paper documents that accountants might use to lay out and mathematically model a corporation's financial state. Bricklin learned about spreadsheets while studying at Harvard Business School. As a computer hobbyist, he recognized an opportunity to build an electronic version of the spreadsheets that his professors used. He realized that an electronic spreadsheet would offer two key benefits. First, because computation (e.g., summing columns of numbers) would be done digitally, it would be a less error-prone process than in the paper-based system; and second, an electronic spreadsheet would allow an accountant or business planner to easily explore options by plugging in different numbers to see how they affected the overall system—the "what if?" functionality that was particularly highlighted in early electronic spreadsheet marketing. Bricklin and Frankston worked together to turn this idea into a working software product, and their VisiCalc application became one of the top-selling applications of the early microcomputer era. VisiCalc was soon joined (and eventually displaced) by other software systems that embodied the same general ideas—Lotus 1-2-3, for example, SuperCalc, and Microsoft's initial offering, Multiplan, which was later replaced with a new product called Excel.

Through these multiple generations of software systems, two ideas have remained central to the notion and to the interface of the spreadsheet. The first is the *grid*. A spreadsheet presents itself as an extensive grid of *cells*, organized into abutting rows and columns like the squares on square-ruled paper. The cell is the fundamental unit for editing—each number, each figure, each text entry is placed within a cell, and those cells are organized into a rectangular grid of rows and columns. The grid is the basis of association, alignment, grouping, and reference. The second central idea is that some cells can be active—their contents are not fixed, but rather are calculated from values in other cells according to a *formula* (say, to compute the average of the figures in a column, or to convert a series of values into percentages). The grid exists to serve the formula; the grid provides a way of naming cells, using a coordinate mechanism so that a formula can link cells together. The formula captures both ideas that were central to Bricklin's original conception—automated calculation and exploration depend on formulae that will calculate results and outcomes based on figures the user enters. The idea of the formula, then, is arguably the idea that drives the design of the spreadsheet as an artifact.

Grid and formula, then, are the two key organizational devices for the spreadsheet. Contemporary spreadsheet software includes many more features—such as advanced mechanisms for graphical displays, integrated programming languages, and connections to databases and the internet—but the combination of grid and formula lie at the heart of the spreadsheet as a digital document form. That is not to say, however, that they are always equally important, or even both used. For instance, although the formula is the mechanism that captures the key design insights that inspired Dan Bricklin to create VisiCalc, many spreadsheets contain little to no calculation at all. Looking at spreadsheets in organizational life reveals many in which no formulae arise, and even the numbers that might be entered are not intended for tabulation or formulation. As spreadsheet software became a standard office tool, spreadsheets became available for many uses—some centered on the formula and some on the grid. For many people, the spreadsheet is a convenient tool for keeping lists and multiple forms of structured or patterned data, even when no calculation needs to be performed over the data. In these applications, the grid—the organizational pattern and the set of operations it provides—plays a central role.

In what follows, I use these two features of the spreadsheet document form, the grid and the formula, as anchors for an exploration of the materialities of the form and the consequences for how work is conducted around it. To ground this discussion, I also draw from some empirical material gathered as part of a larger ethnographic study, one of those within which "spreadsheet events" figure prominently. This research was a collaboration with several colleagues and is reported in much more detail elsewhere (e.g., Mazmanian et al. 2013; Vertesi 2014b; Vertesi and Dourish 2011); most of the details are not immediately relevant here. Some background will be helpful, though.

Our work involved more than four years of immersive team ethnography with a distributed scientific collaboration oriented around a spacecraft in the outer solar system and managed by NASA. The project in which these scientists and engineers were engaged was huge in its scope; the overall process of conception, design, building, execution, data gathering, and analysis has already spanned decades and continues. Hundreds of people have worked on the project, bringing expertise in a huge number of disciplines, from astral navigation to planetary geophysics.

The challenge of planning spacecraft activities is analogous to allocating particle accelerator beam time or telescope time (Traweek 1988; McCray 2000) yet more complex: the engineering requirements, or constraints, of the spacecraft must be balanced against the demands of twelve instrument teams for observational time and resources. Notably, the collaboration is itself organized like a spreadsheet, with each row of the matrix being an instrument and each column being a discipline, and scientists categorized for the most part in individual cells at their intersection.

We conducted ethnographic work at the engineering center for the spacecraft mission, a contracted location staffed with NASA employees. The majority of the scientists were located at different institutions, universities, or research laboratories across the United States and Europe. Three times a year, the team flew in to a single location for face-to-face meetings for one week (Project Science Group meetings, or PSGs). During the PSGs, the team shifted gear to discuss issues of overarching concern, or to set strategic directions for the mission. The predominant tool for both types of activities, Microsoft Excel, and the methods of using it remained the same across meeting contexts.

Spreadsheets—some generated specifically for the occasion, and some that had originally been developed for other purposes (including grant proposals and previous planning purposes)—would often be projected onto screens at the front of the room, focusing the attention of attendees and creating a structure for the work of the group. This work often revolved around prioritization and activity planning—determining what science could be done with the limited time and limited resources available, and what sequences of spaceship operations could be practically achieved. These spreadsheets are generally not highly dynamic and do not depend on a complicated structure of formulae and calculation to do their work.

The notions of grid and formula so central to the spreadsheet's form each manifest their own materialities. I will take each in turn.

The Grid

A spreadsheet organizes and displays data items. There is no inherent reason that these should be aligned on a grid. A database doesn't employ a grid, nor does a word processor or a notetaker. In fact, it is even possible to imagine a spreadsheet application that adopts a more free-form layout mechanism—possible to imagine, but difficult. The grid plays such a central role in how spreadsheets operate in practice, and indeed many people adopt spreadsheets specifically because the layout structure matches needs for lists, tables, and data collections. The grid is fundamental to the materiality of the spreadsheet form; much of what we manipulate when we manipulate spreadsheets is actually the grid—navigating, extending, inserting, deleting, and merging grid columns and rows.

Granularity

The first consequence of the grid is that it is a structure within which the granularity of data is defined. The cell is the smallest manipulable object on the spreadsheet, and so it is the unit of action. Objects can be manipulated as groups, of course, but with different degrees of ease. Rows and columns can be manipulated as well, although less easily than individual cells; some operations can apply to arbitrary two-dimensional blocks, but these tend to be harder or more restricted. Noncontiguous blocks—that is, blocks of data made up of multiple subregions that do not abut or that take a shape other than simply rectangular—are generally impossible to address, select, or act on.

Laying out a spreadsheet, then, involves—implicitly if not explicitly—committing to a level of analysis and engagement with the data. It is a commitment that is not easily revised; reorganizing the level at which a data set is mapped onto the elements of a grid (*refactoring* the spreadsheet, in the language of programming) is well-nigh impossible. When we think about spreadsheets not simply as repositories of data, but also as instruments of analysis, tools of engagement, and structures of participation and collaboration, then we see that these questions of granularity can be highly significant. "Raw data is an oxymoron," observes Lisa Gitelman (2013), drawing attention to how sensor systems, scientific theories and models, and institutional arrangements of data collection have already made their presence felt before the first data item is recorded; spreadsheets too demonstrate commitments to particular plans of action or modes of analysis. This matters in part because spreadsheets are so often the medium of data sharing. Data are shared not least because of the idea that they can be put to new purposes and embedded in new systems or structures of working; indeed, that is part of what it means to *be* data in the first place, that they are independent of particular uses. Yet the granularity by which data are expressed, and the styles of manipulation that are opened up or closed down by the commitments to granularity expressed by the encoding into the grid, call into question the limits of any repurposing.

The Anticipatory Grid

Many of the spreadsheet events we observed at the space project centered on what was called the "tour spreadsheet," used to evaluate and plan science activities on upcoming parts of the mission. During the meeting, the spreadsheet was projected at the front of the room, worked on by a community of team members, and then presented to their colleagues. At the outset, however, the spreadsheet was presented as a series of blanks. The tours (mission flight segments) fit across the top column headers, and the science priorities were listed down the side. The cells themselves, however, were empty. The instructions from management were for each Discipline Working Group to sit down with a copy of the spreadsheet and fill in the section about their mission goals. As the week progressed, the spreadsheets were increasingly filled in, until all team members could present the conclusions of their team's discussion.

A spreadsheet starts not blank but empty. The grid shows a structure waiting to be filled in. Once a spreadsheet contains data, it also displays a structure by which those data will be talked about, debated, and managed. One might start at the top and work one's way down, one might start at one side and work one's way across, one might be driven by the gaps or by high-lights or by numerical values, but whichever way one approaches the data, the grid provides an organizing structure that speaks to what is about to be done.

In other words, the grid *anticipates*—both data and action. With respect to data, the grid does not simply hold information—it also shows where more information would go (and the limits of what would fit). The pattern that the grid imposes on data is an extensible pattern. As a spreadsheet is filled out, the blank cells invite further data entry and show how the pattern will extend itself. With respect to action, the grid anticipates how we will act on information. That is, when a spreadsheet is produced as the coordinating artifact for a meeting, it discloses the structure by which the meeting might be organized—row by row, column by column, in order of some value, and so on. These are anticipative orders in that they advertise what will happen next.

In this way, spreadsheets through their anticipatory properties become an important way of guiding discussion. They serve as a way of grounding conversation, dictating what's part of the conversation and what isn't. They also establish common ground and working priorities. The spreadsheet and its form, therefore, become part of the action. The meeting proceeds as individuals go around the room and add annotations to the empty antici-patory boxes based on their conversations.

One important aspect of anticipation lies in the notion of gaps—spaces among the data, either spaces into which the data will extend or spaces that remain to be filled in.

This structural property echoes aspects of Levi-Strauss's (1955) structural analysis of myth. Levi-Strauss adopts a method that breaks myths down into their smallest sentence elements and then lays them out in a grid to highlight their organizational structure. In his approach, the relationships between elements that the grid expresses are the topic of analysis, rather than the individual components. The space between elements is the space that holds meaning. Further, the gaps in the grid—the elements not repre-sented, the components not found—become structurally important and semantically telling. Similarly, what the grid embodies in organizational practice is an anticipation of completion and a set of structural relations between elements that make them make sense together.

Alignment and Separation

The grid holds things together—but not too close. It aligns but separates. It creates an intersection where cells, rows, and columns can all have identity—and, hence, ownership, authority, and control. The grid, then, separates data, and as it does so, separates responsibilities. But it also brings them into alignment—it abuts them, or it formulates them for comparison and for mutuality. So, for example, a spreadsheet can circulate within an organization with different parties adding their own rows or their own columns into a prescribed framework, so that the spreadsheet accumulates the perspectives of different entities while highlighting the relationships among them (e.g., in the way that they fit into the predefined structure). At the same time, it maintains the individual and separate identities and authorities of the elements of the text.

In other words, in an organizational setting in which different groups come together, an individual or a group can "own"—that is, be responsible for, or act as gatekeeper for—a spreadsheet, or a column of a spreadsheet, or a row of a spreadsheet, or even a cell of a spreadsheet.

Our observations certainly reflected these kinds of alignments. For instance, a tour spreadsheet might be circulated among different groups, gradually being filled out with new data, with each group responsible for a particular column. The columns are structured to be equivalent—each one is organized in the same way—but distinct. What's more, they are held to be aligned with each other but can be viewed as the individual responsibility of different groups. The intersection of different interests, or of different groups, or of different perspectives becomes visible within this grid. In my own academic department, we see this when it comes time to manage applications for graduate study, for example. A spreadsheet appears in which each row is an applicant and each column records some relevant information—areas of interest, test scores, and notes from interviews, for example. Different people care more about different factors; some place greater weight on test scores, some on letters of recommendation. We each have varying degrees of interest in different candidates. Various groups have responsibility for ensuring the accuracy of particular columns of data (some are verified by the campus admissions process, some detail the work of committees, while others describe individual faculty actions).

Collaborative activities are a coming together not simply of ideas or actions, but also of people, groups, and interests. The dual properties of alignment (bringing things into line with each other) but separation (retaining individual identities) provide potential support for this process of coming together.

The Formula

Although, as a digital document, the spreadsheet is oriented entirely around the grid, with the consequences as laid out above, the grid is not uniquely a feature of the spreadsheet as a digital form. The grid of the spreadsheet expands—albeit typically in more flexible ways—on the printed or hand-drawn table, which employs a grid in order to fix and relate data items on paper, on blackboards, or in other nondigital media. However, the same cannot be said of the second key component of the spreadsheet—the formula.

The formula is where computation explicitly enters the picture. Maintaining our focus, though, on the specifically performative and interactional dimensions of digital materialities, I want to explore how formulae arise as objects with which people need to grapple in spreadsheets—how they shape the material form of the digital object, constrain how we can interact with it, and create new structures within the interaction.

Direct Data and Derived Data

We can distinguish between different sorts of items on a spreadsheet. Some—let's call them *direct* objects—are numbers and pieces of text that have been entered directly—"Paul," 2016, 3.14. Of these, some are referred to in formulae—that is, they are the basis of calculations. So, if one of those direct data items—say the number 14,285—was part of a column of numbers, and another cell contained a formula to calculate the average of those numbers, then that 14,285 would be a direct object that is referred to in a formula and so gives rise to another value. Let's call those kinds of direct objects *base* objects and the others *nonbase*. At the same time, as well as direct objects, we have another class of objects that are generated by formulae—let's call those *derived* objects. The number that appears as the average of the column that contains 14,285—the value that is calculated as the average—is a derived object. It's a number that appears in the spreadsheet, but it appears as the result of a calculation rather than because it was entered directly.

With this terminology in place, consider a couple of aspects of the relationship between these different items.

The first is that the spreadsheet is generally designed to mask—visually, at least—the distinction between direct nonbase objects, direct base objects, and derived objects. As illustrated in figure 4.2, if I look at a spreadsheet grid and see the numbers 1, 2, 3, 4, and 10 laid out in front of me, I have no way of seeing whether that fifth number is a direct object (i.e., the number

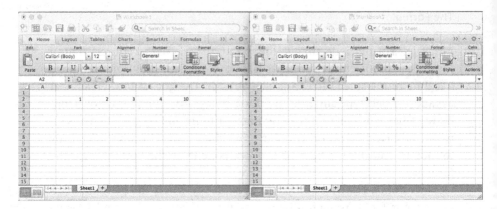

Figure 4.2
In one of these spreadsheets, the number 10 is a numeric literal. In the other, it is the result of a computation. There is no immediate visual distinction.

10 entered into the cell) or a derived object (the result of a formula adding the other four). Nor can I see whether a given number is being used to calculate another. Direct objects and derived objects are made visually identical, and indeed, in many ways, we are encouraged to treat them the same way, even though the conditions under which they come to be there may be very different, the patterns by which they might change are very different, and the kinds of things that might cause them to be erroneous are similarly very different. This is of course intentional: the goal of the spreadsheet is to resemble a paper document in which all figures and objects have the same status. Yet in terms of the material foundations that give rise to the spreadsheet as it is laid out on the screen (or printed on paper)—material issues like fragility, robustness, permanence, and so on—there is considerable variation here.

A second consideration is how elements slip from one category to another. In particular, any object—a direct object or a derived object—can become a base object as the spreadsheet develops. One need not mark out, in advance, one's intent to derive a new value from an old one, nor do anything to the old value in order to make it into a base object. In this, it is largely unlike most traditional programming languages, which distinguish structurally between different kinds of data and different ways in which data objects might be related. This is of considerable significance when we consider the dynamics and trajectories of spreadsheet development—the extent to which a spreadsheet can move from being a collection of data to a generalized tool. A data object is always potentially an abstraction, and its role within the system of dynamic calculations is not fixed or even necessarily certain at the outset.

Further, the relationship between base objects and derived objects is not one-to-one; a single base object can give rise to any number of derived objects, while a single derived object may depend on very many base objects. Consequently, small changes may have broad effects—effects that may not even be directly visible. When we take this together with the visual unavailability of patterns of relationships, we see that the materiality of the spreadsheet—in terms of its brittleness or robustness, and its responsiveness to change—is difficult to gauge or assess for a user or even for a spreadsheet's designer. Just to make things worse, a spreadsheet may not actually have a designer in any regular sense, but rather arise through the slow accretion of modifications and customizations, as documented by Nardi and Miller (1991).

Dynamism and Content

Another issue arises with derived values, this time connected not so much with the structural relationships that obtain between different elements on the spreadsheet, as with the relationships that obtain between the different forms that the spreadsheet might take—as an active spreadsheet on a computer screen, or as a stored document on a disk or in another storage medium. Think again of our simplistic spreadsheet that contains just the numbers 1, 2, 3, 4, and 10. I noted earlier that we cannot visually distinguish between one version of this in which these numbers are all direct values (let's call this variant A), and one in which the number 10 is a derived value (we'll call this variant B). A corollary of this is that, when the spreadsheet is stored in a file, the numbers that appear on the screen—1, 2, 3, 4, and 10—all somehow also appear on the file in variant A, but in variant B, the number 10 does not itself necessarily appear. In a simplistic but illustrative coding, variant A, stored on disk, is roughly something like:

cell(0,0)='1'; cell(0, 1)='2'; cell(0,2)='3'; cell(0,3)='4'; cell(0,4)='10'

That is, it contains a literal description of what is in each cell. In variant B, however, the file must say something like:

cell(0,0)='1'; cell(0, 1)='2'; cell(0,2)='3'; cell(0,3)='4';
cell(0,4)=formula(sum(range(cell(0,0):cell(0,3))

Here, the number that appears on the screen—10—does not appear in the file, because what appears in the file is a reference to the formula that generates the number but not to the number itself (see figure 4.2).

One particular importance of this is that it undercuts or questions our expectations about the nature of electronic documents. Discussions of the move of documents online, or the relative properties of online and offline repositories (e.g., Bannon and Bødker 1997; Trigg et al. 1999; Riles 2006) often point to searchability as a property of digital documents that can have a significant influence on their roles and their use (one that might be positive or negative in different circumstances). Similarly, theorists of documents (e.g., Levy 1994) have concerned themselves with issues of fixity and fluidity in addressing the question of how individuals and organizations might deal with, assess, understand, or act with documents, both physical and digital. However, think about these two concerns in the case of our trivially simple example. Since the 10 is never recorded in the document file itself, it is not searchable (either not at all, or not easily)—no amount of looking through the file will turn up the 10. The only way to search for it is within the framework of the calculation engine itself—so one can load the spreadsheet and search for the number, but one cannot search, Google-like, over a variety of spreadsheets to find the one with the 10 in it. Further, how should we think about the fixity of the 10 in the spreadsheet? On the one hand, it is utterly ephemeral—never stored, calculated again every time the document is loaded or processed, disappearing once more when the document is saved or unloaded or the application window closed. On the other, it is exactly as stable as the 1, the 2, the 3, and the 4, since it is generated from them; as long as they remain the same, so too does the 10.

The point here, with respect to our broader investigation of materialities, is that the different materialities of digital and nondigital spreadsheets do not simply consist in variations along a series of dimensions—more or less searchable, more or less stable, more or less fluid. The materialities of digital and nondigital spreadsheets *simply do not line up*. We can certainly compare them to each other, and we can talk about their relative abilities to respond to particular kinds of action or to support specific forms of practice, but our language about their different properties begins to break down quite quickly, in ways that show the specific materialities that each offers.

Documenting and Connecting

The spreadsheet has one other set of materialities that we have not yet examined. Spreadsheets have all the particular properties analyzed so far— grid-based structures, dynamic content based on formulae, the ability to be displayed at the front of the room and manipulated "on the fly" in spreadsheet events. But they are also digital documents, and as digital documents, they share key properties with other digital documents, not least those concerned with storage and reproduction. Like all digital documents, spreadsheets can be saved, named, stored, versioned, emailed, and copied. They can be uploaded to websites and downloaded to thumb drives.

The very mundanity of these spreadsheet properties makes them easy to neglect. And indeed, there is perhaps little to say about them on their own that has not already been said. What makes them interesting is how they intersect with some of the other properties of spreadsheets as organizational artifacts in practice.

The fact that they can be stored, transmitted, and copied means that spreadsheets used the way that we have described here—the spreadsheets that serve as working documents in meetings—can also leave those meetings. They do so in a number of ways, serving different purposes. In many cases, of course, they serve as records of activity—as documentation of the outcome of the working processes enacted in the meetings. As records of activity, they have a strongly outcome-oriented focus—they do not record debates, positions, or disagreements, and they do not express degrees of tentative accord. To the extent that meeting minutes document processes, spreadsheets document outcomes, which, in outcome-oriented organizations, can often make minutes seem superfluous. The materiality of the spreadsheet as a record of action reconfigures the ways in which we think we need to keep track of what's going on.

In addition to being a record of activity, the spreadsheet in these cases can simultaneously serve as a record of agreement. Consider again the case of the space science meeting. Making the kinds of decisions that those meetings are charged with—determining priorities for science planning in the face of limited opportunities—is a potentially fraught process. While collaborators are colleagues on one big team, they are also people with their own priorities and careers. Collecting data with instrument A means not collecting data with instrument B—and the people who work with instrument B also need to gather data to do their work, develop their models, publish in their journals, and progress in their own careers. The decision about which science is "better" and whose work "deserves" priority is, unsurprisingly, a complicated one, as it would be in any similar situation. So the spreadsheet can function not just as a record of activity but also as a record of an agreement that's been struck. It's in the spreadsheet, so that's what we're going to do.

This brings us to another critical set of properties of spreadsheets as they come out of meetings, which is perhaps less about spreadsheets-as-records and more about spreadsheets-as-templates. As digital documents, things that can be stored and retrieved, spreadsheets circulate not just in space (between people, places, and organizations) but also in time. Indeed, many if not most spreadsheets are not created from scratch but are made by modifying those that have come before. Perhaps the process we're enacting today is the same process we engaged in last year; well, then, let's start from last year's spreadsheet. Perhaps the process we're enacting today is a consequence of last month's process; let's take last month's spreadsheet and see if it provides a structure for what we need to do next.

So we can distinguish between different trajectories here. One is the way in which spreadsheets and similar artifacts become enrolled in the processes of verification, audit, and execution of decisions, moving essentially from one process to another—from a decision-making process, for example, to an assessment process. We saw examples of this in our studies of space science, where the spreadsheets that were generated during planning were then transformed into a "traceability matrix," a tool of project planning and management that is often used to make sure responsibilities are being met and goals achieved. So the very fact that the spreadsheet's grid structure aligns the form of the document with the form of the task—steps, timelines, recipes, and so on—means that the structure can become the baseline for new kinds of organizational documents, and through successive processes of transformation, the spreadsheet can move easily from one process (or one part of the process) to another.

A slightly different way in which this happens is when the spreadsheet becomes a record of prior action that allows for the action to be repeated. Eugenia Cacciatori (2008, 2012) documents cases of this sort in organizational life, Excel spreadsheets that serve as "memory objects" for prior organizational decisions and then become the template for how it should be done next. Documents become records; records become templates; templates become routines; routines become processes.

The idea that digital documents become templates that capture and then enforce regularities is not restricted to spreadsheets, of course. One corporation with which I have worked uses PowerPoint "slide decks" as its principal document format, for everything from project proposals to employee evaluations. These slides are generally never "presented"—nobody stands at the front of a room, laboriously working through the bullet points—but the well-understood genre of the powerpoint presentation structures the way in which information is gathered and entered—direct, punchy, and organized by slides and bullet points, which might themselves later be extracted or rearranged.

However, spreadsheets as a digital material have several properties that lend themselves particularly to this kind of use.

The first is, again, the centrality of the grid, although here in a different way than we have encountered it before. We have seen how the grid offers alignment, anticipation, and coordination, but it is also a means to make structure visible independently of content. That is, the grid is the basis around which the form of a spreadsheet emerges—a sorted table over in one place, a summary in another, here a calculated average, there a summed total. The spreadsheet contains data, but it contains them in a way that structures them for comprehension and for an understood relationship to likely needs and uses. This makes it easier to separate and extract the structure that generalizes across cases, and to turn a spreadsheet that was produced on one occasion of a process into a tool for reproducing that process.

The second is, perhaps unsurprisingly, a consequence of the formula. The formula expresses constraints and relationships between data items independently of the values that are present. It says "this cell should always contain the average of the data in that column," independently of the actual data items. It encodes futurity, separating things that might change (the data items themselves) from things that should not (the relationships that will hold between cells).

Since one never explicitly *needs* to use formulae, we can ask why, on some occasion, we might. Why use a formula to calculate the average rather than just calculating it ourselves and entering the data directly? Why add two numbers with a formula rather than just writing down the sum? Why use a formula to count the number of occurrences of a data item? Convenience is certainly one reason, although sometimes a formula is more complicated to enter than an obvious number. Avoiding errors might be another reason, although it's easy to make a mistake in a formula and hard to track it down again. But a third, perhaps overriding reason to use the formula is that we expect that the primary data may change. What we want is not a number, then, but a way of making sure that the number is always up-to-date. Using a formula turns the spreadsheet from a catalog of data items into an operable tool—from a collection of text and numbers to an application that can be used to achieve some end, over and over again in different cases and with different collections of data. The use of the formula is a way to express that the spreadsheet will continue to do its job even as its contents change; it is a way that stability is produced within the document form.

Formula and Grid

Formula and grid, then, are the source for the specific materialities of spreadsheet forms—their granularity and robustness, their transmissibility and fluidity, their dynamics and interactional limits. These materialities in turn shape and constrain the ways in which spreadsheets are used within organizations, institutions, or social settings, to do work, to achieve collective ends, to generate alignment, and to get things done. As a representational form, the spreadsheet comes with commitments to particular structures that create not only a way of seeing data but also a way of working with them.

Spreadsheet Alternatives

When we talk of spreadsheets as the digital materials incorporated into presentation-based meetings, as I have described, it is worth exploring the question, "spreadsheets rather than what?" That is, if we think about the configurations of these meetings in comparison to alternatives—those artifacts other than spreadsheets might be imagined to be an anchor of these meetings—then we may be able to see what specific features of the configurations are important, and what is signaled by them. At the same time, of course, and as we have seen, spreadsheets exist within an ecology of data representations—not just alternatives but also parallel forms that circulate within organizations and within institutional practices in ways similar to—but crucially not generally the same as—spreadsheets. Again, it is useful—particularly in understanding practical materialities—to think through the space of alternatives and see where the specificities of spreadsheets matter.

Spreadsheet rather than powerpoint. As documented by Knoblauch (2013), one of the primary technologies that anchors large meetings of this sort, and that is twinned with the same room and projector setup, is a powerpoint presentation. These sorts of presentations have become so much the norm in business, academic, and scientific settings that the presence of the spreadsheet instead is a marked condition of difference and something to be examined. The key difference, of course, between a meeting anchored by powerpoint-style presentation software and a meeting anchored by a spreadsheet is the spreadsheet's malleability. Some presentation software (e.g., Adobe Reader, which is often used in full-screen mode to run presentations) provides no facilities for updating or editing the document at all; other presentation software (e.g., Microsoft's PowerPoint) distinguishes between "editing mode" and "presentation mode," so that in presentation mode, the document remains fixed. The meetings we have described are focused on document editing; the use of spreadsheets focuses attention on the idea that what is going on is not simply communication but deliberation, and that the document that anchors the meeting is one to be not simply produced but transformed within the context of the meeting itself.

Spreadsheet rather than word processor.   If the goal is simply to focus on editing rather than on display, then one might imagine that other editing tools, such as a word processor, could be used (or even a powerpoint-style tool running in edit mode). Most word processors have facilities for editing tables and grids of the sort that we have observed (they do not incorporate the automatic processing or formula facilities of conventional spreadsheets, but as noted, those facilities are frequently not used in the spreadsheets that anchor these meetings). The tables that can be managed in a spreadsheet, however, tend to be larger and more complex than those that can be easily handled in a word processor or in a presentation tool. Further, the specific manipulations of a grid that a spreadsheet provides—splitting, windowing, and so on—are features of spreadsheet software but not of word processor or presentation software. This suggests then that the complexities of both data and interaction specifically support the use of spreadsheet software rather than alternatives.

Spreadsheet rather than whiteboard.   If the central concern is that the meeting be anchored by grid-organized data, and that data be editable and updatable, one might imagine that electronic tools are not needed at all, and that a blackboard or whiteboard at the front of the room—or even a large wall-mounted sheet of paper—would be sufficient. This would allow for a grid to be prepared and then filled-in, and (in the case of the whiteboard or blackboard) to be revised as the discussion develops. Again, we might note the problems of complexity that were suggested by the comparison to a word processor, but thinking of what the spreadsheet provides over the whiteboard highlights another important aspect of the meeting, which is that what it produces is not only a set of decisions but a distributable, archival artifact that expresses those decisions. That is, the spreadsheet has a life both before and after the meeting—it can be prepared, shared, and collectively produced in advance, and it can be stored, archived, e-mailed, and distributed electronically afterward. While the document anchors the meeting, its lifetime extends beyond that meeting, and connects the meeting to other aspects of organizational life.

Offline rather than online spreadsheets. Finally, here, although I have spoken generically of "spreadsheets," the meetings that my colleagues and I observed used one particular spreadsheet software package in particular—Microsoft's Excel. As part of the Microsoft Office software suite, Excel is a leading software product that is widely distributed and available on both Mac and PC platforms, so it is unsurprising perhaps that Excel would be the spreadsheet of choice (other than, say, Numbers, part of Apple's iWork suite.) It is still useful to consider, however, what Excel offers over alternatives, and one of the most intriguing alternatives is the spreadsheet functionality available in cloud-based services, in which spreadsheets are hosted on servers to support collaboration among distributed groups. Given that in spreadsheet-based meetings we have observed, meeting participants will often have a copy of the same spreadsheet open on their own laptops for ease of viewing, one might imagine that an online server-hosted spreadsheet would be a more convenient tool. An online spreadsheet would be a "live" view of the master document, maintaining synchrony automatically. It would be widely available not just for viewing, but also for editing, allowing more than one person to update the document at once. It would be automatically archived, and it would be even more widely available than an Excel document, which, although it can be edited on both Macs and PCs, cannot always be edited (and sometimes not even viewed) on mobile devices such as tablets and phones. However, what Excel critically provides here is a single point of control. As a single-user tool, Excel, projected at the front of the room, configures the room around a single spreadsheet that is being edited by just one person. An online spreadsheet might allow anyone to edit, but in doing so would open up control of the document from a single person representing the collective perspective of the group to the many individuals or constituencies within the group, who each might have their own ideas of how things should develop. In other words, the very feature of an online spreadsheet that is often touted as its central advantage—that it can provide multiple simultaneous viewers and editors—is a disadvantage here, to the extent that it disperses the collective attention and collective voice of the group as a whole.

Spreadsheet Materialities

In the previous chapter, the discussion of emulation revolved around what makes those representations effective in specific systems. There, the relationship between different representational systems—those of the programs of both emulating and emulated computer, for example, or those that link a program and its execution—proved useful in illustrating the question of representational materiality and its link to systems of practice, in that case, the practices of programming and system design. In this chapter, links between representation and practice have again been at the forefront, although in the case of the spreadsheet, the scales of action and the terms of reference are quite different. Here, acts of representation are those engaged in by end-users, not by programmers, and indeed end-users are the primary focus of the software design. Here, too, they must be embedded in other forms of professional or working practice, such as the work of planetary scientists, but also the work of accountants, managers, reviewers, professors, or other people who encounter spreadsheets as things they use to get their work done. Here, we have seen collective processes—those of groups gathered together, those linked by organizational collaborations, or those linked by professional practice—playing a more significant role. And here we have seen a greater role opportunity for a form of emergent, collaborative practice to arise—not formalized in advance but developed as needs require, as people figure out how they want to put the technology to work to meet their needs. Representation remains at the center of the picture, but the picture changes significantly. New material constraints emerge as important, but the fundamental ideas of the digital as material are much the same, brought into this new domain.

Whereas chapter 3's discussion of emulation focused especially on the technologies that make digital representations work, here our attention has turned more toward human and organizational practices around digital materials. I have sought to draw attention to how we work with digital materials, and how we craft bridges between their capacities and potentials on the one hand, and our needs and expectations on the other. Sometimes, of course, this is a process of figuring out what those capacities and potentials are, and of revising (or discovering new) needs and expectations. Neither is entirely predefined. Our own requirements and demands shift over time, but even fixed software systems can be used in new ways, embodied in new systems, deployed in new networks, and paired with new components, which mean that the software system itself is highly malleable too, even without resorting to end-user programming (Nardi 1993). The materialities of the digital help set the terms for the emergence of specific kinds of human and organizational practice, but they do not define it nor are they always immutable.

The spreadsheet case has also provided us with a place to start unpicking and documenting specific materialities. The goal is not so much to produce a catalog as to figure out how to adopt a useful analytic perspective that helps us see where different kinds of materialities arise in the encounter between people and technology. Again, as emphasized in the opening chapter, the goal is not simply to say, "Look, the digital is material" but rather to uncover in what ways, and with what consequences, particular digital forms have particular material properties—not just to dub them material but to analyze them as exhibiting materialities. We have seen several: granularity, as something that is largely fixed when the spreadsheet is initially designed; the dynamics of reference, and the way that it governs the responsiveness of the application and the relationship between what is on-screen and what is stored; the mutability of object forms, and the consequences for our expectations of fixedness and fluidity in the data we encounter; the clustering of different kinds of collective reference, and the implications for how a complex problem might be mapped onto a grid; transportability as a key feature of how not just data but also responsibility and record move around; alignment as a tool for maintaining relations between independent data objects and their referents; and so on. These specific materialities become visible and consequential in the analysis of the encounter between people and spreadsheets. They begin to illustrate what matters when we adopt a materialist stance toward the digital.

In the next chapter, I adopt a similar stance toward a different technological assembly, that of the database. Like spreadsheets, databases are a generic form rather than a specific application, although, also like the spreadsheet, a range of conventions applies. Unlike spreadsheets, databases are often barely visible to end-users, embedded within information processes, network service back ends, and other places where they are hidden from the view of end users as infrastructure, at least until they break down (Bowker and Star 1999). Databases can be read as the core technology of our contemporary digital life; their materialities, then, are ones that may shape more than might be apparent at first glance.

5   No SQL: The Shifting Materialities of Database Technology

If spreadsheets, the topic of the previous chapter, open up for us the ways in which representational materialities might be braided together with social practice, databases do so in a way that is even more thoroughgoing. Databases are not objects of direct user attention in quite the same way as spreadsheets; fewer people spend their time interacting with them directly. On the other hand, databases are core technologies that support and lie behind so many other systems, from e-commerce websites to university teaching schedules, blogging platforms, and online libraries. Of the twenty-seven browser tabs open on my computer as I write this paragraph, at least eighteen of them show websites backed by databases. Databases route our e-mail and our tax documents, deliver maps to our phones and jury summonses to our doors, and track our deliveries and our flights.

Databases, then, are not simply a widely deployed technology; they are the basis on which corporations, government agencies, and other institutions relate to us, and perhaps too the way in which we relate to them, to each other, and to the world around us. As recordkeeping becomes increasingly digital, we increasingly understand, talk about, think about, and describe the world as the sort of thing that can be encoded and represented in a database. When the database is a tool for encoding aspects of the world, the world increasingly seems to us as a collection of opportunities for "databasing"; and as Michael Castelle (2013) notes, the forms of databasing in which we engage are ones that are entwined with the structures and patterns of organizational life.

Databases have been of interest to researchers in software studies since the early formulations of that research program. Recall from chapter 2 that databases particularly play a central role in Lev Manovich's (2001) analysis of new media forms in *The Language of New Media*. Manovich proposes that the database is the central cultural form of the twenty-first century, as the novel was for the nineteenth and film for the twentieth. In talking of, say, film as a cultural form, Manovich means more than simply that film was an important media category; he argues instead that filmic or cinematic concerns—visuality, narrative, montage, diegesis, linearity, point of view, and so on—are cultural or symbolic tropes by which we "read" media. Similarly, when he suggests that the database is becoming a new cultural form, he means that the database animates a new set of considerations of form, aesthetic, and structure in cultural production.

The fundamental move from the cinematic form to the database form is a move from narrative and linearity to relationality. The database has no inherent narrative structure; there is no natural sequentiality to objects in a database. What structure the database provides is one of relations—between objects and their properties, from object to object, and so on. Manovich's concern is not with the media themselves but with their symbolic forms (so, for example, he cites the films of Peter Greenaway as being database-like), but he uses the notion of the database particularly to unpack the form of "new" or digital media. So, for instance, hypertext and video games are both database-driven forms in his analysis. Hypertext eschews conventional linear text for a more free-form exploration of associations as one moves from element to element clicking on links. Video games open up narrative sequences and depend on associations between actions and responses in the game world. These are both cases of the database form, in Manovich's analysis.

While noting aspects of the history of databases and their structures, Manovich deliberately sets to one side the question of just what the database is. He focuses on form rather than on mechanism, emphasizing collection and relationality as key elements of the database, in whatever way they are implemented. Manovich's argument is concerned with the abstract form of data-driven media rather than with the materiality of database representations. Nonetheless, the compelling force of his argument supports a materialist investigation that takes seriously the question of just what the database is and does. If we read databases as doing more than structuring cultural and aesthetic production and see them also as thoroughly embedded within organizational, institutional, and state processes, then the nature of the database as a representational tool, including its capacities, gaps, and limits, comes to matter. Accordingly, this is the topic for this chapter.

As it happens, we find ourselves at an especially interesting techno-cultural moment with respect to just this inquiry, as recent years have seen some radical reconsideration of the relationship between database functions, infrastructural arrangements, and informational practice, which make it particularly appropriate to inquire further into how the notion of associative media might be grounded in specific notions of the database and specific materialities of digital forms. Some of this has come about through the development and deployment of very large-scale web-based data platforms (e.g., DeCandia et al. 2007); some has come about through the burgeoning interest in so-called big data technologies (e.g., Alsubaiee et al. 2014). Examining the materialities of the database form uncovers a range of historical specificities that help contextualize broader arguments about digital media, and that also illuminate the significance of contemporary shifts, dislocations, disruptions, and evolutions.[1]

With that as a backdrop, the goals for this chapter are threefold. First, I set out to examine the specific materialities of the database form in the sense that Manovich and others have examined. That is, I show how the specific kinds of relationality expressed in database forms are historically and materially contingent. Second, I explore some contemporary developments in which the evolution of hardware platforms, database technologies, and media experiences are tightly entwined, partly in order to illustrate the relevance of an argument based in media materiality and partly to document a slightly different pattern emerging in the context of large-scale networked digital media of the sort increasingly familiar to us online. Third, I use this case to expand the broader argument developed so far about the consequences of digital materialities, extending it from the interactional to broader concerns about the way in which digital media forms are knitted in with institutional action.

Database

The term *database* is often used ambiguously. This is not simply a complaint about, say, the black boxing or deferral of the term in Manovich's analysis, but is true in the technical domain too, where the term has different uses at different times. Purely within that domain, we can distinguish between three levels at which the term is sometimes used.

The first level is simply a collection of data. In informal parlance, the term *database* is sometimes used simply to denote the amassing of data or information, perhaps synonymously with *data set*. Yet, database, as a technical term, is not merely a quantitative measure of data.

1. This approach is in line with the forms of analysis that Manovich has subsequently developed, although he has focused his attention largely on the applications involved in the production of contemporary digital media rather than on core infrastructures like database technology (Manovich 2013).

A database as used in computer science, under a second level of description, is a collection of data that is, critically, encoded and organized according to a common scheme. As we will see, databases may employ different sorts of schemes or arrangements for their data, including record structures, tree structures, and network structures. Arranging data into a common format makes each data item amenable to a common set of operations—data items can be sorted, compared, collated, grouped, summarized, processed, transformed, and related because a common format is employed. At this level, then, the database comprises two components—the data and some description of the organizational scheme by which they are formatted.

The third common use of the term *database* is to refer to the software system that implements this relationship between data format and data. In computer science, these are more formally called database management systems (DBMS). Software systems like Oracle Database (often just called Oracle), FileMaker Pro, and MySQL are database management systems—that is, they provide programmers and end-users with the tools they need to describe data formats and to process data collections according to those formats.

In summary, a database management system implements a database, which organizes a collection of data. The term *database* is variously used to refer to each of these three elements, although it is useful and important to distinguish between them. In particular, the common data formats, incorporated into databases and implemented in database management systems, are worthy of more attention.

Data Formats and the Relational Model

The primary challenge of database development is the identification of a common format for data items or objects. If a database is to encode information about people and their belongings, for example, how should we represent people, and how should we represent the objects they possess, and how should we represent the relationship between the two?

Aspects of this problem are specific to particular databases and applications; for instance, representing people and their belongings will probably be done differently by an insurance company than by a moving company. Other aspects of the data modeling problem, though, are more generic. Different database management systems and database technologies have offered different styles of representation. The challenge is to find an approach that is rich enough to handle all the different applications that might be developed and uniform enough to handle each of them in the same way.

The most common approach in contemporary database systems, in widespread use since the 1970s, is called the relational model (Codd 1970). In a relational system, data are organized into tables. Each column of a table encodes information of a particular sort—for instance, a table might have one column for someone's name, and a second column for their social security number. Each row of a table encodes a relation (hence the name *relational*) between data items; for instance, one row expresses the relationship between the name "John Smith" and the social security number 123-45-6789, while another expresses that relation between the name "Nancy Jones" and the social security number 987-65-4321. A relational database might comprise many different tables, which together relate different items of data to each other—within a single database, for example, one table might relate names to social security numbers, a second might relate social security numbers to years and tax returns, while a third relates years to total tax receipts. Such a model has many useful properties. First, it fulfills the requirement that it be flexible enough to accommodate a wide range of applications within a single generic data model. Second, it allows a small number of operations to be defined that apply across those tables (insert a new row, remove a row, find all rows with a specific value, update a value in a row, etc.). Third, it corresponds to a mathematical description (the relational calculus) that can be used to analyze the properties of specific operations. Fourth, it supports a particular set of optimizations (database normalizations) that can be shown to improve system performance.

Since its introduction in the 1970s in IBM's influential System R, the relational model has become the dominant one in commercial and independent database technologies (Astrahan et al. 1976). In parallel, the Structured Query Language (SQL), a programmable notation for database access and manipulation that was designed in concert with the relational model, has, similarly, become both a conventional and a formal standard for database programming. The fact that IBM introduced the relational model will be important to our story here, given that in the 1970s, IBM was simultaneously in the business of hardware design, software production, and bureau computer services. Before we return to that question, though, we should place the relational model in more context by noting that, although it became the dominant model, it was never the only one. Alternatives exist—some that predated the relational model, and some that have been developed since. Examining these alternatives briefly will provide some context for understanding the materiality of relational data processing.

Alternatives to the Relational Model

For comparative purposes, let's briefly consider alternatives to the relational
data model. The goal here is not to be exhaustive, by any means, but to set
out some alternatives as a basis for exploring the specific materialities of
different forms as they arise in real systems. I focus on three models in
particular—hierarchical, network, and attribute-value approaches.

In a hierarchical model, the fundamental structure is not a table, as
in the relational model, but a tree (and in particular, the inverted trees
common in computer science, with a single object at the "top," or *root* of
the tree.) Objects are connected in tree structures, which look rather
like family trees; each data object is potentially the *parent* of a number of
other objects, which can in turn be parents themselves. A tree is a recursive
data structure in that each subcomponent—that is, the collection of elements grouped under any given data node—is itself a tree. A tree structure
supports a range of operations, including moving up and down the
tree, moving and merging its *branches*, and performing searches over sub-
units. Just as a relational data model does not specify any particular relationship between the objects that are placed in a table, so too the hierarchical
model does not specify what relationship is implied by the "parent/child"
relationship. It might describe part/whole relationships (as in the phyloge-
netic tree that organizes organisms into species, genus, family, and so
forth), or it might describe institutional relationships (such as a tree of organizational reporting relationships or of academic advisers and graduate
students).

As figure 5.1 illustrates, a network model relaxes the constraints even
further. In a network model, data objects are connected to each other in
arbitrary structures by links, which might have a range of *types*. One sort of
link, for instance, might be an IS-A link, which connects an object representing something in the world with an object representing the kind of
thing that it is. The statement "Clyde is an elephant," for example, might
be encoded in the database by an IS-A link that connects a "Clyde" object
to an "elephant" object, which might find itself similarly linked by objects
representing other elephants while it also connects via a different sort of
link, a HAS-A link, to objects representing "tail," "trunk," and "hide." The
result is a network of interrelated objects that can be navigated via links
that describe relationships between objects and classes of objects. As in the
hierarchical model, links have no predefined meaning; just as database programmers creates a series of objects that match the particular domains they
are working with, so too do they develop a set of appropriate link types as
part of their modeling exercise.

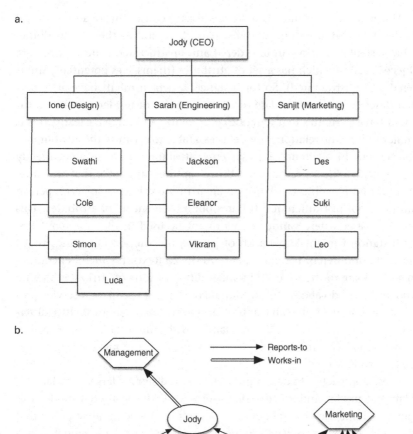

Figure 5.1
Representing data in (a) hierarchical and (b) network data formats

Although network models relax the linkage constraints of a hierarchical model, the attribute-value systems relax them still further. An attribute-value system comprises an unordered and unstructured collection of data objects, each of which has a set of attributes (themselves potentially unordered and unstructured). So for instance, a person might have attributes that describe nationality, date of birth, and city of residence, while a car might have attributes that describe color, make, and model. Clearly, this is similar to how the relational model uses a table to organize the attributes of objects, but in attribute-value systems, attributes are associated directly with specific objects, rather than being captured in a table that will store data for multiple objects. That is, in an attribute-value system, each person can have not just different attributes but a different *set* of attributes. This matches cases where various items might be used in disparate contexts; for instance, I might know a lot of people, but the sorts of things that I know about different people depend on the contexts in which I encounter them or relate to them, so I remember different sorts of attributes about a student than I do about a professional colleague, a friend, or a service professional. The attribute-value approach is very broad, and in slightly different contexts, it goes by different names; with minor variations, it is also known as entity-attribute-value and as key-value, although the core ideas are the same.

These approaches to data representation and storage largely predate the relational model. Indeed, the development of the relational model was motivated not least by the desire to develop a unified approach, one that provided a stronger separation between an abstract data model and a machine-specific representation, which was seen to be a problem of network models, for example. Further, Codd's efforts in building his relational database systems on top of an algebraic foundation that could be reasoned about mathematically made it attractive for high-performance and high-reliability settings. The alternative approaches persisted, however, particularly in settings like artificial intelligence (AI) research, where they were seen as more "natural" approaches that could be used to model human knowledge practice. Indeed, hierarchical and networked models are more likely to be seen now in AI textbooks than in database textbooks, while attribute-value mechanisms were seen as so foundational to AI research that they were incorporated into basic infrastructures like the Lisp programming language (Steele and Gabriel 1993).

In the relationship between these alternative forms, though, we can find the first hint of how specific materialities of representational models necessitate an elaboration of Manovich's argument about databases as cultural forms. The fundamental element on which Manovich's database analysis rests, the relationship between abstract descriptions and specific data items, clearly is a feature of the dominant model of data representation, the relational model, but not an inherent feature of databases per se. It is more specifically grounded not just in the digital in general but in particular kinds of computational platforms—and as those platforms shift, the foundations of his analysis do too. Before we consider those shifts, though, let's examine some of the specific materialities of the relational form.

The Materialities of Relational Data

One key feature of the relational model, in comparison to the others, is the separation it creates between the structure and the content of a database. The structure of the database—technically known as a schema—defines the set of tables and the columns of the table, along with the types of data (such as numbers, dates, and text items) that each column will contain. The content of the database is the actual data that get stored in each table—the data items that make up each record. Defining or constructing a database is the process of setting up the database schema. Subsequently using the database is the process of adding, removing, updating, and searching the data records that make up its content. The separation is both temporal and spatial. It is spatial because the database schema is represented separately from the data; it is temporal because the schema must be set up before any data can be entered (and because, in many cases, the schema is difficult or impossible to change once data entry has begun.)

In hierarchical databases and network databases, by contrast, there is no separation between structure and content. In these models, data items are directly related to each other; in the relational model, the relationships between items are encoded in their mutual relationships as defined by the database schema. Hierarchical and network databases—as well as attribute-value systems—do not (in general) reify structure and manage it as a separate concern.

Relational databases derive several advantages from the separation of structure and content. First, the separation means that database operations are made uniform, because they will all fit with a predefined structure. Second, it allows the system to optimize database performance; since it knows in advance what sort of data will be processed, efficient algorithms that are specialized to defined structures can be employed rather than more flexible algorithms that tend to be less efficient.

The significance of the separation between structure and content lies in the radical differences in their malleability. Content is infinitely malleable; indeed, that is the point of the database in the first place. The openness, flexibility, and extensibility of a database lie in the content that fits within the schema. That schema itself, however, is much more rigid. While there are mechanisms in most relational databases for columns to be added to or deleted from the database structure, such changes are limited and invalidate data contents, limiting their uses still further.

One of the features of the database as a generic form—as a tool, as a research product, or as a platform for collaboration—is its provisionality. Manovich celebrates the database's resistance to narrative, in comparison to film and literary forms; the database, he argues, is open to many different narratives since the user can traverse it freely. In addition to this narrative provisionality, it also offers an archival provisionality, since the database can be extended and revised, its contents continually updated; indeed, we generally think of databases as dynamic and evolving rather than fixed and complete. For instance, we saw in the previous chapter how spreadsheets are incorporated into patterns of punctuated archiving more easily than databases. Narrative and archival provisionality, however, are primarily associated with content. The structure of a relational database is much more resistant to change. So the database is provisional, but only with limits; it is open ended, but only in the terms originally laid down in its structure. It invites new users in, as viewers, as editors, and as contributors, but the structure of the schema largely defines and constrains the conditions of viewing, editing, and contributing.

When we consider the materiality of database forms, then, we need to consider it in light of the principle that we encountered in chapter 1: the database is composed entirely of bits, but those bits are not equal. Some are more easily changed than others; some carry more significance than others; some exhibit more flexibility, and others more rigidity. A database is not simply a collection of bits, any more than an airplane is simply a collection of atoms. If the database is malleable, extensible, or revisable, it is so not simply because it is represented as electrical signals in a computer or magnetic traces on a disk; malleability, extensibility, and revisability depend too on the maintenance of constraints that make *this specific collection* of electrical signals or magnetic traces work as a database; and within these constraints, new materialities need to be acknowledged.

The significance of the materialities of relational data does not lie solely within the domain of its structural forms. Those structural forms come too with specific procedural demands; indeed, the ability to encode data and the ability to operate on those encodings are twin aspects of the relational model. In fact, it is in the area of database processing that we find the seeds of contemporary shifts in database materiality, so I turn now to the question of processing relational data.

Processing Relational Data

Relational databases model their data in tabular form. Like a row in a printed table, a single entry in a table describes a relation among items of data. Basic operations on these tables include changing an item of data, inserting a new relation (that is, a row in the table), or deleting a relation. Yet, many of the actions that we might want to perform in an application using the database involve more than one database operation. For instance, transferring money from one bank account to another might involve changing the values of two different relations in a table (the relation describing the balance of the originating account and the relation describing the balance of the destination account). These multioperation actions are problematic because they create the opportunity for inconsistency, from the application's point of view (e.g., a point at which the money exists in both accounts, or in neither account), if the action should be interrupted partway through, or if another action should be carried out simultaneously. Accordingly, databases are designed to cluster primary actions together into *transactions*, which group basic operations into indivisible logical units that correspond to application actions.

In traditional relational databases, the execution of transactions is held to what are known as the ACID properties. ACID is an acronym for the four fundamental properties of transaction processing—atomicity, consistency, isolation, and durability. These are the properties that a processing system for relational database transactions must maintain:

Atomicity means that transactions are carried out as an indivisible unit—either the entire transaction is performed, or none of it.

Consistency means that the database is in a consistent state at the end of the execution of each transaction (and hence, before the execution of any other).

Isolation means that transactions are executed as if each is the only transaction being performed in the system at a time, or in other words, the execution of any transaction is independent of, or isolated from, the concurrent execution of any other transaction.

Durability means that once a transaction has been executed, its effects are permanent. A user may choose to change the data, but no internal action of the database will "undo" a transaction once it is committed.

The ACID properties were first defined by James Gray (1978, 1981). They have become the touchstones for database implementation so that, as new execution models and new software architectures arise, maintaining the ACID properties ensures the consistency and effectiveness of applications designed to rely on database functionality. While ACID is not the only database consistency regime, it is the most widely adopted model, particularly for high-reliability applications.

The ACID properties describe the constraints that govern the execution of transactions within a relational database system. In doing so, they establish a link between the relational data model—which, for Codd, was characterized by both its universality and its mathematical foundations—and a processing model, which pays more attention to algorithms and performance. Although the terms are used almost interchangeably to refer to conventional database processing (given that almost all relational databases are transactional, and almost all transactional databases relational), they draw attention to different aspects of the systems.

Castelle (2013) has pointed to transactional processing as an important link between organizational practice and technological systems, compellingly suggesting that this is one important consideration in accounting for the success of the relational model. My immediate concern here with the transactional model is in terms of the link it provides from the relational model to specific execution contexts and their material arrangements.

The Materialities of Relational Data Processing

As I noted earlier, the relational model was developed by researchers at IBM, and first enshrined in an IBM software product, System R. System R was notable for many reasons; it introduced the first version of the programming system (SQL) that is most commonly used with relational database systems, and it demonstrated that the relational model could be implemented efficiently. In many ways, it is the progenitor of the vast majority of contemporary database systems.

IBM, however, was not only a software provider; it was also an influential hardware developer. IBM's hardware was both sold and rented to clients, while at the same time it also provided bureau computer services. Database services were a critical component of IBM's business. With a new data model and transaction processing framework in hand, then, IBM was also in a position to develop its computer architectures to enhance performance in executing relational database transactions, and to define the benchmarks and measures by which database systems would be evaluated.

Indeed, we could reasonably argue that the identification and definition of the ACID properties enabled, or at least fueled, the development of the database field, or what we might call the ACID regime, which encompasses both the software and the hardware developments that enable high transaction-throughput systems. The ACID properties provide a processing framework for relational data, and turn attention to transactions-per-second as a measure of system performance. Further, they set the context for the development of hardware features (cache lines, storage system interfaces, etc.), which are themselves assessed by their effect on benchmarks. The database industry adopted as an initial measure of performance a benchmark (known as TP1) that had originated inside IBM, so that the relational data model, the ACID processing framework, the design of hardware to execute it efficiently, and the use of a standard model for evaluating performance in terms of transactions became mutually reinforcing.

In the ACID regime we find at work highly interwoven sociomaterial configurations. High-performance database architectures are designed to take advantage of the latest hardware and machine architecture developments, while hardware designs emerge to support the needs of database software implementations. Similarly, database systems are developed to meet the needs of business and commercial applications, needs that commercial applications develop around the capacities and possibilities of database systems. The material configurations of database technologies—the architectures of hardware platforms and the capabilities they offer when twinned with appropriately designed software systems—can be seen as woven into the very fabrics of organizational life and commercial arrangements, if we see the cost of database communications and integration as a component of the "transaction costs" that Ronald Coase (1937), in his classic paper, outlines as fundamental to the shaping of organizational structure in a market economy. Coase argues that there are costs associated with the execution of transactions in a marketplace, beyond the basic price of goods and services. As an analogy, if I want to depend on an external agency to clean my house, I have to make my house "cleanable" by a third party, for instance, by separating fragile items from regular household goods (something that takes time and hence costs money). Or, to delegate my travel arrangements to a travel agent, I need to go through the process of explicating my previously implicit and subtle preferences about airlines, flight times, preferred routes, and layover arrangements. On this basis, Coase shows that the question of whether a particular function (say, document management in a law firm, catering facilities in a university, or IT support in a government agency) should be supported in-house or should be outsourced to the marketplace depends on the relationship between the costs of actually providing the function and the transaction costs involved in letting the market handle it. In highly technologized operations, database interoperation is certainly a relevant factor; not only are there transaction costs involved in establishing the compatibility of two databases, but there may also be costs associated with the loss of, or monitoring of, the ACID properties when functions are divided across two or more distinct database systems. But this means we can trace a bidirectional relationship between, on one hand, computer system structure and, on the other, the organizations that employ them.

Shifting Materialities

So, the notion of the "database," which has occupied the attention of theorists in the software studies movement, needs to be unpacked. Databases abound; different data models have disparate constraints and are differently adapted to hardware platforms that are themselves evolving.

The current moment is a particularly interesting one for investigating this topic, precisely because a number of the elements are currently undergoing some reconsideration. Although there have always been alternatives to the dominant relational model, a recent specific and coordinated shift in business models, application demands, database technologies, and hardware platforms are reframing the database in ways that highlight the relevance of a material reading of database practice. Two trends have contributed to this. The first is the harnessing of distributed processing for internet services; the second is the increasing interest in big data applications.

We can start to understand this by thinking about questions of performance. What does it take for database performance to improve? One source of improvements is on the software side, with the development of new algorithms and data structures that allow database processing to be optimized. In parallel, though, hardware changes have been extremely important. So, another source is the higher performance of new processor designs, as well as the steady—at least until recently—progress characterized by Moore's law. A third is improved memory and input/output architectures that can shunt data between storage systems and the processor at higher rates.

The most significant performance improvements in recent years, however, have been associated with the introduction of some form of parallelism, in which multiple operations can be carried out simultaneously. Some of the earliest parallel computers were those that introduced the ability to perform operations on more than one data item at a time. *Vector*, or *array*, processors that began to appear commercially in the 1970s were optimized for processing large amounts of data in fairly predicable ways; they are often applied in scientific computing where large amounts of data need to be subjected to the same amounts of processing (e.g., in signal analysis or in simulations of physical phenomena). These tend to be of less immediate value for database processing, however. Instead, database technologies have often depended on forms of parallelism where separate instruction streams can be carried out at once.

These forms of parallelism are commonly characterized by the degree to which other resources are shared between the data streams. At the smallest level, a single processor might have multiple functional units that can operate simultaneously, often for integer or floating-point mathematical operations, for example. Here, everything is shared, right down to the instruction stream, but different parts of different instructions might be executed at once. At the next level, *multicore processors*—processors that include multiple "cores," or independent subprocessors—share all the resources of a computer system, including memory, cache, and input/output devices, but might be executing multiple instruction streams or multiple programs simultaneously. Almost all contemporary personal computers and smartphones employ multicore processors. At the next stage of parallelism, multiple processors might be connected and share access to the same memory, perhaps via a shared bus; or, at the next stage, multiple processors might have their own memories and their own buses but be connected to the same storage devices (e.g., disks).

At each step in this progression, less and less is shared between the parallel elements of the system. The ultimate expression of this is known as *shared-nothing* architecture, in which a computer system is forged out of a range of independent computers linked by a network. Shared-nothing architectures have arisen in different areas but have been driven particularly by the need to support web applications with potentially millions of simultaneous, loosely connected users all over the world. Databases, on the other hand, were not one of the core application areas for which people adopted shared-nothing architectures (although, as it happens, the term *shared-nothing* was coined by database researcher Michael Stonebraker in an early article that pointed out the benefits and the problems of this architecture for database design [1986]).

In the early days of the web, large-scale shared-nothing clusters, often comprising standard desktop PCs, proved a useful way to address these applications, since they can be easily scaled up or down (by adding or removing computers) and lend themselves well to serving many users simultaneously.

The challenge, of course, is to coordinate the action of these devices and to be able to program them to operate in concert. In 2004, Google engineers Jeffrey Dean and Sanjay Ghemawat published a description of the programming model on which Google bases its software services (Dean and Ghemawat 2004). The mechanism, known as MapReduce, was not in itself startlingly novel, and yet, in context, it has proved to be tremendously influential. The context here includes contemporaneous descriptions of a compatible distributed file system (Ghemawat et al. 2003), the highly visible success of Google itself, and the shift in hardware platforms associated with Google and Google-like services. Google's approach to hardware is not to rely on high-performance mainframe systems, but rather to harness massive numbers of medium-powered computers, often stock PCs. This approach has been adopted by many other corporations. MapReduce provides a programming model and an infrastructure that allows computations to be distributed across and coordinated among these large and variable computing clusters. Arguably, at least for a range of applications, systems like MapReduce provide high-performance computing platforms without the massive capital investments required for high-performance hardware. The devil lies in the details, though, and in particular here the details of the hedge "for a range of applications."

The basis of the MapReduce mechanism lies in tackling problems in two steps, called *map* and *reduce*. The *map* step transforms a single large computing task into a set of smaller tasks that can be conducted independently, each producing a single result; the *reduce* step takes the results of those separate computations and combines them into a single solution. In the MapReduce programming model, the challenge for the programmer is to encode a problem in terms of these map and reduce operations. So, for example, to find the most frequently occurring set of words in a document, we might map the main goal into a set of parallel tasks, each of which will count up the instances of single words, producing an array of individual word counts, and then reduce this by selecting just those most-frequent words in which we are interested; or if I wanted to count up the number of nail salons in a city, I might break the city up into mile-square sections, count up the salons for each section concurrently, and then sum up the results. What we achieve through this mechanism is a degree of scalability; that is, our task can be executed on different-sized clusters of commodity computers depending on the size of the data set.

This achievement comes at a cost, though. One component of this cost is the differential support for applications. Some tasks fit more naturally into the MapReduce model than others, and so some aspects of application functionality may have to be sacrificed to fit this model. For instance, the mechanism used to count nail salons in a city cannot be used to count roads, because roads will cross the boundaries of smaller regions; the decisions are not independent when the decomposition is spatial. A second, related component is the degree of consistency achievable within the system—a system based on MapReduce and the independent but coordinated operation of many small computing systems may not be able to achieve the degrees of consistency achievable under the ACID regime. Here again the concern is that there is no communication between the processing units handling each mapped task until the reduce stage is performed.

MapReduce has been influential in at least two ways. First, it is the fundamental mechanism that powers Google's own services, including not just web search, but mail, maps, translation, and other services that many people rely on day to day. Second, it has strongly influenced others; for instance, an open-source implementation of the MapReduce model, called Hadoop, has been adopted as a core infrastructure by a wide range of internet corporations, including eBay, Facebook, Hulu, and LinkedIn.

Like the ACID properties, MapReduce is a single component in a larger system, but a component that encapsulates a larger regime of computational configuration. MapReduce as a programming model is associated with particular styles of hardware provisioning (flexibly sized clusters of medium-powered, interconnected computational devices) and, in turn, with a particular approach to data storage. In the cluster-computing or cloud-computing model associated with the MapReduce regime, traditional relational storage, as an application element, is often displaced by associative storage characterized by large, informally organized collections of data objects linked by broad associations. If bank accounts are the canonical example of data managed in the ACID regime, then Facebook's collection of photographs are the canonical example of associative storage—a large-scale informal collection of "tagged" data objects in which consistency demands are low (if some temporary inconsistency arises between two users' views of a collection of "images of Paul," the consequences are not particularly problematic). Again, like the ACID regime, we find an entwining of technological capacity and commercial use, mediated in this case not only by the development of hardware platforms by computer manufacturers, but also by the provision of commercial computational facilities by service providers like Amazon, Rackspace, and SoftLayer. Software like Hadoop makes feasible computational services deployed across scalable clusters of computational nodes; the combination of these systems, along with virtualization technology, allows scalable cluster resources to be sold as commodity services, simultaneously making new hardware configurations commercially productive; and the availability of these services enables the development of new sorts of cloud computing applications characterized by distributed access, low degrees of integration, and loose consistency. Once again, these trends are mutually influential, and are also linked to the emergence of particular genres of user experience, as in the proliferation of social networking and informal-update notification services—the essential framework of what is popularly called "Web 2.0."

So what happens to the database in a MapReduce world? As we have seen, the relational data model, and the ACID-based transactional execution model that it supports, co-evolved along with mainframe computing platforms, but MapReduce is part of an alternative platform, based on heterogeneous clusters of commodity processors connected by networks. Formal ACID properties are difficult to maintain in these inherently decentralized systems, since the consistency that ACID requires and the course-grained parallelism of MapReduce cluster computing are largely incompatible. Two strategies emerge in response to this. The first is to build data storage platforms that replicate some of the traditional execution model but relax the constraints a little, as represented by systems like Spanner (Corbett et al. 2012), to be discussed in more detail later. The second is to abandon the relational/transactional model altogether, an approach that has resulted in a range of alternative data management platforms like MongoDB, FlockDB, and FluidDB, as well as research products such as Silt (Lim et al. 2011) and Hyperdex (Escriva, Wong, and Sirer 2012). Collectively, systems of this sort are sometimes called NoSQL databases (e.g., Cattell 2010; Leavitt 2010; Stonebraker 2010), an indication of their explicit positioning as alternatives to the relational-transactional approach (since SQL, the Structured Query Language, is the canonical way of programming relational-transactional databases).

So, while the arrival of MapReduce as a programming model for a new platform architecture triggered significant innovation and transformation in database technologies, this is not all about MapReduce by any means.

These new database platforms lend themselves to effective and efficient implementation on a new class of hardware architectures, but they by no means require it. Rather, they implement an alterative to the relational model that can be implemented across a wide range of potential platforms. Rather than being tied to particular hardware arrangements, they embody instead a different set of trade-offs between expressiveness, efficiency, and consistency, and propose too a different set of criteria by which data management tools should be evaluated. By reevaluating the trade-offs, they also support a different set of applications—ones in which responsiveness, distribution, informality, and user interaction play a greater part.

What we see braided together here, then, are three separate concerns. The first is the emergence of an alternative architecture for large-scale computer hardware. The second is the development of an alternative approach to data management. The third is the rise of a new range of applications that take a different approach to the end-user aspects of data management. These three concerns develop in coordination with each other, in response to each other, but with none as a primary causal factor—a constellation, in Adorno's sense. A material reading of this constellation focuses on its specific properties as they shape representational practice and the enactment of digital data.

Data without Relations

The term *NoSQL database*—a members' term redolent with moral valence— does not refer to a single implementation or conceptual model, but rather refers to a range of designs that, in different ways, respond to perceived problems with the relational approach. These problems might be conceptual, technical, pragmatic, or economic, and different problems provoke different design responses. One should be careful, then, in generalizing across them. When we take them together, however, we can see some patterns in both the motivation for alternatives to the relational model and in the forms those alternatives take. These patterns begin to point to the types of relationships between representational technology and representational practice that were among our original motivations.

Key considerations that drive the development of NoSQL databases include the need to conveniently incorporate them within a MapReduce framework, implemented on loosely coupled clusters of individual computers rather than on tightly coupled or monolithic architectures. Developers have also sought data models that more closely conform to the conventions of contemporary programming languages, especially object-oriented languages, and processing models that relax consistency constraints in exchange for the higher performance that can be obtained when parallel streams of processing no longer need to be closely coordinated. These considerations are not independent; for instance, the processing costs of transactional consistency are higher in loosely coupled distributed systems, while object-oriented data models and programming frameworks are regularly employed in cloud-based and Web 2.0-style programming systems (themselves frequently built on cluster-based servers rather than on large mainframes).

One of the most common approaches to NoSQL data management is an attribute-value system (also sometimes known as a key-value system). Whereas the fundamental element in the relational model is the table, which describes a relationship among data items, attribute-value systems are built around data objects, which frequently represent directly elements in the domain being modeled (e.g., people, pages, apps, or photographs). Associated with each object is an unstructured collection of data values, each of which is associated with an identifying term, or *key*. So, if I want to associate myself as the owner of a particular data object, I might link the value "Paul Dourish" to the object, using the key "owner." This, of course, is the same basic attribute-value model that we saw earlier in the discussion of prerelational models. It is a model that was largely displaced by relational databases, but that becomes interesting again in the context of new system architectures.

The expected pattern of interaction is that programs will take an object and look up the value associated with the key (e.g., to see what value represents the "owner" of an object); finding whether a particular value is associated with an object without knowing the key is frequently inefficient or not even possible. The central database operations here are to add a new key/value pair to an object, to update the value associated with a key for an object, or to retrieve the value associated with a key for an object. In some implementations, pairs of keys and values are associated directly with an object, as described above; in others, there may be no anchoring objects but just an unstructured collection of key/value pairs.

There may be many objects in such a database, but generally no formal structure collects them together. Similarly, there is generally no formal structure that describes what keys are associated with what objects. While a particular program might employ convention (such as using an "owner" key, for example), keys and values are generally associated directly with objects rather than being defined in schemas to which objects must then conform. The data are "unstructured" in the sense that no formal structure governs or limits the keys that can be associated with an object.

This arrangement has a number of properties that meet the particular needs outlined above. Since objects are relatively independent, they can be distributed across different nodes in a cluster of computers with relative ease; similarly, key/value pairs are independent of each other and can also be distributed. Furthermore, operations on each object are independent and can be distributed across a range of machines with relatively little coordination. There are, then, different ways that an attribute-value system can be managed in a MapReduce framework fairly easily; operations can "map" over objects, or they can "map" over keys, and in both cases, operations can be performed that take advantage of the MapReduce approach with little overhead. The relative independence of objects and of keys from each other is also a convenient starting point for a replication strategy that takes advantage of distributed resources, especially in applications that read data more often than they write. The Dynamo system, a distributed attribute-value system designed and used by Amazon.com in its web service applications, was an early and highly influential example of a NoSQL database that operates in accordance with this model (DeCandia et al. 2007).

While attribute-value systems are a common approach to NoSQL databases, other approaches attempt to retain more of the relational model and its guarantees within evolving technical contexts. Google's Bigtable (Chang et al. 2008), for instance, is an internally developed infrastructure providing database services to many of Google's applications and is itself deployed on Google's distributed infrastructure. To take advantage of this environment, and to provide high availability, Bigtable databases are distributed across several servers. Bigtable provides a tabular format but does not provide the traditional relational database model. It provides no transaction facility for clustering database operations into larger blocks that maintain the ACID properties. Further, given the importance of questions of locality (that is, how data are clustered) and of storage (whether data are small enough to store in main memory for faster access, or must be stored on a disk)—both of which are considerations that traditional database systems explicitly hide from applications and application programmers—Bigtable provides application programmers with mechanisms to control them.

The designers of a follow-on system, Spanner (Corbett et al. 2012), turned explicit attention to attempting to recover those elements of traditional relational databases that had been lost in the development of Bigtable, including transactional consistency and relational tables (or variants on the same). Similarly, one of the advantages that they list for Spanner over Bigtable is its use of an SQL-like query language—that is, one that is similar to the query language introduced in IBM's System R, and which, over time, evolved into a national (ANSI) and international (ISO) standard.

The desirability of transactional semantics and an SQL-based language reflect a different form of materiality that is beyond the scope of the immediate argument here—the way in which particular standards, expectations, and conceptual models are so deeply entwined with programming systems that, despite the vaunted flexibility and malleability of software, some interfaces emerge almost as fixed points due to their ubiquity. More relevant here are the alterative materialities of relational and key/value approaches to databases, and their consequences.

From Databases to Big Data

In parallel with the growth of NoSQL databases, MapReduce technology, and distributed web services, the other huge influence on contemporary research and practice in database technology has been the arrival of big data as a paradigm for technology, business, and science (Kitchin 2014; Boellstorff et al. 2015). *Big data* is a marketing term as much as a technical one, and clearly one could question the criteria on which its definition depends (how big does your data need to be before they can be called big data?), but as a paradigm, one can certainly identify some key characteristics that distinguish its contemporary manifestations. Big data typically involves large-scale information processing and pattern recognition over large, dynamic, and evolving data sets that often represent real-time accounts of human and natural systems—credit card transactions, voting patterns, health data, meteorological events, chemical sensor readings, and the like. Advocates characterize the data sets over which big data systems operate in terms of "the three Vs"—volume, variety, and velocity.[2] *Volume* characterizes the most obvious feature of big data systems—that they involve processing large amounts of data. However, it is not simply the volume that is important. *Variety* captures the fact that the data items may be of quite different types. Rather than integrating uniform records, big data systems often integrate data of diverse sorts and from diverse sources. Finally, *velocity* concerns the rate of data production. In many ways, this

---

2. Highlighting the potential uncertainty or inaccuracy of data, *veracity* is sometimes included as a fourth V. Boellstorff and colleagues have "three Rs" (Boellstorff et al. 2015), and Deborah Lupton, "thirteen Ps" ("The Thirteen Ps of Big Data," *This Sociological Life*, May 11, 2015, https://simplysociology.wordpress.com/2015/05/11/the-thirteen-ps-of-big-data). The alphabet is big data's playground.

is the most significant consideration. Big data systems are in many cases dealing not with data *sets* but with data *streams*—sequences of data items that are being produced in real time and that may arrive in rapid succession. If one imagines, for instance, attempting to respond in real time to credit card transaction data (to detect potentially fraudulent transactions), stock market trading data (to analyze trading patterns), or highway traffic sensor data (to manage the flow of vehicles onto freeways), then one can immediately see first that data might be arriving extremely quickly and second that processing them cannot depend on warehousing and offline analysis.

As we saw above in discussing the pressures that drove the development of NoSQL databases, these characteristics of big data systems stress the foundations of traditional relational and SQL-based database systems. The need to be able rapidly to scale up as data volumes grow has meant that, as with the web services cases above, shared-nothing hardware platforms (parallel platforms without large shared disks or shared memories, like the clusters for which MapReduce algorithms were developed) have also been the usual platform for big data technologies. Yet, where many web services could be built using custom technologies, those same technologies work less well in more exploratory forms of data analysis. So, early big data system developers often found themselves looking for the kinds of systematized query and data manipulation mechanisms that SQL provides. Query tools like Facebook's Hive or Yahoo's Pig provide SQL-like data management languages over MapReduce systems. According to colleagues of mine at UC Irvine who have been examining these questions, "well over 60 percent of Yahoo's Hadoop jobs and more than 90 percent of Facebook's jobs now come from these higher-level languages rather than hand-written MapReduce jobs" (Borkar et al. 2012, 46).

Building on these experiences, they have been developing a system called AsterixDB that represents a database science response to big data problems (Alsubaiee et al. 2014). The AsterixDB developers distinguish between two aspects of big data processing systems—the analytic/computational engine, often powered by batch-processing MapReduce engines like Hadoop, and the storage engines, such as NoSQL database systems (Borkar et al. 2012). They note, as we have seen, that these often operate in tandem, but they observe that their mismatches are sources of inefficiency and inflexibility. Traditional database technologies, after all, combined storage and processing as an integrated whole; the architectural style of big data systems, on the other hand, has yoked together components that were often designed independently and with different goals, and the separations between them means that efficiencies from one part of the system cannot necessarily be passed on to others.

Citing the need to reintegrate these components, they have developed a new platform—what they call not a DBMS but a BDMS (big data management system)—that seeks to support multiple different query and storage paradigms but to do so with tight integration and direct support for streamed data as well as stored.

Like the rise of NoSQL data stores, designs such as that of AsterixDB reflect a clash between the representational materialities of traditional databases with contemporary platforms, applications, and architectures. The reorganization of software architectures to better match both storage and processing needs to architectural arrangements and the properties of large-scale data sets point toward specific material properties of both databases and their implementations.

Database Materialities

Given the principle that we need to attend not just to materiality broadly construed but to specific material properties that shape and are shaped by representational practice, what properties are significant in the rise of NoSQL databases and related new approaches? I deal with four here—granularity, associativity, multiplicity, and convergence.

Granularity

As we saw in the case of spreadsheets in the previous chapter, granularity concerns the size of the elements that are the objects of attention and action within the system—and, in turn, with the entities they might represent. Here again, granularity seems critical. Relational databases deal in terms of three different scales of action—data values, relations, and tables. Different commands in the SQL control language will act directly on entities of these different scales (the UPDATE instruction operates on data values, for example, while INSERT operates on relations and CREATE TABLE operates on tables). These matter because representational strategies—that is, how a social or physical object or phenomenon in the world might be represented both in database notation and as a stream of bits—have consequences for what might be simple or difficult to perform in a particular database. For instance, when the scalar arrangements at work make it easy to address streets and houses as individual objects in a system, then it is relatively easy to build systems that reason about, for instance, postal routes. If, on the other hand, a house must always be represented in terms of a collection of rooms, then it becomes easier to reason about heating systems but harder to reason about property rights.

These considerations are, in part, an aspect of the art of programming and reflect the design choices of those who build databases, but they are constrained by and shaped in response to the representational possibilities and material consequences of underlying technologies. As a representational and notational issue, then, granularity is a consideration that directly relates specific aspects of database technology implementation (such as cache size, memory architecture, query plan generation, and programming language integration) with the representational "reach" of databases (including the question of what sorts of objects in the world they might represent, what forms of consistency can be achieved, with what temporalities they can be tied to dynamic events, and how easily they can be updated). Where relational databases focus primarily on relations—that is, on recurrent structural associations between data values—NoSQL databases tend to focus on objects; and where the relational form sets up a hierarchy of data values, relations, and tables, NoSQL databases tend to operate at a single level of granularity, or where they provide clustering mechanisms, they do so to give the programmer control over aspects of system performance rather than as a representational strategy.

Associativity

Related to the material questions of granularity is the question of *associativity*. How do different data objects cluster and associate? What binds them and allows them to be manipulated as collections rather than as individual objects? Here, again, we see a difference between the relational model and NoSQL approaches, a difference that has consequences for representation and manipulation in database-backed technologies. In relational systems, data objects are associated through patterns in data values. This takes two forms. Within a table, such associations happen by bringing objects together according to the values stored in one or more columns within a table. So, for example, one might use the SELECT statement to identify all managers whose salaries are over $80,000, or to find all the books published by MIT Press, or to look for all the stellar observations made between particular dates. In all these cases, a table is searched and particular columns are examined to find which entries (relations) will be returned for further processing. The second form uses data values to cluster data across multiple tables. Here, distinguishing features are often used to bring relations together. For instance, if I have a table that relates people's names to their social security numbers, and another table that relates vehicle license numbers to the social security numbers of the vehicle's owners, then I can use the social security numbers to create a new, amalgamated table that relates people's names to the license numbers of their cars. Or, again, if one table maps product UPC codes to prices, and another maps UPC codes to supermarket sales, I can use the UPC codes to link prices to sales and find the total "take" at the checkout. Here, patterns in data values are used to link and associate records across different tables.

The attribute-value systems of most NoSQL entities, though, operate largely in a different manner. Here, we have two quite dissimilar forms of association.

The first is the association of a value to a data object. This is similar to that of database relations, but it differs in a critical way—here, values belong to particular objects directly, rather than being instances of an abstract relationship (which is how they manifest themselves in the relational model, which, as we have seen, separates data from their generic description in a schema). Keys and values (which are perhaps similar to column names and data values in the relational model) are closely associated with each other, while different values (similar to related values) are loosely associated, even for the same base object. This alternative arrangement results in a different pattern of data distribution and consistency (see below), and affects how those data might be moved around in a particular implementation (including how they might be migrated between different nodes or even different data centers).

The second form of association in the attribute-value system describes how a base object is linked to another. In some systems, the value associated with a key can be a pointer to another object. This allows objects to be "chained" together—connected in patterns that relate a first object to a second, and then a third, and then a fourth, and so on. This is reminiscent of the *networked* data model that we encountered earlier. Indeed, attribute-value systems are regularly used to implement such networks because of their other key difference from relational systems—the absence of the schema as an abstract description of data structures. Network structures map naturally and obviously onto the interaction patterns of web-based applications, including social networking applications; they provide poor support, though, for analytic applications, which need to summarize, sort, and aggregate information across data items. Once again, as in other cases, the question is not whether particular operations are possible or impossible, but whether they are efficient or inefficient, easy or difficult, or natural or unnatural within particular programming frameworks. In questions of associativity, as in other material considerations, the structural and notational properties of data stores involve commitments to particular models of processing and contexts of information system development and deployment that make visible the relationship between technological infrastructure and social contexts.

Multiplicity

As databases are used to coordinate tasks and activities that are distributed in the world, as performance becomes a key consideration, and as computer systems are increasingly constructed as assemblies of many processing elements, database designers have come to place a good deal of reliance on replication—the creation of replicas of data items that can be made available more speedily by being present in different places at once. Replication is especially useful for data that are read more frequently than they are updated. Updating replicated data involves considerably more work than replicating data that are stored centrally, but for data that are to be read frequently, being in two places at once can be extremely helpful.

As we have seen, data models (such as the relational model, the network model, and the hierarchical model) are notational strategies by which aspects of the everyday world are encoded in computer systems. Replication, as a way in which database systems attempt to optimize their performance, arises within the structure offered by a data model. What can be replicated, then, is not "the information about my bank account" or "the files relating to my book" but tables and relations, or whatever data objects make sense to the database, rather than to its users.

In exploring the problems of granularity and associativity, then, we found ourselves exploring the way in which data objects become "live" inside the system. Fundamentally, the concern is that the database be both a representational form and an effective form; that is, databases provide a notation that people use to represent and reason about the world, which is simultaneously an engineering artifact that directs and structures the operation of computer systems. The data model points in two directions, which is precisely why the materialities matter.

Multiplicity extends our previous concern with granularity to consider how different representational forms lend themselves to disparate implementation strategies, including varied strategies of replication, and hence to diverse approaches to system performance. Here again we find ourselves in territory where "the database" must be more than simply a formal construct; it is also a specific object with specific manifestations that make it effective for particular uses in individual contexts. *Multiplicity*—the ability to act coherently on multiple manifestations of objects that, from another perspective, are "the same"—reflects this concern with the particular and with the different constraints associated with diverse approaches to database form (Mackenzie 2012).

In particular, approaches to multiplicity speak to the opportunities for partition—that is, for a system to operate as multiple independent entities, either briefly or for an extended period. A simple case might be a database that continues to operate even when your computer is temporarily disconnected from the network (implying that there may be, for some time at least, replicas of data on your own computer and on a server—replicas that may need to be resolved later). Users of cloud services are familiar with the problems of synchronization that these replicas imply (to be discussed in more detail in a moment). More generally, what this suggests is that the granularity with which data are modeled is also an aspect of the granularity of access and even of the digital entities that one encounters (e.g., whether a laptop appears to be a device independent of the server or the cloud infrastructure to which it connects).

Multiplicity and the management of replicas is typically seen as a purely "internal" feature of the database—an implementation detail that is irrelevant to, and often to be hidden from, other aspects of the system, its interface, and its function. It is seen, too, as independent of (and hence indescribable in terms of) the notational system of representation implied by the underlying data model. Nonetheless, these material considerations "bleed through" in interaction.

Convergence

Multiplicity opens up the question of consistency, and consistency opens up the question of convergence. In distributed databases, convergence describes how temporary inconsistencies, such as those that arise when part of the database has been updated while other parts have not, are eventually resolved; that is, how different paths eventually converge on a single consistent outcome. We can think of this as the stabilization or normalization of diversity and disagreement; databases that converge are those that eventually resolve partial inconsistencies into a consistent whole.

With respect to a materialist analysis, two aspects of convergence are particularly worth examining. The first is the question of bounded consistency and the relationship between databases and the software systems that use them; the second is the question of the temporalities of convergence.

Bounded consistency refers to the way in which a particular system might be able to accommodate a certain degree of inconsistency. For instance, in a banking system, absolute consistency is typically required for account balances, but minor deviations in the spelling of a customer's name might be tolerable, at least for short periods. So, if a customer conducts a money transfer at an ATM, the details must be immediately and consistently available within the rest of the system; but if he talks to a teller to correct a spelling mistake, it may be sufficient that this information make its way to the central system before the end of the business day.

A software system often incorporates both a database system for storage and some application-specific components that manage the specific details of that application. For example, a computer game might rely on a database that records the details of objects and places, and then on an application-specific component that implements the rules of the game. When we speak of bounded consistency, we are often talking about the relationship between these two components. To what extent can inconsistency in the database component be tolerated by the application logic? Where, then, does the boundary between those components fall, and how rigorous is the separation between them?

Traditional relational database systems, with their transactional semantics, embody one answer to these questions. Transactional semantics guarantee that no inconsistency is ever "visible" to components outside the database (including to other pieces of software). Users or software clients request that the database perform some operation, and the database carries this operation out while guaranteeing observable consistency. In other words, the guarantee of consistency is also, inter alia, a commitment to a separation between the database and other components. The communication channel between the components is narrow. When we begin to allow bounded consistency, we also "open up" aspects of the operation of the database to external scrutiny and widen the channel of communication. This has implications for other aspects of the fabric of the software system, including choices of programming languages, production environments, and the physical distribution of software components across sites; the more tightly coupled are application logic and database function, the more constrained are the choices.

The temporalities of convergence—that is, the temporal rhythms and dynamics of data consistency—further illustrate the entwining of materiality and practice in databases. At the lowest level, we must pay attention to propagation times and network delays that are consequences of the distribution of data across multiple nodes in a data center, or between different data centers (or even between different components in an apparently "monolithic" computer, which is always, of course, constructed from many components, including a hierarchy of storage systems from registers to disks, with different temporal characteristics). A little more abstractly, we must pay attention to the computational complexity of the algorithms that will resolve conflicts, which themselves depend on how the data are structured. But perhaps more important than the simple question of "how long will it take?" is the question of "how do the temporalities of convergence relate to the temporalities of use?" For example, while applications that serve interactive users are typically slow in comparison to computer performance (since most systems can perform thousands of operations in the literal blink of a human eye), nonetheless we can observe radically different temporal dynamics when a database is serving up tagged photographs in a social networking application versus when it is serving up objects to be rendered in three dimensions at thirty frames per second in a multiplayer game.

Further, the temporalities of database resolution mean that sometimes, from a user's perspective, time can seem to flow backward. That is, to achieve convergence, it may be necessary for a system to *undo* conflicting operations that, from a user's perspective, have already been completed. In other words, convergence is not simply a question of resolving inconsistency, but one of doing it in a way that makes apparent sense, and that sense might be subject to a temporal logic on the part of human users; similarly, the temporality of this process must be compatible with the dynamics of human experience or other forms of external action within the relevant domain.

Like the other properties that have come before, then, problems of convergence shape the choices available in how different elements are assembled to form a system and highlight the constraints that structure them. Temporally and structurally, convergence highlights the nature of coupling between different components, including the coupling between digital systems and the world beyond. It casts doubt, then, on any simple reading of "how digital systems operate" or "what databases do" by suggesting that particular manifestations of the digital, shaped by and giving rise to material arrangements, must be understood in their specificities.

Material Consequences

Looking at spreadsheets in the previous chapter provided an opportunity to see how representational materialities provide a framework around which organizational action evolves. The specific forms by which data can be manipulated structures in turn the kinds of discussions that we can have around those data and the kinds of purposes to which they can be put.

Saying "it is stored in a database" or "databases keep track of our data" fails to capture the complexity or reality of contemporary information contexts. How the database operates shapes what the database entails as a means of managing or a form of control.

Databases are more flexible than spreadsheets, of course, and they are less commonly visible as user interfaces. On the other hand, the central role they play as tools of computerized administration means that their materialities are all the more significant. Brubaker and Hayes (2011) document, for example, the ways in which aspects of human identity are mapped onto database structures in online settings, and with what consequences; Haimson et al. (2016) have focused particularly on issues surrounding sexual identity transition, for example, and the problems that arise when database constraints impose themselves on how we communicate with institutions or present ourselves to each other. Similarly, launching off from the analyses that people like Denis Wood (1992) have offered of the ways in which maps are used to persuade, communicate, shape understandings, and reinforce power, Curry (1998) shows how geographical database systems, with their own representational commitments, are similarly partial and problematic. A confluence of broad concerns—from data-driven *audit culture* as a form of accountability-driven organizational management (Strathern 2000), to contemporary interests in big data and the opportunities around statistical machine learning—place the database increasingly at the center of many areas of personal, organizational, and civic life. In much the same way as we should be wary of the claims to objectivity in the term "raw data" (Gitelman 2013), we should be alert to the implications of database infrastructures as representational tools. The materialities of database technologies shape the kinds of "databasing" that can be done and imagined. Databases, then, have a remarkable power that reaches in two directions, inward toward architectures and outward toward society, systems, and services.

On the one hand, we can see a mutually constitutive relationship at work between hardware platforms and data representation systems. The essence of computational representations is that they are *effective*, that is, that they can be operated and operated on to achieve particular results. This effectiveness is dependent on the relationship between the representations and the material tools through which those representations are manipulated, that is, computational engines (computers and processors) and storage engines (disks and memory architectures). In turn, their structures are also materially realized; we need to pay attention to the material considerations in building computational resources, which include power, air conditioning, size, structure, and distribution. The von Neumann architecture—the basic design principle of computer systems since the 1940s, which we encountered in the opening chapter—separates processing elements that operate on data from storage elements that record them, in turn placing considerable emphasis on the linkages between processing and storage. Similarly, the question of *interconnects*—how different elements of computer systems are linked together—has arguably become the central question of high-performance computer design over the last several decades (Hall et al. 2000; Al-Fares et al. 2008; Greenberg et al. 2008). What we see here is that the considerations that shape these architectural elements, including such "brute material" elements as the propagation of electrical signals over distance and the heat dissipation requirements of densely packed computational elements—are intimately entwined with the data representational schemes that can be achieved.

On the other hand, we also see how data representational schemes—with all their constraints—play a similar mutually constitutive role in the applications to which they provide services. The capacities of effective representations and data storage facilities suggest and support particular kinds of application functions, while application scenarios contextualize and drive the development of infrastructures and the packaging of infrastructure services as toolkits and frameworks. In particular, the rise of Web 2.0 has been associated with a series of new forms of data storage and manipulation service that eschew the ACID properties of traditional high-performance relational databases in favor of alternatives that prioritize responsiveness over consistency in the face of alternative implementation infrastructures.

The questions of stability, consistency, and granularity that have occupied our attention here concern the internal operations of digital systems, but to the extent that those systems are used to model, monitor, control, and account for entities in the world, they can also "leak" out. Databases are often points of mediation between each of us and the institutions with which we interact, and as such, features of the database, including temporal patterns and structural patterns of its operation, begin to manifest themselves in the how those institutions operate and in how they understand the world—and us. In what Miller (2003) calls "the virtual moment," the model of the world (in the database) suddenly drives rather than documents human phenomena, so that the materialities of that model make themselves visible through the ways in which the model drives institutional action. If organizations can act only on the data they have, then the limits of databases—the limits of their representational capacities, their dynamics, and their scope—also become constraints on action in the world. As Bowker and Star (1999) have comprehensively argued, phenomena that cannot be measured and recorded cannot be acted on; so, for example, pressing the case for research into HIV/AIDS required first that AIDS become a usable classification for mortality. The database might not itself be visible in the foreground, but the effects of its structures are nonetheless consequential.

So, while the spreadsheets that were the focus of attention in the previous chapter were generally visible and projected onto meeting-room screens, databases are often hidden from view. Even more hidden from view are the network protocols that are the focus of the next two chapters, although, once again, the materialities of protocols as representational systems have important consequences for how we communicate, share information, and connect.

6   The Materialities of Internet Routing

In July 2013, a nondescript office tower in downtown Los Angeles set a new local real estate record. The building is named One Wilshire, although that name is somewhat misleading because, although it sits where Wilshire Boulevard begins at South Grand Avenue, its street address is actually on South Grand. When it changed hands for more than $430 million, it commanded the highest ever price per square foot for real estate in the downtown core.[1] One would think that such a price must be justified by the building's luxurious amenities, commanding views, or prime location, but yet it has none of these, at least by any conventional measures. The building directory at the security desk in the marbled lobby begins to hint, though, at what might be unusual about this building, as the companies it lists are uniformly telecommunications providers—Verizon, Covad, Level 3 Communications, and more. It is one of the most wired buildings in the world.

For a building thirty-five stories tall, One Wilshire houses very few people, but it is far from empty. Its space is given over almost entirely to data centers and computer server rooms, colocation facilities and network equipment, with the high-speed network spine as critical to the building's operation as are its architectural supports. The facility's key resource and raison d'être, though, is the "meet-me room" on the fourth floor, an oppressive warren of telecommunications equipment in locked cages, connected overhead by a dense, tangled mesh of bright yellow single-mode fiber-optic cables. One Wilshire's meet-me room is a major internet connection point, also known as an IPX, or internet packet exchange. This particular IPX is one of the densest in the United States. Buildings like One Wilshire are the physical sites where the digital networks of corporations like NTT, AT&T, British Telecom, and Level 3 are connected together. These are the points at

---

1. Roger Vincent, "Downtown L.A. Office Building Sells for Record $437.5 Million," *Los Angeles Times*, July 17, 2013.

which digital messages flow from one operator's network to another: where the "inter" of the internet happens.

One Wilshire is a literally towering emblem of what I referred to earlier as the "brute materiality" of the online world—the fact that the "virtuality" of online practice is grounded in servers that take up real space, consume natural resources, and are connected by physical cables that follow distinct paths. The brute materiality of digital communication infrastructures has been unearthed and scrutinized in many insightful scholarly accounts, including some documented briefly in chapter 2. For example, Lisa Parks (2012) has written about spatiality and territorialization in terms of the footprints of the satellites by which global communications are made real (and distinctly local); Nicole Starosielski (2011) has examined the network of undersea cables snaking across the ocean floor and the flows of capital, expertise, and people that follow their paths; Steven Graham and Simon Marvin (2001) have discussed what they call the "splintering urbanism" that comes about when different networks and infrastructures create different experiences of urban space; and Kazys Varnelis (2008) has examined Los Angeles in terms of its manifestations of networked infrastructures (including specifically One Wilshire).

In line with the interest in representational materialities taken in earlier chapters, my goal here is not simply to contribute to the analysis of brute materiality, but to examine the nature of the specific materialities of the digital forms stored on those servers and transmitted on those wires. In this chapter and in the next, I treat the internet as a historically and technologically specific object—not just as a network in general, but as a particular social, cultural, and economic foundation with distinct technological manifestations and constraints. This entails a focus on the specific protocols on which contemporary internet arrangements are founded. While writers like Alexander Galloway (2004) have examined the politics of network protocols, and others such as Milton Mueller (2010) have written about the institutional arrangements that bring them into being and maintain them, I want here to consider protocols as material that needs to be matched with and understood in relation to the brute infrastructural materialities that we encounter in places like One Wilshire.

In this chapter, I focus in particular on the topic of internet routing—the protocols and mechanisms that, first, allow digital data to traverse a complex, heterogeneous, and dynamic internet, and that, second, distribute the information that allow this traversal to be accomplished. Crucially, our attention here is directed toward the materiality of internet *routing*, not the materiality of internet routers nor the materiality of internet routes. That is, this chapter is concerned not with the physical infrastructure as such—the cables, the servers, the switches, the buildings, and so on—but with the processes at work there.

None of these is a static element, and for the purposes of this chapter, I take a historical perspective that highlights the different perceptions of problems and possibilities that have characterized internet development at various moments. Looking at the evolution of protocols, network topologies, and organizational arrangements over time also gives us a window into the evolution and development of the institutions within which the network is embedded. This highlights that although we glibly refer to "the internet" as a singular object, it is no one thing—it is something that evolves, grows, adapts, and has to be captured in its historical specificity; and it is something that can be open and decentralized at one level and highly authoritarian, hierarchical, and regulated at another.

Internet Transmission and Routing

Although we talk casually about "the internet" or "the network," the very terms *internet*, *Internet Protocol*, and *internetworking* point to a more complicated reality, which is that the apparently singular Internet actually consists of multiple networks. In fact, this is the whole point. The crucial feature of internet technology is that it provides a way for data to move between multiple networks, potentially of quite different sorts. What we call the internet is a collection of networks linked together—local area networks on a college campus, long-distance networks operated by commercial providers, cellular networks maintained by mobile service operators, Wi-Fi networks in homes, and so on—in such a way that data can move easily from one to another.

The internet is a *packet-switched* network. This means that messages from one node to another are broken into small units, or *packets*. Packets from different points on the network might be transmitted on a shared network link, retaining their separate identities. The benefit of this approach is that it allows for more efficient use of network links than if they were dedicated, even temporarily, to transmissions from one particular host to another.

The internet is also a *datagram*-based network. A datagram service is a particular way of using packet switching. In a datagram service, each packet carries its own information, and packets are delivered independently. This means that the network can route each packet to its destination individually, without regard to packets that came before.

Most datagram networks are also, by design, unreliable. They do not guarantee delivery of packets to a destination in the same order as they were sent; for instance, to avoid congestion on a particular link, some packets might be sent via an indirect but more lightly loaded route, causing them to arrive out of order. Further, unreliable datagram networks do not even guarantee delivering a packet at all; so-called *best effort service* means that a network will try to deliver a packet but might fail to do so. Most commonly, this will be a result of congestion on a highly trafficked link; rather than store up all packets waiting to be transmitted, a network node might simply *drop* (delete) the packet (often sending a notification back to the originating host that this has happened). The French research network CYCLADES (Pouzin 1975) was the first to explore a datagram service in which hosts, not the network itself, would be responsible for reliability.

This is the division of labor in the protocols called TCP/IP, which are arguably the defining feature of the internet. Although they are often referred to collectively as TCP/IP, they are actually two different protocols, the Transmission Control Protocol (TCP) and the Internet Protocol (IP), designed to operate in concert. IP offers an unreliable datagram service that delivers packets from source to destination with a promise only of best effort. TCP uses the IP service to deliver packets, but it introduces extra mechanisms to reorder and reassemble packets, to detect drops and to request retransmissions, and to produce the effect of a smooth and reliable transmission service out of the unreliable service offered by IP. Not all applications require the complexity that TCP offers, and some are built directly on IP; applications make use of the service layer that best corresponds to their needs.

Packets

Networks might not seem the most fruitful area for an investigation of representational materialities, but as in most other areas of digital system design, representation and the manipulation of forms are crucial and pervasive.

Figure 6.1 shows the structure of a data packet being sent via TCP/IP. These show the packet *header*, which stores information about addressing and processing. The actual content of the packet is the *data* section at the bottom. The *layering* of network protocols—application-oriented services at the top, with TCP below that, itself running atop IP, and then perhaps Ethernet underneath—manifests itself "on the wire" in the form of a series of encapsulated encodings, where a particular packet on an Ethernet will be formatted according to the Ethernet standard, and then contain a *payload*, which is formatted according to the IP standard, which will itself contain a payload formatted according to the TCP standard, and so on. So, if the

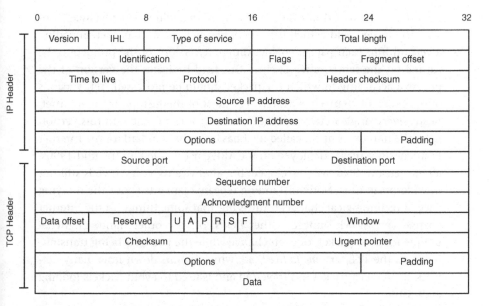

| 0 | 8 | 16 | 24 | 32 |

IP Header

Version	IHL	Type of service	Total length	
Identification		Flags	Fragment offset	
Time to live	Protocol	Header checksum	
Source IP address				
Destination IP address				
Options			Padding	

TCP Header

Source port	Destination port			
Sequence number				
Acknowledgment number				
Data offset	Reserved	U A P R S F	Window	
Checksum	Urgent pointer			
Options			Padding	
Data				

Figure 6.1

TCP and IP packet header format. The first four *bits* of an IP packet (top left) specify the version of the IP protocol according to which it is encoded; the next four specify the IP header length (IHL) in units of thirty-two-bit words, followed by eight bits for the service type, and sixteen for the total packet length, and so on. The first six lines of this table are the IP header and are included for every IP packet on the internet; the next six (beginning with "source port") are the TCP header, included when the IP packet is carrying data from a TCP-encoded stream.

packet illustrated in figure 6.1 were part of a web request, then the data section would itself be formatted according to the protocol standard for HTTP, the hypertext transfer protocol.

The figure shows both the TCP and IP headers, and thus indicates a packet that is part of a reliable TCP stream carried over IP. There is no need here to go over the detail of what each field of the header means. What matters is the idea of format and structure as encoded in these standards. The standards specify the order in which information is presented and the interpretations of this information; they provide encodings of relevant parameters. They also place limits on the size of various fields, perhaps most visibly and consequentially those that specify addresses (thus creating the problem of IP address exhaustion—Richter et al. [2015]), but also those that specify packet lengths, ports, fragmentation details, and so forth. While the *options* sections of both the IP and TCP headers are variable in length, each other element is a fixed size.

Different fields exhibit different sorts of variability. For instance, consider the *version* field, which is the very first field in an IP packet. Encoding a version into each packet enables different versions of the protocol to be carried on the same network, since this field indicates the version of the protocol according to which the packet should be processed. Yet, versions of the protocol change very rarely. For most of the history of the internet, nearly every single network packet has had a single number in this version field: the number four. So-called IPv4 has been the standard for the Internet Protocol since IP was deployed on the ARPANET in 1983. In the mid-1990s, a new version, IPv6, was developed, but after twenty years, IPv6 is still not in widespread use.[2] Notwithstanding repeated laments about the dizzying pace of technological change, it turns out that some things on the internet change very slowly indeed. Other fields, on the other hand, might be unique for each packet, or even change while the packet is being transmitted (e.g., the TTL, or *time-to-live* field, which counts down how many network segments a packet has traversed and is used to avoid packets looping endlessly).

This in turn echoes an earlier observation: everything is bits, but not all bits are equally significant. Some parts of the TCP/IP header space are vital (e.g., the addressing information), while other parts are used little or not at all (e.g., the *identification* field, which has largely only experimental uses, and the *padding* areas, which are entirely unused, if they are present, and serve only to ensure that later data blocks begin on thirty-two-bit boundaries).

Most technical descriptions of TCP and IP focus on just this level of description—header formats and how they are used to ensure the smooth flow and timely delivery of information. What is, of course, entirely missing from this is content—the part that humans presumably care about. Content is most often a chunk of data up to the limits of one protocol or another—an IP packet can be up to 65,000 bytes in length, for example, but Ethernet limits packets to 1,500 bytes, so IP packets traveling over Ethernet will be broken into those smaller units. In some cases, though, a packet's content might be a single byte—perhaps just a single character being entered onto a line of text remotely. The ratio of header size to payload size becomes important, then, as a measure of the efficiency of the transmission. Techniques for "header compression" were needed when dial-up

2. Versions 1–3 were experimental precursors to the widely-deployed IPv4. Version number 5 was assigned to the experimental Internet Streaming Protocol, which was never conceived of as a replacement for IPv4.

telephone lines were common ways to connect to the network, because otherwise too much of the available bandwidth was devoted to the house-keeping information associated with packet headers (Jacobson 1990).

This brings us to one further aspect of the materiality of protocol representations, which is their manifestation "on the wire" (or in the air, in the case of wireless connections). Packets are transmitted at different rates, depending on the transmission medium and adapters being used. They are generally transmitted one bit at a time, with each bit taking a finite time. Since signals propagate at a particular speed in each medium, packets "spread out" in the medium. They have length that can be measured not just in bytes but in millimeters. Their length is not normally a design consideration, but it may come to be one, for instance, when reflections or "echoes" cause interference. Network protocols are material in their representational forms as well as, and perhaps even more explicitly, in transmission.

Routing

Where TCP is designed to focus on reliable transmission, the challenge for IP is to get information from source to destination. *Routing* refers to the function whereby IP packets get from their source to their destination, or more accurately, from the network to which their source computer is connected to the network to which their destination computer is connected, across these different networks. Packets might have to traverse multiple other networks to get from one to the other, those networks might be of dissimilar types, they might be owned and managed by different authorities, and there might be multiple alternative routes or paths. In this model, a single "network" is an individual span of some kind of digital medium, and so it might be quite small. For instance, it is not uncommon for an average American home network to incorporate three different networks—a Wi-Fi network, a wired network (into which your Wi-Fi router is connected), and another "network" that constitutes the connection between your broadband modem and the service provider (perhaps over a telephone line or a television cable). Each transmission from your laptop to the outside world must start by traversing these three separate but connected networks. Similarly, there are many networks inside the internet infrastructure. From where I sit writing these words in an apartment in Boston, the Unix *traceroute* utility reveals that traffic destined for my previous sabbatical spot in Melbourne, Australia, crosses more than twenty networks; it travels first over networks owned by Comcast in Massachusetts, New York, Illinois, Colorado, and California, where it moves onto networks operated by Zayo before connecting to networks run by Telstra on behalf of the Australian Academic Research Network consortium, passing through multiple sites in New South Wales before reaching Victoria and then the University of Melbourne itself. Routing is the process by which packets are correctly directed across these different network connections to reach their destination. Internet routing depends on three key ideas—gateways, routing tables, and network addresses.

Gateways (also known as routers) are central elements in routing. A gateway is essentially a computer that is connected simultaneously to two or more networks, and thus has the capacity to receive packets via one network and then retransmit them on (or *route them* to) another. For instance, a domestic broadband modem is connected to your home network and to your service provider's network, and thus can act as a gateway that moves packets from one to the other; when it receives a message on your local network that is destined for the wider internet, it will retransmit it on the connection that links it to your service provider, where another router will see it and retransmit it appropriately. Most laptops and desktop PCs have the capability to act as gateways if they are connected to more than one network simultaneously, although most gateways are actually dedicated devices (like your broadband modem or, on a larger scale, routers made by companies such as Cisco or Juniper Networks). A gateway, then, can route packets from one network onto another. To do so, though, it requires information about how the network is organized.

The second key element, then, is the information that a gateway needs to successfully route packets. In general, this information is captured by the *routing tables* in a gateway. A routing table comprises a list that associates destinations with networks. These can be thought of as rules that say, "If you see a packet that is destined for network X, send it to gateway Y." When a gateway receives a packet, it looks up these rules to determine which of the networks it is connected to should receive it. Note that a rule of this sort does not imply that gateway Y is directly connected to network X; it might simply be that another gateway reachable through Y is one step "closer" to network X. Routing in TCP/IP, in other words, is decentralized. There is no central authority where the topology of the network is entirely known, nor any single point from which all networks can be reached. Rather, a packet makes its way across, say, the twenty "hops" from Boston to Melbourne through a series of individual decisions made at each gateway it passes. A packet is passed from gateway to gateway according to routing tables that move it closer to its destination, until it finally is delivered to a network to which its destination host is directly connected.

This brings us to our third concern with network addresses. Routing tables would become impossibly large if they needed to store routes for each host connected to the internet. Instead, they record routes to networks, not to individual hosts. This requires in turn that some means be found to identify and name networks. A typical IP address (the familiar four-byte number like 128.195.188.233) identifies a particular host, but some part of the address is seen as numbering the network to which that host is connected. The precise mechanism by which networks are numbered is discussed in more detail later, but for now, it is sufficient to note that routing tables do not record routes for every single host address, but rather record routes for networks (e.g., 128.195.188.0, a network to which the host 128.195.188.233 might be connected.)

Bearing these considerations in mind, let's proceed to another level of the analysis of routing, which concerns the protocols that govern the distribution of routing information.

Routing Protocols and Network Structures

Efficient and effective internet routing depends on information about local network topology being available to routers. As we have seen, however, the decentralized nature of the internet means that there can be no single source of information about the structure of the internet. Routing is wayfinding without a map; it is based instead on local decisions made from the best available information. Just as routing decisions are made in a decentralized manner, the sharing of information on which those decisions are based is similarly decentralized. Routers periodically exchange information about available network connections and routes, to update each other's tables. Routing protocols define how information about network topology and available routes—the information that routers stores in their routing tables and use to make routing decisions—spreads through the network.

There is no single universal routing protocol. Different protocols exist for particular needs, and various protocols have predominated at different historical moments. I examine three protocols here—the Routing Information Protocol (RIP), the Exterior Gateway Protocol (EGP), and the Border Gateway Protocol (BGP). These protocols constitute something of a historical progression, although not a strong periodization, since all persist in different settings. For our purposes here, though, they provide entry points into different aspects of the entwining of representational materiality and institutional arrangements.

The Routing Information Protocol

One of the earliest internet routing protocols, and one of the most widely deployed, is RIP, the Routing Information Protocol. RIP's widespread adoption in the 1980s and 1990s derived not from its technical superiority but from the fact that it was implemented by the *routed* (pronounced "route-dee") software distributed with 4BSD Unix software, popular in academic environments, and later with derivatives such as Sun Microsystems' SunOS. In fact, this software was, for some time, the only available specification of the protocol: there was no formal description or definition, merely the behavior of the implementation. Not only was RIP an early protocol for exchanging internet routing information, but it was heir to a longer legacy; RIP is a variant of the routing information protocol that formed part of Xerox's Network Service protocol suite (XNS), which itself embodied ideas originally developed as part of Xerox's Pup and Grapevine systems (Oppen and Dalal 1981; Birrell et al. 1982; Boggs et al. 1980). Pup and Grapevine had been developed at Xerox PARC, which is located only a few miles from the campus of Stanford University, where Vinton Cerf, one of the inventors of TCP/IP, served on the faculty during the early 1970s. The designers of Pup participated in research meetings that Cerf hosted at which a good deal of groundwork for successful internetworking was laid. They had also, prior to their work on Pup, gained considerable experience with the early ARPANET design (e.g., through Robert Metcalfe's development of ARPANET interfaces for computers at MIT and at Xerox). Accordingly, there was much intellectual exchange among these different groups and different technical developments (see chapter 7).

A router running RIP will periodically (every thirty seconds, in the original design) broadcast a description of its routing tables to other routers that it knows about. The information that a RIP router provides is essentially its own perspective on the network—that is, it describes how the network looks from its own vantage point. RIP provides two pieces of information about each of the routes it advertises, its destination and the *hop count*. So, a route advertisement in RIP is, roughly, a statement that says "network #54 is 3 networks away from me." Hop count—that is, the number of routers or network segments to be traversed in order to reach the destination—is used as an approximate metric of distance. Some networks might be fast, and some slow; some might cover long distances, and some short. These distinctions are not, however, captured in the hop count, which provides a more rough-and-ready basis for decision making about the most efficient route. Using hop counts also allows routers to detect and avoid loops that might arise when two routers each advertise a route to the other.

Although the RIP message format allocates thirty-two bits to record the hop count, allowing it to indicate a range of values from zero to more than four billion, only numbers in the range zero to sixteen are used. A value of sixteen indicates an "infinite" hop count, used to signal that a network is unreachable. Accordingly, an internet in which routes are communicated solely via RIP can be no more than fifteen networks "wide"—that is, a packet cannot be routed across more than fifteen segments—unless other measures are taken. In practice, this makes RIP useful primarily in smaller networks that are themselves connected using different routing protocols; the global reach of "the Internet," in other words, is premised on such specificities.

The limits of hop count that follow from the protocol design are one way in which representational materialities influence or constrain the development of broader technological arrangements. At least two others posed significant limitations for the development of the network.

The first concerns how the protocol requires that routers regularly exchange routing information with each other. The spread of this information through the network is crucial to the network's operation, and the need to remain up-to-date in a network that is continually changing means that routing information may need to be updated regularly. As the network grows, however, so do the routing tables, with the consequence that an ever-greater proportion of the network's capacity is consumed by the exchange of routing information, especially if routing tables are updated as often as once every thirty seconds, RIP's typical update interval. In other words, the materialization of the routing protocol that matters includes not only the representational constraints of the protocol's structure but also the way in which the protocol is manifested as an ever-expanding volume of signals on wires.

The second, related issue arises in the internet routers themselves, which must store the information about network routes. Routers often have more limited capacities than host computers, including more limited space in which routing information can be stored. As the network grows, so do the network routing tables (at least in the absence of other mitigating designs, some of which will be discussed shortly). Routing tables, then, have to be understood as data representations that consume capacity in network routers as well as capacity in the network itself.

RIP's constraints mean that it has long since been abandoned as a wide-area routing protocol. The fifteen-hop limitation, for example, is untenable in the contemporary internet. That isn't to say that RIP has disappeared. It persists in limited deployments, for example, as a so-called interior

protocol—that is, one that might operate inside smaller networks connected to the global internet via some other protocol, such as those to be
discussed in a moment.[3] We could read the failings of RIP (at least as originally designed) to support the scale of the contemporary network in terms
of a well-worn narrative, that of the "success disaster"—a technological success so significant that it exceeds the limits of the imagination of its pro-
genitors.[4] A similar story is often shared regarding internet addresses, once
imagined as a plentiful resource but now in very short supply as more and
more devices are connected to the network. My goal here is not to tell such
stories, which have a teleological character that I want to avoid. Instead, I
want to take this account of RIP, first, as embodying a series of ideas about
network operation that persist even when the protocol itself has faded into
the background, and, second, as describing a baseline against which later
developments can be contrasted in such a way as to make the persistence of
these ideas clearer. We can do this by looking at the ways in which later
protocols introduce new ideas about network organization that respond to
or reflect the perceived failings of the earlier protocols.

The External Gateway Protocol and Autonomous Systems
RIP is an early internetworking router information protocol, but, particularly in the wide-area (rather than local) networks, more elaborate routing
protocols have been the norm. Tracing through a sequence of these protocols also provides an account of an unfolding understanding of routing
problems and routing needs, as well as the evolving institutional contexts
of internetworking. EGP, the Exterior Gateway Protocol, is an important
part of that institutional development.

As with RIP, the core of the EGP is a mechanism by which routes are
shared from one router to another. Also like RIP, hop count is used as a
rough-and-ready measure of distance, although unlike RIP, routes of
more than fifteen hops can be expressed. EGP expresses the "distance" to
particular destinations relative to specific identified gateways (rather than

3. Indeed, the most recent version of RIP, known as RIPng, is designed to operate
over the most recent version of IPv6, a successor protocol to IP that is still not widely
deployed at the time of writing. RIP seems destined to persist in some form or other
for a long time to come.

4. Vinton Cerf and Robert Kahn's (1974) original paper presenting the TCP/IP architecture and protocols famously states, "The choice for network identification (8 bits)
allows up to 256 distinct networks. This size seems sufficient for the foreseeable
future."

implicitly from the sending router.) The protocol is also more fully featured than that of RIP, particularly with respect to issues of active network management and administration. For instance, there is an explicit component by which new neighboring gateways can be identified and polled; by contrast, this structure in RIP is left as a matter of configuration.

The official EGP specification was published in 1984 (Mills 1984). EGP displaced an earlier protocol known as GGP, the Gateway-to-Gateway Protocol, itself a close variant of RIP. EGP, as its name suggests, was explicitly designed as an *exterior* routing protocol; that is, it was designed explicitly to support coordination between networks rather than within networks. The distinction between interior and exterior routing regimes is a reflection of the experience with the emerging and growing internet during the period of rapid growth of different institutionally supported infrastructures (like CSNET, which became operational in 1981, and NSFNET, which became operational in 1985—see chapter 7). Local area networks tend to have different properties than long-haul networks, including much faster transmission rates; similarly, their users—often computer scientists conducting research—might need to be able to implement different routing strategies and deploy different routing technologies to meet local needs. This led network developers to conceptualize internetworking in a slightly different way, with an emphasis on the autonomy to be granted to different constituent networks.

This concern with autonomy leads to one of EGP's most significant innovations, institutionally if not technically, which is the introduction of the idea of an autonomous system (often abbreviated AS). An *autonomous system* is made up of a set of networks and hosts that fall under a single administrative authority, generally the network of a particular corporation or institution like MIT, Facebook, or the U.S. Department of State. The owners of an autonomous system are the people who have control to organize their network and set policies about how it's to be used. An autonomous system is generally considerably larger than a technical network, since an AS encompasses many networks and computers that fall under a single administrative authority. The value of autonomous systems for networking is that they allow routing protocols to operate at a different level. Two different problems can be identified—mechanisms for managing routes and routing information inside an AS, and mechanisms for managing routes and routing information between autonomous systems. EGP addresses inter-AS routing; it defines how routing information is shared and distributed between autonomous systems. Other protocols (or, in the case of statically configured networks, no protocols at all) might define how routing information moves around inside autonomous systems; since these systems are by definition autonomous and independent, each AS can determine its own best way of distributing routing information.

What we should note about an autonomous system is that it is not a purely technical arrangement, but an institutional one; being defined by the limits of administrative authority, it names an entity whose identity is rooted in social and institutional arrangements. Routing under EGP is a sociotechnical affair; routes are defined not between networks but between autonomous systems. In the contemporary Internet, autonomous systems have numbers (known as ASNs) assigned by a central authority, and the objects of attention in routing are these autonomous system numbers. Where a protocol like RIP concerns itself with how information should be moved from one network to another, a protocol like EGP concerns itself with how information should be moved from one autonomous system to another—that is, from one institutional entity to another or from one administrative domain to another. This internet is not so much a network of networks as a network of institutions (Gorman and Malecki 2000; Malecki 2002).

So, the intended purpose and conventional use of EGP are different from those of RIP. RIP is not committed to particular forms of use, although its constraints limit the conditions under which it can be deployed. EGP on the other hand is designed specifically to connect autonomous systems. Accordingly, EGP is designed to be used with particular conventions about which routes should be advertised and which should not; these conventions are not encoded directly in the protocol, but rather the protocol is designed under the assumption that administrators will be conscious of them. Indeed, *administration*, in the form of support for defined zones of authority, is a feature of EGP in a way that is simply not present in RIP.

EGP has one other important institutional feature, which is that it supports only hierarchical network topologies. EGP distinguishes between interior and exterior networks, or between network fringes and a network core, and is designed to run in the core. This hierarchical arrangement in which a core provides the fabric that connects other networks is central to EGP's design, and leads to a hierarchical or treelike arrangement of network centralization. While this form of centralization arose as a practical management reality in the creation of the early internet, it is of course antithetical to the key idea of a decentralized, distributed network in which information might follow many different paths from one point to another, ensuring robustness in the face of damage or congestion. The issue of network centralization as a function of both technical and institutional arrangements is one to which I return later; first, though, I examine the successor to EGP and a major contemporary routing protocol, the Border Gateway Protocol.

The Border Gateway Protocol, CIDR, and Policy Routing

EGP is largely an obsolete protocol. At the time of writing, the major routing protocol employed on the internet is its replacement, the Border Gateway Protocol (BGP). As the name suggests, BGP is an exterior routing protocol, employed on routers at the "borders" of autonomous systems, a concept that it carries over from EGP.[5] BGP is more sophisticated than EGP along a number of dimensions, including its capacity to support more diverse network topologies and its support for network administration.

BGP is currently in its fourth instantiation (sometimes called BGPv4 or BGP4, but I will simply use the abbreviation BGP here). Each version has incorporated into the protocol and the configurations that support its implementation new features that, as we saw with EGP, weave together representational materialities, organizational priorities, and institutional constraints. I discuss two here.

BGP, Classless Routing, and the Politics of Address Exhaustion In 1993, changes were introduced to the way in which internet routing worked. The new model—called CIDR (pronounced "cider"), or Classless Inter-Domain Routing—extended and built on conventions of *subnet routing*, which had been in operation for some time, but adopted them as the basis of a new model of routing that would apply across the internet (Fuller et al. 1993). CIDR was a response to a growing problem for internet routers, particularly core routers, which was the size of routing tables. The large number of networks meant that routing tables were growing, with three consequences. First, the storage demands on each router were growing significantly, beyond what had ever been imagined; second, the processing time necessary to sort through the routes was also growing; and third, the process of transmitting the routing tables (via protocols like EGP) was becoming unwieldy because the routing tables were so large.

CIDR was known as *classless* routing because it replaced an earlier scheme of network addressing that distinguished between three *classes* of networks, classes A, B, and C. Class A network addresses were distinguished by just

5. BGP can also be used as an interior protocol, although it is most commonly used in an exterior context.

their first eight bits, so that, for instance, all addresses that begin 13.x.x.x belong to Xerox Corporation. Holding a class A network allocation meant that one had control of a total of 16,777,216 separate internet addresses (although a handful are reserved and cannot be used). Class B addresses were distinguished by their first two bytes (sixteen bits); addresses in the range 192.168.x.x, for example, are class B addresses designated for private use. Each class B allocation includes 65,536 addresses (with the same caveat). Class C network addresses were distinguished by their first three bytes, and provide 256 addresses (again, minus a handful).

In the original scheme—which by contrast with classless routing became known as *classful* routing—the three classes of addresses served two simultaneous functions. They were the units of routing, because, as discussed above, routes direct packets toward networks rather than to individual hosts; and at the same time, they were also the units of allocation. If a new entity needed some address space—perhaps a university, a government, a company, or an internet service provider—then it would be allocated one (or more) class A, class B, or class C addresses. This conflation of two functions then resulted in two interrelated problems that classless routing could, it was hoped, solve. The technical problem was the growth of routing tables; the political problem was the growing scarcity of address space.

In classful addressing, networks are either class A, class B, or class C; the division between the network portion of an internet address and the host portion occurs at an eight-bit boundary, so that in a class A address, the thirty-two bits of an IP address are divided into eight bits of network identifier and twenty-four bits of host, rather than sixteen and sixteen, as for class B, or twenty-four and eight, as for class C. Classless addressing introduced a mechanism whereby the boundary between network and host portions could be made more flexible.

This mechanism would address the technical problem, the growth of routing tables, by allowing smaller networks to be coalesced into a single network that was still smaller than the next class up. This was especially important for class C addresses. A class C address covers only around 250 possible hosts. For many organizations that didn't need a whole class B address, a class C network was too small. So many organizations would be allocated many class C network addresses—each of which would require individual entries in routing tables. By creating the opportunity to have, say, ten bits of host space (for around 1,000 hosts) rather than eight bits—a new arrangement not possible in traditional classful routing—classless routing could shrink the size of the routing tables by dealing with networks at a new level of granularity.

It also addressed, to some extent, the political problem. The introduction of classless routing may have been sparked not least by the troublesome growth of routing tables, but it directly addresses another regular concern around internet management and governance, the question of address allocation and exhaustion. The original strategy for internet address allocation was based on address classes, with class A addresses particularly prized among large organizations. This resulted in various well-known inequities of allocation, such as the fact that MIT (with the class A network address now known as 18.0.0.0/8) had more allocated addresses than China.

Classful address allocation suffers a second problem, which is address wastage. Xerox, for instance, was allocated the class A network 13.0.0.0, although it seems unlikely that they would use all 16 million available addresses; however, at around 65,000 addresses, the next step down (class B) was deemed likely too small. No effective mechanism was available for smaller allocations. It remains the case, even in a world of classless routing, that the IP address space is continually approaching exhaustion, even as we know that wastage goes on within the already allocated blocks (Wang and Crowcroft 1992; Mueller 2010). Again, this is also happening within the context of deep historical iniquities in address allocation as noted above.

The politics of network address space allocation and the dynamics of routing table growth and exchange are dual aspects of the same material configurations. The political and technical issues are not so much twin problems as different facets of the same problem, which is that in the interests of efficiency and effectiveness, networks are the primary units of route determination. When we see these in a material light—that is, when we see route advertisements as things that have size, weight, lifetimes, and dynamics—then the political problems become material too.

Policy Routing in BGP There is a second social foundation for contemporary routing arrangements. The Border Gateway Protocol supports (indeed, is designed around) what is known as *policy-based routing* (Breslau and Estrin 1990; Estrin and Steenstrup 1991). The fundamental insight here is a simple one: in a world of autonomous systems, packet forwarding and routing decisions should be based not simply on the availability of a point of interconnection between networks, but on policies set by those who exercise administrative control over the networks. Administrators can require particular kinds of traffic flow along particular routes. There are many reasons that one might want to make such decisions, including security, monitoring, efficiency, active network management, and quality-of-service guarantees. Policies, similarly, can be defined to discriminate traffic based on different criteria, including point of origin, point of destination, type of data being transmitted, or available network capacity. Perhaps unsurprisingly, studies of policy routing show that in practice, they result in *route inflation*—that is, that policy-compliant paths are often longer than the shortest path a packet could follow. Hongsuda Tangmunarunkit and colleagues (2001) report that, at the time of their analysis, 20 percent of paths were longer by 50 percent or more. Significantly, this suggests a shift in the conception of route optimality. Where to be "optimal" once meant to follow the shortest (or fastest) path, it now means to follow the path most compliant with organizational considerations.

Policy routing can be used to shape how the network routes traffic, as well as to ensure that autonomous systems have defined points of entry and exit. Routing, in this model, becomes less a matter of topology and interconnection, and more a matter of institutional relations. The mythos of the internet is its open, amorphous, and adaptive nature. Such celebrations of openness as John Gilmore's famous proclamation that "the Internet treats censorship like damage and routes around it" is grounded in this idea that the network will adapt to damage and interference, whether accidental or intentional. To an extent, of course, this is entirely true; but it is certainly not as true as it was in the earlier days of the internet, and it is true now only to the extent that new routes conform to the organizational and institutional policies of the relevant network authorities. Censorship, in the contemporary internet, is a simple matter of policy—as protesters in Egypt discovered in 2011 (Srinivasan 2013). As we will see shortly, in a discussion of network peering, routing policies are driven as much by economics as by technical characteristics (Rayburn 2014). An adequate account of the political economy of network technologies, then, needs to go beyond questions of ownership, equity, and access, incorporating an understanding of the relationship between this and the materiality of network routing—the material constraints that network routers need to manage (such as the explosion of network topology data and the need to move from networks to autonomous systems) and the material instantiation of economic relationships in protocols like BGP.

Material Considerations

As a lens, routing protocols like RIP, EGP, and BGP provide us with a view into contests over network arrangements as they develop over time. They provide us with an idea of the debates and the problems over which development has stumbled, but also reveal a series of constraints, conditions, and expectations that are eventually encoded in the network's basic operations. I have read these as material in the sense that I have developed throughout this book, thinking both of the representational constraints and the expressive possibilities of the digital forms through which our own experience of information technology is produced. This has brought us to an examination of questions of structure, topology, and institutional relations, among other topics. If we step back from the protocols in particular, though, some broader material considerations come into view. Starting on familiar ground, with questions of granularity, and ending with more recent network developments, I want to examine three of these here.

Granularity and Networks as User Objects

This discussion has been based on a set of technical conditions that govern what "a network" is, in internet terms—not an abstract large-scale entity ("the Internet" rather than the ATM network) nor an autonomous system ("UC Irvine's network") nor even the entities of common experience ("my home network"), because none of these is the sort of "network" of which the internet is a connective fabric. Rather, the "networks" that the internet connects are particular media arrangements—lengths of coaxial or fiberoptic cable, wireless signal fields, tangles of twisted pair wires, and so on. These networks are technical entities but not user entities.

Or, at least, not usually. The vagaries of routing can also result in the infrastructure of network arrangements becoming visible and even important as a question of user interaction. Amy Voida and coauthors (2005) document an interesting and unexpected case, that of music sharing within a corporate network. In IP, a network is not only the unit of routing, but also the unit of broadcast; that is, a protocol mechanism allows messages to be delivered to all the hosts on a particular network. This in turn means that networks can become visible as marking the boundaries of broadcast-based sharing. In the case documented by Voida and colleagues, participants in a corporate network came to realize aspects of its internal structure—that is, the way that it is composed of multiple subnetworks connected via routers—through the patterns of visibility and invisibility that they can perceive through the use of music sharing in Apple's iTunes application. iTunes can allow people on a network to share music with each other, and the corporate participants in the study took advantage of this facility. They began to encounter problems, however, that resulted from the network topology. A friend's music might be unexpectedly invisible, for example, if the friend was on a different network, or someone's music might "disappear" if that person was relocated to a different office, even within the same building. The network topology itself became visible as a routine part of their interactions, and suddenly the material arrangements that underlay the notion of "the network" became an aspect of the user experience.

What is significant here is the collapse of the network stack: the tower of abstractions that separates the physical medium from internetworking protocols, and internetworking from applications. Suddenly, in this model, the specific material manifestation of IP networks—as runs of cable, governed by signal degradation over distance and the number of available sockets on a switch—need to be managed not only for the network but also for the users. Network engineers and researchers have long recognized that the abstractions of the network stack may be a good way to talk about and think about networks but are a less effective way of managing or building them (see, e.g., Clark and Tennenhouse 1990). Yet, the intrusion of the material fabric of the network and its routing protocols into the user experience is a different level of concern. If granularity is a core material property, one that shapes the decomposition of the network into effective units of control, then Voida and colleagues highlight the way in which this materiality manifests itself in multiple different regimes.

Centralized Structure and Network Power

The mythology of the internet holds that it was designed to withstand nuclear assault during the Cold War era, both by avoiding centralized control and by using a packet-switching model that could "route around" damage, seeking new routes if any node was lost. Whatever the status of that claim,[6] it is certainly true that one of the defining features of the internet is its variable and amorphous topology. Unlike networks that rely on a fixed arrangement of nodes, such as a ring formation in, for example, the Cambridge Ring (Hopper and Needham 1988), the internet allows connections to be formed between any two points, resulting in a loosely structured

---

6. It's true that Paul Baran's (1964) original report on packet switching was inspired by the nuclear assault scenario, and that the developers of the Internet recognized the originality and value of this approach to network design; however, the extent to which the Internet or its ARPANET predecessor was designed with this goal in mind is highly questionable. Baran, as it happens, didn't call his invention packet switching; that term was coined by British computer scientist Donald Davies, who independently arrived at the same idea while working at the National Physical Laboratory in Teddington, England. Baran had used the more awkward "distributed adaptive message block switching."

pattern of interconnections (what computer scientists call *a graph*). The absence of formal structure and the avoidance of critical "choke points" or centralized points of control is arguably one of the essential characters of the internet. Nonetheless, our examination of routing and routing protocols reveals a more complicated situation at work.

What is revealed by the history of routing protocols is the fact that it's one thing to design a network and its protocols, and quite another thing to build, grow, and develop it. The distinction between these two concerns matters, because each of these domains of activity, and each of their institutional structures, has a significant influence on the end result.

The traditional origin narrative of the internet traces its proximal history to the ARPANET effort, which provided much of the impetus, and funding, for both a network design and an initial implementation. As we have seen, some argue that, since the ARPA funding agency was an arm of the US Department of Defense, the ARPANET to some extent reflects military concerns with both command-and-control and risks of attack. Perhaps more significant, though, is the fact that, as an ARPA project, the ARPANET was designed to link ARPA-sponsored institutions. Universities that were not conducting ARPA-sponsored research were not incorporated into the ARPANET. This caused other US computer science departments, conscious of the ARPANET networking research program but unable to participate, to worry about being left behind in the ongoing research endeavor. A group of them proposed a similar networking effort of their own, under the name CSNET. CSNET is discussed in more detail in the next chapter, but it's worth pausing at this moment to make the argument that, from an infrastructural point of view if not from an intellectual one, CSNET has a reasonable claim to being a more significant progenitor of the contemporary internet than ARPANET does. The CSNET consortium of universities sought support from the US National Science Foundation (NSF) to build their network, using the same network protocols that had been designed for the ARPANET. It was the CSNET backbone (rather than the ARPANET backbone) that eventually formed the basis of NSFNET, an internet linking NSF-sponsored research institutions; and it was the NSFNET backbone to which commercial network carriers began to connect, and the management of which was itself eventually turned over to private industry in the moment that essentially birthed the commercial internet.

What I want to draw attention to in this story, though, is the notion of "backbone" itself—the idea that the network might be conceptualized as a combination of local networks, regional networks, and long-distance networks, each of which might be built by, sponsored by, and funded by different kinds of institutions and organizations. This arrangement is not a consequence of the network's design, as such, but it is a consequence of the historical processes of bringing the network into existence, and—as we saw with EGP—these kinds of historical patternings can subsequently find themselves expressed in the network protocols and technologies themselves.

The gradual emergence of the internet resulted in an informal but technologically grounded set of institutional relationships between different "tiers" of network service providers. There are, essentially, three sorts of network carriers. *Tier 1* providers operate international networks that span the globe and provide the major channels of network connectivity. *Tier 2* providers have large national or international networks, but without the reach of the tier 1s. *Tier 3* providers may just be regional; they don't operate their own large-scale networks but must buy network provision from the larger operators (Gorman and Malecki 2000).

The true defining feature of tier 1 providers, though, is not the topology or reach of their networks, but the scope of their institutional power. Tier 1 providers—of whom there are no more than twenty—are network providers so powerful that they can agree to engage in what is known as settlement-free peering with other tier 1 providers. *Peering* is an agreement in which networks carry each other's traffic (they are "peers" in the network); *settlement-free* peering is a bilateral agreement in which no money changes hands (Laffont et al. 2001). When two network providers engage in settlement-free peering, they are saying to each other, "I agree to carry traffic that originates on your network, and you agree to carry traffic that originates on my network, and we won't charge each other for the privilege." Tier 2 and tier 3 network providers, on the other hand, lack this same reach and what Manuel Castells calls network power; they need to pay for the right to connect to tier 1 networks (Rayburn 2014).

These precarious peering arrangements, in which the flow of network traffic becomes hostage to commercial arrangements, highlights the very centrality of tiered network arrangements at work in a network whose avowed modus operandi is decentralization. We can observe the alignments between technical considerations, like the shift toward autonomous systems as a solution to the problem of route proliferation, border-oriented routing protocols as a way to manage interinstitutional relationships, network tiers as a way of concentrating traffic flow and thus market significance, and settlement-free peering as a way to reinforce network power. The representational materialities of network routing tables and the protocol expressions that describe, manage, and control them become comingled with institutional and commercial arrangements even within a network whose design embraces principles of openness, interconnection, and adaptation (Mansell 2012).

A More Content-Centered Network

When talking about internet routing, one talks primarily about network topology and structure—how the elements are connected, what sorts of interconnections provide bridges from one network to another, how administrative authority is asserted over different aspects of the network, and similar topics. What is notably absent from this discussion is content—the actual information that is flowing across the network. Internet routing protocols operate independently of particular forms of content (such as text, voice, video, data files, web pages, and so on), and so content may seem to be irrelevant to a discussion of routing, or even to a discussion of the interrelationships between commercial and institutional concerns and technical concerns. In recent years, however, matters of content have come to play a significant role that, again, opens up new ways of thinking about network topology and institutional relations.

One particular driver of this has been the need to be able to provide internet subscribers with speedy access to large volumes of data, particularly data that need to be delivered in real time. A simple case, for example, is on-demand video streamed from services such as Netflix or Amazon. Recently published figures suggest that movies and television shows streamed from Netflix constitute a staggering 34 percent of network traffic at peak hours. Not only is this a huge volume of data, it is also a volume of data that must be delivered promptly and evenly if an acceptable viewing experience is to be achieved; jittery or interrupted video will be deemed unacceptable by customers. While web pages can be delivered at uneven rates as long as the service is not unacceptably slow, video content places different demands on the network. For content providers like Netflix, then, or other people who need to deliver large volumes of data directly to customers with strong constraints for both volume and timing, the somewhat unpredictable operation of shared, long-haul transit networks poses a problem.

The result has been the development of content distribution networks (CDNs). CDNs are technological arrangements designed to deliver large volumes of data at high speed directly to end-users and network consumers. The technology of CDNs is not significantly different from that of other parts of the network infrastructure, but the topology is different. A CDN solution for Netflix, for example, would comprise significant amounts of digital storage connected directly (or almost directly) to the distribution networks of internet service providers, with multiple copies of each data file maintained in different regions or localities. Netflix may be headquartered in Los Gatos and Apple in Cupertino, but when I view a movie on Netflix or listen to music via the Apple Music service, the data that are streaming to me originate much closer to me than those cities, via content distribution networks that maintain nearby copies of popular movies and albums that don't need to travel over long-haul networks.

As Laura DeNardis (2012) notes, this produces a shift in networking topologies that begins to break down the traditional distinctions between tier 1, tier 2, and tier 3 providers, and does so in ways that are driven primarily by concerns about content rather than topology—an interesting shift. Some tier 1 providers, such as Level 3 Communications, also operate content distribution networks on behalf of customers. Other CDN corporations developed their own infrastructures specifically to provide CDN services—Akamai, one of the early providers, is an example. Nevertheless, the move toward CDNs in general is a move that attempts to reframe the institutional relationships among different classes of carriers. Broadly, it is a move that suggests that instead of purchasing transit capacity (the capacity to transmit data over long distances), one might instead purchase locality (the capacity to locate data close to the point of need). In light of the tropes of virtuality and placelessness that animate so much discussion of the internet and its use, this is a particularly intriguing shift.

Protocols as Mechanism

Craig Partridge's (1994) book, *Gigabit Networking*, provides a comprehensive overview of the technical issues involved in running networks at gigabit speeds (that is, at data transmission rates of more than one billion bits per second). Yet, in opening a discussion on the use of the TCP/IP protocols, the author finds himself presented at the outset with an odd challenge. The challenge is that, while it is clear that network technologies can transmit data at gigabit speeds—indeed, much faster—it was not at the time universally accepted that IP-based networks could run at that speed. Skeptics argued that the protocol itself—the set of conventions and rules about how data should be formatted and how they should be processed when being sent or received—made gigabit speeds impossible. As we have seen, data in IP networks are processed as discrete packets, each with their own addressing information, and packets are processed independently by the network. The challenge for running IP (or any protocol) at gigabit speeds is whether a network router can process a packet before the next one arrives. As network transmission rates increase, the time available to process any given packet decreases. Advocates for alternatives to IP would argue that IP couldn't "scale"—that is, that the overhead of processing the protocol data was too great, and that IP packets could not be processed fast enough to make effective use of a gigabit network. Partridge begins his discussion, then, by laying out specific software code that can interpret and forward IP packets and then painstakingly demonstrating, instruction by instruction, that this code could be executed by a network router operating fast enough to enable gigabit transmission rates.

The very fact of Partridge's demonstration—and, more to the point, its necessity as a starting point for his discussion—highlights some significant issues in how we think about networking technologies. These are issues that might seem self-evident to computer scientists and engineers, although their very obviousness might blind us to their importance; to others who write, talk, and think about networking technologies, though, they may seem unusual. First, the demonstration highlights the idea that what the network can do is not the same as what the transmission lines can do, although we often talk about them as though they are the same thing—that is, a transmission line might be able to transmit data more quickly than the "network" can. Second, the demonstration highlights the fact that different network protocols can have different properties not just in terms of their formal properties but also in terms of their practical capacities—a protocol does not simply imply rules and conventions in the terms that Galloway (2004) opens up, but is also subject to analyses that focus on weight, length, and speed. Third, it draws our attention to the relationship between the *internals* of a network (the practical manifestations of how it operates) and the *externals* (what it can do for us and how).

For Partridge, the capacities of the network need to be understood in terms of multiple materialities—the execution rate of network routing code, the complexity of IP header decoding, and the sheer raw speed at which IP packets flow down a wire. In practice, a protocol can be too complex—too *heavy-weight*, in technical parlance—to achieve desired characteristics. The possibilities of the protocol need to be seen in light of other capacities, other materialities, and other technical arrangements. Similarly, protocols limit possibilities. They are designed to make certain undesirable situations impossible. The nature of what makes particular situations "undesirable," though, is much more than simply technical, even when we use technical levers to control and manipulate the range of possibilities. Protocols, in their shapes and capacities, produce both technical and

institutional arrangements simultaneously. In tracing the entangled histories of protocols, topologies, network conventions, institutional arrangements, commercial exchanges, and representational strategies, I have
sought to demonstrate the impossibility, or implausibility, of talking about
one without talking about the others.

Networks and Representational Materialities

Taking just the case of network routing, we have been able to see at work a
series of ways in which representational forms—encodings and the constraints or range of available manipulations—contribute to the shaping of
issues of use, experience, and policy.

First, for example, the degree to which topology and temporality are
entwined finds its resolution in the representational materialities of routing. As networks grow, the rates at which they change also accelerate. Every
time a computer is unplugged, and every time a laptop wakes up and connects to its Wi-Fi network, the topology of the internet changes. In a small
network, this might only happen occasionally, but on the global internet,
it is an unceasing source of flux. The gradual evolution of network protocols is in part a response to this, creating ways to limit the impact of these
changes and the need for others to know what has happened. The pace of
change in network structure is one material character of the infrastructure,
and protocols play a key role in mediating between infrastructural flux and
institutional action.

Second, we have seen a direct relationship between the representational
forms in which network routes can be expressed and the bounds and scales
of network activity. From the fifteen-hop limit in RIP to the acceptable formulations of policy routes in BGP, representational practice sets the limit
on what is doable and expressible in the network as an operational entity,
and enables the emergence of zones of social, organizational, and institutional autonomy and dependence.

The third consideration to which we should be directed is that of decentralization, deferment, and delegation. The decentralization of internet
operations—the fact that packets are routed without appeal to a central
authority, and that internet policy is driven by what is called the *end-to-end*
model, which argues for placing control at the edges of the network—is one
of the most widely acknowledged features of the internet as a specific technology (Saltzer et al. 1984; Gillespie 2006). However, one of the things
that an examination of internet routing throws up is that the flexibility of
decentralized routing depends on many other components that may
not have that same degree of decentralized control. Galloway (2004) has

detailed what kinds of commitments to collective agreement are implied by decentralization within a regime of protocol-driven interaction. We might also point to questions of network addressing and topology as places where decentralization operates within a framework of deferment of authority and delegation to others.

At the same time, however, we must also bear in mind a fourth material consideration that this analysis suggests, which is the need to distinguish between protocol, implementation, and embodiment. The distinction between protocol and implementation is well recognized; that is, we understand, analytically, the distinction between those formal descriptions of how systems interoperate on the one hand and the specific pieces of software that implement those protocols on the other—the fact that protocols are rarely complete, for example, or at least that implementers have discretion in the choices they make about the extent to which deviations from the protocol will be accepted. The distinction between protocol and embodiment, though, speaks to a different issue. It highlights the fact that a protocol might be clear, well-defined, and effective in design, and yet be ineffective or inoperable in practice—for example, when routing tables are too large, when network connections are too slow, when routing hardware lacks the computational resources needed to process the protocol, or when the protocol is poorly matched to local conditions. A failure of protocol-connected systems is not in itself a failure of protocol, or even necessarily of implementation; specific embodiments, not just of infrastructure but crucially also of the protocol itself—data on the wire—also matter.

The broader, programmatic point is that a materialist concern with the internet needs to be engaged not just with what "networks" are, but rather with what this particular network—as a specific case, and as one among a range of alternatives—might be. That is, it is not enough to argue for the critical role of decentralization, or to examine the formalized disengagement afforded by protocols, or to note the geographical siting of infrastructure. Rather, a materialist account must examine just how that decentralization becomes possible, what specifically the protocols do and how, and how specific forms of spatial and institutional arrangements become possible in *just this* Internet—one that is materially, geographically, and historically specific. In this chapter, routing and routing protocols have been a means to open up these questions, in particular by placing contemporary arrangements in the context of historical antecedents. In the next chapter, I attempt a different form of contextualization by looking toward non-Internet networks as alternative conceptions of the possibilities and problems of digital communication.

7   Internets and Othernets

Using a reading of routing protocols, I highlighted in chapter 6 how internet structure and its institutional arrangements emerged in concert with representational materialities and the encodings of digital objects within the network's own transmissions. The structure that emerged troubles our conventional understandings of what the internet is and how it operates. Part of the difficulty in assessing the operational possibilities of internet technologies is the lack of alternatives that might support a comparative analysis. In chapter 6, a historical reading made such an analysis possible by allowing us to think about different protocols and their different concerns. This chapter widens the focus somewhat to look not just at routing but also at other aspects of network behavior, adopting a different comparative approach that looks across different kinds of networks in order to see the contemporary internet as one among a range of possibilities.

The Internet?

Part of my motivation here is to respond to the kinds of statements about the internet's operation that one encounters regularly in both academic discussions and the popular press. When people argue, for example, that "the Internet treats censorship as damage and routes around it" (Elmer-Dewitt 1993), quite what is it that they have in mind? Or again, if one believes that the internet is a democratizing force as a result of its decentralized architecture (Dahlberg 2001), or that it's a platform for grassroots community building rather than mass media messaging (Shirky 2008), how should these statements be read?

One focus of valid critique for comments like these is their casual treatment of topics such as democracy, censorship, broadcasting, or community (e.g., Hindman 2008). However, the term that I want to focus on in these statements is "the internet." When we attribute characteristics to the internet, specifically, what do we mean? Do we just mean "digital net-works"? Do we mean digital networks that implement the internet proto-cols, and if so, which protocols do we have in mind? Or do we mean the one very specific network that we have built—*the* Internet, *this* Internet, *our* Internet, the one to which I'm connected right now? Or something else entirely?

To make this argument more concrete, let me begin by describing two cases from my own working history, two digital transitions that illustrate the complexity of talking about the internet as a force for decentralization.

The first of these transitions occurred in the early 1990s when I worked for Xerox. Xerox had been a pioneer in digital networking. Early research on Ethernet and distributed systems constituted an important precursor to the development of the Internet Protocol (IP) suite, and research systems such as Pup (Boggs et al. 1980) and Grapevine (Birrell et al. 1982) had sub-sequently given rise to a protocol suite called XNS (Xerox Network Ser-vices), which was the basis of a line of digital office systems that Xerox sold in the marketplace. Xerox's own corporate network spanned the globe, linking thousands of workstations and servers together using the XNS pro-tocols. In the 1990s, as Unix workstations began to dominate the profes-sional workstation market, and as the arrival of distributed information services such as Gopher, WAIS, and the web spurred the accelerated growth of the internet, many inside Xerox became interested in using TCP/IP on internal networks too. Particularly at research and development centers, small groups began to run TCP/IP networks locally and then increasingly looked for ways to connect them together using the same leased lines that carried XNS traffic between sites. What began as renegade or guerilla actions slowly became organizationally known and tolerated, and then formally supported as TCP/IP became a recognized aspect of internal corporate net-working within Xerox.

XNS was a protocol suite designed for corporate environments. Although technically decentralized, it depended on an administratively centralized or managed model. The effective use of XNS was tied together by a distributed database service known as the Clearinghouse, which was responsible for device naming, address resolution, user authentication, access control, and related functions (Oppen and Dalal 1981). Users, servers, workstations, printers, e-mail lists, organizational units, and other network-relevant objects were all registered in the Clearinghouse, which was implemented as a distributed network of database servers linked via a so-called epidemic algorithm by which they would keep their database records up to date

(Demers et al. 1988). Access control mechanisms distinguished administrators, who could update Clearinghouse databases, from regular users, who could look up names but couldn't introduce new ones. The Clearinghouse service was central enough to the operation of XNS services that this administrative access was needed for all sorts of operations, from adding new users to installing new workstations.

By contrast, the TCP/IP network and the Unix workstations that it often linked were administered in a much more distributed fashion. For the Unix machines, users could be defined locally for each computer, and similarly, workstations could maintain their own machine addressing and network routing information. Even when systems were interconnected, much less coordination was required to get machines connected together effectively in the IP network than in the XNS network. As a result, the rise of the IP network provided a route by which people could to some extent become more independent of the corporate IT management structure through which the XNS network was operated. Since XNS was the dominant technology for organizational communication, it wasn't entirely possible for people using TCP/IP to "route around" the corporate network, but it started to provide a certain amount of independence.

The second transition was also a transition to IP, but in a very different context. This transition was in progress while I worked at Apple in the late 1990s. As at Xerox, the rise of the internet in general was reflected in the increasing use of TCP/IP in a network that had originally been put together through a different network protocol—in this case, AppleTalk. AppleTalk was a proprietary network suite that Apple developed to connect Macintosh computers; it had evolved over time to operate over the Ethernet networks commonly deployed in corporate settings, although it had originally been developed for linking computers together in relatively small networks. One important feature of the AppleTalk networking protocols is their *plug-and-play* approach, which allows a network to be deployed with minimal manual configuration. For example, AppleTalk does not require that network addresses be preassigned or that a server be available for network resource discovery; these features are managed directly by the networked computers themselves. Accordingly, setting up AppleTalk networks requires little or no administrative intervention. TCP/IP networks, on the other hand, do require some services to be set up—DHCP servers must be deployed to allocate addresses, name servers to resolve network addresses, and so on. (In fact, the contemporary networking technologies known as Bonjour, or Zeroconf, are mechanisms designed to reintroduce AppleTalk's plug-and-play functionality into TCP/IP networking.) So, where the transition from

XNS to TCP/IP was a decentralizing transition at Xerox, one that increased people's independence from corporate network management, the transition from AppleTalk to TCP/IP at Apple moved in the other direction, creating *more* reliance on network infrastructure and hence on network administration.

These examples illustrate two important concerns that animate this chapter. The first is that statements about "the internet" and its political and institutional character suffer for a lack of contrast classes. The internet may well be decentralized—but compared to what, exactly? More decentralized internetworks could be imagined and have existed. We might be able to make some more fruitful observations if the "internet" we are trying to characterize weren't such a singular phenomenon. In what follows, I briefly sketch some cases that might serve as points of comparison, providing for more specific statements about contemporary phenomena by showing how they might be, and have been, otherwise. The first concern, then, is to provide a framework within which the characterizations can take on more meaning. The second concern is that the singular nature of the internet makes it hard for us to distinguish the conceptual object of our attention, the object that we are characterizing. Given that the internet—the specific Internet to which we can buy or obtain access today—is generally the only internet we have known, it's hard to pin down just what object it is that we are characterizing when we talk about, say, decentralization. Do we mean that a world-spanning network-of-networks is inherently decentralized? Or is decentralization a characteristic of the specific protocols and software that we might use to operate that network (the internet protocols)? Or is it rather a characteristic of the specific network that we have built, which doesn't just use those protocols, but implements them in a specific network made of particular connections, an amalgam of undersea fiber-optic cables, domestic Wi-Fi connections, commercial service providers, and so on? Is it *our* internet that's decentralized, while we could still imagine a centralized one being built? Or—even more interesting perhaps—is our internet actually less decentralized than it might be, failing to achieve its own promise (if that's something we want)?

To provide the resources to think about these questions fruitfully, I will approach the topic from two perspectives. The first is to briefly catalog some alternatives to "the" internet. Some of these are entirely alternative networks; some are small components of the broader internet that do not always operate in the same way as the whole. The second is to take in turn some key aspects of network function—routing, naming, and so on—and examine their contemporary specificities, with particular focus on the relationship between specific commercial and technical arrangements and the openness or range of possibilities encapsulated by the network design. Taken together, these allow us to develop an understanding of the landscape of potential network arrangements within which our current arrangements take their place, and perhaps more accurately target or assess statements about what "the internet" is or does.

Othernets

Our starting point is what I have been calling "othernets"—non-Internet internets, if you will. My concern is with networks as technological arrangements, although from a phenomenological or experiential perspective, one might reach a different understanding of "othernets." Communication and media scholars have argued convincingly that the notion of a singular internet that is the object of everyone's experience is no longer useful (Goggin 2012; Schulte 2013; Donner 2015; Miller et al. 2016). The variety of ways to gain access to online resources (via fixed-line infrastructures and desktop computers, or via a mobile phone), the variety of ways to make use of those resources (via web browsers or via apps, for example), and even the range of different services that make up each person's own particular set of conventional usage sites (Facebook? LinkedIn? QQ? Odnoklassniki? Twitter? Weibo? Instagram? Venmo? Snapchat? Kakao?) suggest a much more fragmented and enclaved experience of digital services than is allowed by the notion of "the" internet.

These concerns notwithstanding, my interest here is in the technological arrangements by which internetworking is brought about (although a technological reading might similarly support the phenomenological one). My non-Internet internets are other sorts of networks, some of which predate the contemporary internet, although many persist. Some of these are networks of a similar style that happen to use different protocols; some of them are radically different arrangements. Some of them are global networks, and some more localized; some are specific networks, and some are ways of thinking about or approaching network design. What they do for us here, though, is flesh out an internetworking space of possibilities, one that helps to place "the internet" in some context.

Before we can begin, though, we need to ask a seemingly simple question: what is a network? One would imagine that there is an easy answer to this question, although in fact it is not quite as clear as it might seem at first blush. Clearly, networks connect computational resources that are distributed in space, allowing information of some sort to flow between different devices. That account is straightforward but perhaps too all-encompassing, since the relationship between my computer and its keyboard might be described as a network that fits the description. Indeed, there might even be times when it makes sense to think of the array of devices connected to my computer as a network, but this is not one of them. So perhaps we should be more specific and require that the devices being connected by a network be more widely distributed than simply different parts of my desk, and identifiable as individual "devices" in some sense. That helps but is still overly inclusive; it might encompass a mainframe or large minicomputer with links to so-called dumb terminals throughout a metropolitan region, for example. (A *dumb terminal* has no computational capacity of its own; it simply transmits keystrokes and displays characters sent via a serial line to a remote computer.) For the purposes of this discussion, I will focus on networks that link together independent computational devices, that is, devices that can run programs themselves and that can, in principle at least, be used for computational tasks even in the absence of the network (much as I can continue to run programs on my laptop even when I am disconnected from the internet). If dumb terminals connected to a mainframe computer have no computational capacities of their own, then a network, by contrast, links devices that are themselves usable as computers.[1]

Why ask this question at all? There are a few reasons that it's worth talking about. I raise it, first, to point out that it's not entirely straightforward: partly because the term has evolved over time, partly because it's a matter of perspective and utility, and partly because there are different conditions that one might want to impose. I raise it too because it shows that a user's perspective on how networks relate to devices turns out to be important; the question is perhaps not just what is a network but what it means to treat something as one. Finally, I also raise the question because there are some historically interesting cases that, while interesting, do not fit.

One of these is the remarkable Cybersyn system that Stafford Beer designed for the Allende government in Chile in 1971–1973, and which has been compellingly analyzed by Eden Medina (2001). Cybersyn was envisioned as a system to regulate and manage the Chilean economy with a particular focus on manufacturing and transportation, based on Beer's

---

1. It should be noted that the early ARPANET did provide a means for terminals to be connected to hosts via Terminal Interface Processors, or TIPs, which were variants of the IMP devices through which hosts connected to the network. However, the primary entities networked via the ARPANET were the IMP-connected hosts themselves.

cybernetic management principles (Pickering 2010). It was never fully implemented, since the development effort was interrupted by the coup that brought down the Allende government, although the system was partially functional and was used to help manage resources during a national strike. Even in its fullest design, though, Cybersyn was a system but not a network; it collected information through a string of terminals and telexes to be placed in factories around the country, but these connected to a single computational facility in Santiago. By contrast, OGAS, the Soviet "proto-internet" whose history is told by Benjamin Peters in his remarkable book *How Not to Network a Nation* (Peters 2016), was intended as a network, with computer systems managing factory production throughout the country, linked together to distribute information and regulate output; like Cybersyn, though, OGAS never got off the ground.

A more complicated case is that of Minitel, the French videotex service (Mailland and Driscoll forthcoming). Minitel was a hybrid of a true network (linking computers) and a mainframe model (providing access through simple video terminals). Minitel subscribers gained access to the system through simple terminals that, in the first instance, were given away free of charge by France Telecom. These terminals would connect to a system access point (known as a PAVI) through a standard telephone line. The PAVI would then provide an interface through which people could access services hosted on other computers maintained by third-party service and information providers. There is a network here, in the sense defined earlier; it operated according to the X.25 protocol suite. The end-user experience, however, was of a dial-up mainframe-style service. One reason that Minitel is worth examining, even if it does not quite meet the definition of network that I have set out here, is that while the original French system was a remarkable success, the effort to reproduce the service in the San Francisco Bay Area under the name 101 Online was a dismal failure, as documented by Mailland (2016).

Minitel itself was remarkably successful. While similar systems in other parts of Europe failed to make inroads with subscribers, Minitel, launched as a trial service in 1978, connected an estimated 25 million users in France by the late 1990s (out of a population of 60 million). It was the first successful mass-market digital information infrastructure. Minitel provided a huge array of services, including telephone directory listings, online banking, weather reports, stock prices, travel reservations, astrology, package and freight shipment, sports information, and, of course, pornography.

Given the remarkable success of the system in France, it is perhaps unsurprising that its operators thought to branch out overseas, and that

Silicon Valley and the San Francisco Bay Area would have seemed an obvious place to start. In 1991, France Telecom launched 101 Online, the US version of Minitel, beginning by targeting European expatriates, hoping they might be familiar with the service, and giving terminals away to influential figures such as journalists and cultural entrepreneurs in the hope of bootstrapping content and attracting interest. Within eighteen months, though, the system had foundered entirely. Mailland (2016) explores different reasons for its failure, some of which are simply errors of management and clashes of personality. Others concern timing, and the idea of rolling out a service that required specialized terminals at a time and in a place where personal computers were already a significant household presence. More interesting here, though, are the consequences of architecture: the way in which technological arrangements, including control over content, network capacities, questions of interoperability and compatibility, and organizational structure matched with the local ethos of technology use. Mailland uses this case to reflect on the problems of oft-repeated claims about the relative capacities for innovation in the private and public sector:

In France, Minitel, the epitome of a high-modernist statist model, had been explicitly designed to support the development of a private hardware and content-creation sector. The resulting implementation choice was to decentralize the hosts and allow creators control over their content. In contrast, in the US, the private-sector implementation of the same technology led to closing the network by centralizing all content on the network operator's mainframe and only allowing the network operator to edit content. In this case, leaving it to the private sector to make implementation choices stifled innovation. (2016, 20)

Minitel straddles the boundary between network and server. Other networks provide clearer contrast cases to the contemporary internet.

Fidonet

A bulletin board system (BBS) hosts messages and discussions, generally on a quite simple technology platform, such as a conventional home PC with a modem, which allows people to call into the platform over regular phone lines to read and post messages. In the United States, where local phone calls were generally free, bulletin board systems flourished in the late 1970s and early 1980s, as the home computer market grew. With very simple software, people could communicate by dialing in to the BBS at different times and posting messages that others would read later. While one certainly could make a long-distance call to connect to a BBS, most BBS use was local to take advantage of toll-free calling, with the result that most BBS activity was highly regionalized.

Fido was the name of the BBS software first written by Tom Jennings in San Francisco in 1984 and then adopted by others elsewhere in the United States. Before long, Fido was updated with code that would allow different Fido bulletin board systems to call each other to exchange messages; Fidonet is the name of this software and of the network of BBS systems that exchanged messages through this mechanism.[2] Fidonet's growth was explosive; from its start in 1985, it had around 500 nodes by the end of 1985, almost 2,000 by 1987, 12,000 by 1991, and more than 35,000 by 1995. Each of these nodes was a BBS that served tens to hundreds of users, who could exchange e-mail messages, files, and discussions on group lists.[3]

Fidonet's design was (with one critical exception) radically decentralized. Based as it was on dial-up rather than on an infrastructure of fixed connections, it employed a model of direct peer-to-peer communication. The Fidonet software was originally designed with a flat list of up to 250 nodes; a system of regions, zones, and networks was introduced within a year of the original software when it became clear that the system would soon grow beyond that capacity. This structure, which mapped the topology of the network geographically, provided a message routing structure that reduced costs (by maximizing local calling and by pooling messages for long-distance transfer) but with a minimum of fixed structure; direct communication between nodes was always central to the Fidonet model. The structure essentially exhibited a two-level architecture: one of conventional structures (that is, the conventional pattern of daily or weekly connections between sites) and an immediate structure, made up of those nodes communicating with each other right now. (The internet—being made up in its current form primarily of fixed infrastructure and broadband connectivity—largely conflates these two.)

Before the introduction of regions and net, Fidonet had used a single "flat" list of nodes, which was directly maintained by Jennings. The introduction of regions and nets allowed for a more decentralized structure. This

2. In other words, much like "the internet," "Fidonet" is a label both for the potentialities of the software infrastructure and for the only known case of its implementation.

3. This count of Fidonet nodes year by year is offered by BBS: The Documentary (http://www.bbsdocumentary.com): 1984: 132; 1985: 500; 1986: 938; 1987: 1,935; 1988: 3,395; 1989: 5,019; 1990: 7,503; 1991: 12,580; 1992: 18,512; 1993: 24,184; 1994: 31,809; 1995: 35,787.

was simultaneously an addressing structure and a routing structure, linked together—the structure of the network was also the structure that determined how messages would make their way from one place to another.

Fidonet was built around a file transfer mechanism that would allow files to move from one node to another. Other facilities could be built on top of this mechanism, such as electronic mail. From the user perspective, the discussion groups known as *echoes* were a major feature of Fidonet. Echoes allowed users to post messages that would be distributed to all users on the system interested in a topic. A "moderation" mechanism allowed echo managers to discourage off-topic posts, but this was post-hoc (rather than an approach that required explicit approval before a message was sent out). As in systems such as the WELL (Turner 2006), the topically oriented discussion forums provided by echoes were the primary site of interaction and community building across Fidonet (although unlike the WELL, Fido echoes were networked rather than centralized).

Usenet

Usenet is a somewhat informal term for a worldwide network of computers linked by a series of mechanisms built on top of a facility provided by versions of the Unix operating system (Hauben and Hauben 1997). The facility was known as uucp, which stands for "Unix-to-Unix copy." In Unix's command-line environment, "uucp" was a command that enabled users to copy files between computers. It was designed by analogy with the standard "cp" command for copying files; just as users might use "cp" to copy a file from a source to a destination filename, they might also use "uucp" to copy a file from a source to a destination, where either the source or destination file location was in fact on a different computer.

As with Fidonet, uucp was developed as a basic user file-copy facility that people realized was general enough to support other facilities as extensions. For instance, uucp could be used to support e-mail messaging between sites, exchanging individual messages as files that the remote system would recognize as drafts to be delivered by e-mail locally. The same mechanisms that named remote files, then, might also be used to name remote users.

Since Usenet had been initially designed simply to provide a user interface to a dial-up mechanism for file exchange, it provided no global naming mechanism to identify sites, files, objects, or users. Rather, its naming mechanism was a sequence of identifiers (separated by exclamation points, or *bangs*) that explained how a message should be routed. So, for instance, the path "seismo!mcvax!ukc!itspna!jpd" directs a computer to deliver the file first to a computer[4] called "seismo," at which point the path will be rewritten to "mcvax!ukc!itspna!jpd"; subsequently, it will be delivered to a computer called "mcvax," then to one called "ukc," and so on. The user is "jpd," whose account is on the computer "itspna." To send a message correctly, then, required that one knew not only the destination, but the entire route that the message should take—the series of peer-to-peer connections that must be made. Each path describes a direct connection; our example bang path only works if "mcvax" is one of the computers that "seismo" regularly connects to directly. One couldn't, for instance, route a message along the path "seismo!ukc!itspna!jpd" because seismo only dialed in to certain other computers, and ukc was not one of them.

Two aspects of this are worth noting. The first concerns the dynamics of network structure in the presence of this route-based addressing mechanism. Route-based addressing via bang paths means not just that you need to understand how your computer is connected to the network; everybody needs to understand how your computer is connected to the network if they want to reach you, and they need to understand how all the intermediate computers are connected to the network too. This arrangement does not allow, then, for frequent reconfiguration. Should seismo stop talking to mcvax, then every person using that connection as part of their routing process would find their routes broken.

The second noteworthy aspect, a partial consequence of the first, is that within the open, pairwise connection structure afforded by Usenet, a backbone hierarchy of major sites soon arose, at first through conventional practice and later through explicit design. These were sites that engaged in significant data transfer with each other or with other groups, including ihnp4 at AT&T's Indian Hill site, seismo at the Center for Seismic Studies in northern Virginia, and mcvax at the Mathematics Centrum in Amsterdam, which effectively became the primary trans-Atlantic gateways, and national sites such as ukc at the University of Kent at Canterbury, which effectively became the gateway to the United Kingdom. Significantly, some of these also served as well-known nodes for routing purposes; one might quote one's email address as "...!seismo!mcvax!itspna!jpd," with the "..."

4. To be slightly more accurate, it directs the local machine to deliver this message along the connection locally labeled as "seismo." Two different computers could have two different labels for links that both actually connect to "seismo"; there is no service that ensures uniform naming, and the mapping of names to links is entirely local. However, conventional practice—for the preservation of operator sanity—was that links and machines were generally named consistently.

essentially meaning "whatever path you regularly use to reach here." As in other examples, then, the design of the network is unstructured but the practice requires a commitment to some form of well-understood centralization.

Uucp mail, with its explicit use of bang paths, was not the primary or most visible aspect of Usenet, however. A distributed messaging service, which came to be known as Usenet news, was first deployed in 1980, using the same underlying uucp mechanism to share files between sites. Unlike e-mail messages directed to specific users, however, articles in Usenet news were open posts organized into topically organized *newsgroups*. Via uucp, these would propagate between sites. Usenet connected many of the same academic and industrial research sites that came to be incorporated into ARPANET or its successors, and so over time, internet protocols became a more effective way for messages to be exchanged, at which point, Usenet newsgroups were (and continue to be) distributed over TCP/IP rather than uucp.

BITNET
BITNET was a large international network that linked primarily academic institutions. BIT, at different points in its history, was said to stand for "Because It's There" or "Because It's Time." Established in 1981 with a link between the City University of New York and Yale University, BITNET grew through the 1980s and early 1990s, linking almost five hundred institutions at its peak (Grier and Campbell 2000). BITNET was created using NJE, a remote job-entry mechanism provided as part of IBM's RSCS/VNET protocol suite—essentially, a mechanism that allowed one to send a program to be executed remotely by another computer. The very foundation of BITNET in the notion of "remote job entry" signals that it was heir to a legacy that predates interactive and time-shared computing; naming computer program executions "jobs" speaks to the language of large-scale, computer-center batch computing, often in the form of punch card operations redolent of the 1960s. The computers that BITNET linked, then, tended not to be the midsized departmental minicomputers of ARPANET but large-scale IBM mainframes, the sort that a university might house in its computer center in order to provide a general-purpose computational resource to an entire campus. Similarly, then, while ARPANET nodes were often located in computer science departments or research facilities, BITNET typically provided facilities housed in larger and more formal institutional settings. Although the NJE protocol was an IBM design, it was not limited to IBM computers. Nonetheless, IBM computers predominated on BITNET,

and the others that participated (e.g., DEC VAX systems running VMS) still tended to be large-scale machines offering a general computing service to a broad academic population.

In line with the batch processing tradition, BITNET's facilities were not based on direct, real-time connections between hosts or between users, but rather employed a "store-and-forward" mechanism over a hierarchical arrangement of network nodes. That is, an e-mail message to be sent to a remote user would be forwarded in its entirety to one host and then another, step by step, through a hierarchy of local, regional, and national nodes (as with Usenet).

Perhaps the most lasting legacy of BITNET in the contemporary online world is the term LISTSERV. While many networks (and indeed nonnetworked systems) had provided facilities for redistributing e-mail messages to multiple recipients in order to create announcement and discussion lists, BITNET provided an automated mechanism for managing these distribution lists, called LISTSERV. Although the LISTSERV software is long gone, the name *listserv* persists in several ways—as a generic term for e-mail distribution lists, as a label for specific discussion lists (e.g., "the materiality listserv"), and in the convention of using "-l" as a suffix for distribution list addresses (e.g., "aoir-l," "cultstud-l"). The LISTSERV software operated in the context of BITNET, which meant that listservs were always hosted on BITNET hosts, but listserv participation was not limited to BITNET users; through gateways between BITNET and other networks, users from beyond BITNET could also participate in listserv discussions, giving listservs a visibility beyond the reaches of the network itself.

X.25

During the 1980s, a number of public data networks based on a series of protocols known as X.25 offered competition to the emerging TCP/IP internet standard. Following conventional practice, I use X.25 here as the umbrella term for a panoply of related protocols that defined different but related elements of this networking infrastructure, including X.3, X.28, X.29, and more, which were developed and defined by the CCITT (the Comité Consultatif International Téléphonique et Télégraphique, now part of the United Nations International Telecommunications Union). CCITT was a standards body made up of national telecommunications operators, and many (although not all) of the providers offering X.25 services were traditional telecommunications and telephone companies.

X.25 is a packet-switched service, but unlike IP, it offers a reliable delivery packet service, in the context of "virtual calls," which makes it look, to a networking application, as though it were actually a circuit-switched service. The virtual call model reflects the background of most network operators as telephone companies; it also provided to the operators a natural model for charging. Unlike TCP/IP, X.25 uses packet delivery only internally; there is no datagram service.

In the UK, JANET, the Joint Academic Network, was an X.25 network that provided connectivity to academic institutions, including the University of Edinburgh, where I undertook my undergraduate studies and was employed as a system administrator for a speech technology research center. In consequence, my memories of X.25 are not limited to perusing protocol specifications, but also include the process of getting down on my knees to stretch my arm through an open tile in a raised machine room floor to feel for the power switch that would let me reboot the troublesome network interface. (Brute materiality is never far away.) Contemporaneously, British Telecom offered a commercial X.25 service called PSS. In the United States, one of the major X.25 providers was Telenet, a commercial network provider that had spun off from ARPANET activities at Bolt, Beranek and Newman, Inc., which had built much of the core ARPANET technology under a contract from ARPA; Telenet's president was Larry Roberts, previously of ARPA. Telenet's service predated X.25; indeed, aspects of the X.25 standard were derived from Telenet's research (Mathison et al. 2012), and Telenet migrated toward the standardized service.

X.25 itself names just the data transmission protocol that corresponds to the lower levels of the network stack. X.25 network services tended to be offered commercially within the context of other defined sets of user-oriented services. The UK JANET network, for instance, offered a range of services defined by protocols named for the color of the covers of their specification documents, including Blue Book (file transfer) and Grey Book (electronic mail); these standards had been developed in the context of an earlier British academic network called SERCNet. This arrangement made the development and deployment of new services on top of X.25 networks a slow process. An alternative use of X.25 was as network channels that were treated like virtual cables and used for the transmission of different sorts of network protocols. CSNET, for example, used Telenet service as one of its component networks, over which it would transmit TCP/IP packets.

Some aspects of X.25 service were displaced by other telecommunication facilities, such as Frame Relay; others, especially more user-oriented services, were displaced by TCP/IP networking. X.25 networks still operate in a range of industrial settings, though, particularly in banking and finance; many bank automated teller machines (ATMs) make use of X.25 networks.

XNS

XNS, the Xerox Network Services protocol suite, has already made an appearance here, in the tale of network transitions with which I opened the chapter. XNS had its origins in Pup, the PARC Universal Packet, an early 1970s research project at Xerox PARC (Boggs et al. 1980).[5] At a point where PARC researchers were internally making use of several different packet-oriented network services, they wanted to create a unified structure in which a single packet could move among different and heterogeneous networks. Initial implementations included Ethernet, the Data General MCA network, and the ARPANET. Pup itself offered an unreliable datagram service that provided internetworking across these varied substrates, although the term was often used to encompass the full range of protocols that might be offered over and through the Pup service, including reliable byte streams, remote file access, file transfer, and printing.

Research on Pup predated the design of TCP/IP and influenced it, albeit through somewhat indirect means. PARC researchers participated in the 1973 meetings at Stanford from which the TCP/IP designs emerged. Pup was already in service at this point, but Xerox's lawyers refused to allow the researchers to reveal or discuss it; their participation was limited to asking questions and pointing out potential problems. In Michael Hiltzik's (1999) account of the history of Xerox PARC, he quotes John Schoch, one of the Xerox participants and Pup designers, reminiscing about the meetings:

Somebody would be talking about the design for some element and we'd drop all these hints. ... We'd say, "You know, that's interesting, but what happens if this error message comes back, and what happens if that's followed by a delayed duplicate that was slowed down in its response from a distant gateway when the flow control wouldn't take it but it worked its way back and got here late? What do you do then?" There would be this pause and they'd say, "You've *tried* this!" And we'd reply, "Hey, we never said that!" (Hiltzik 1999, 293)

Inside Xerox, Pup subsequently provided the basis for a large-scale distributed messaging and communication infrastructure known as Grapevine, one of the earliest wide-scale (international) corporate distributed systems efforts (Schroeder et al. 1984).

XNS evolved from Pup during Xerox's efforts to create a viable commercial product around the outputs of PARC's research. Given the histories, the technical analogies between XNS and TCP/IP are reasonably clear. Both provide an unreliable datagram service at the network layer, which can be

5. Although technically an acronym, Pup is normally written with only a capital initial.

encapsulated in packets on a range of media, with higher level protocols providing reliable byte streams, network services like file transfer, terminal connections, and other user-oriented services. Some specific details vary—the routing protocols, for instance, and the specific range of defined services—but there are strong resemblances.

The most significant distinctions are those that were briefly described in the discussion of network transitions at the opening of this chapter. The XNS protocols are essentially defined around a database system called the Clearinghouse (Oppen and Dalal 1981). Although there would be many Clearinghouse servers on most XNS internets, they collectively implemented a single database that named each valid network object—each computer, each server, each printer, each e-mail inbox, each e-mail distribution list, and each user. In order to operate on the network, a workstation, server, printer, or user would need to be identified uniquely in the Clearinghouse database. Further, the names of objects were indexed by organizational units—my own first XNS user account was not simply "Paul Dourish" but "Paul Dourish:EuroPARC:RX," identifying not simply me, but my position in the organization (and therefore automatically providing clustering and collective management of resources associated with a particular organizational unit). This account did not simply identify me within my organizational unit; it identified me to any computer anywhere within Xerox and its corporate affiliates linked to the same corporate internet (like Rank Xerox and Fuji Xerox, joint venture companies through which Xerox operated in different regions of the world). This global database was the basis on which all XNS services operated; it was the basis on which computers were identified, users were logged in, and credentials were established.

Such a global database is quite different from the TCP/IP model, but this is hardly surprising; XNS, after all, was an enterprise network product, and so one could expect or even demand much greater uniformity in operations, management, and administration. Some of the facilities that this uniformity provides, however, are ones that many have argued are needed for the contemporary internet (e.g., single sign-on to services across the network), making it a useful point of comparison.

DECnet

Digital Equipment Corporation (DEC, or just Digital) was a leading designer and vendor of minicomputers through the 1970s and 1980s. Indeed, many of the computers connected to the early ARPANET/internet were DEC machines, especially systems in the DEC-10, DEC-20, PDP, and VAX ranges, which were widely used in the academic research community. At the same time, DEC had its own networking system, delivered as part of its RSX and VMS operating systems. This network system, known as DECnet or the Digital Network Architecture (DNA), was initially introduced in the mid-1970s as a simple point-to-point connection between two PDP-11 minicomputers. Subsequently, the network architecture evolved to incorporate new technologies and new capabilities. The design and development of DECnet was largely contemporaneous with the development of the internet protocols. The last fully proprietary versions were DECnet Phase IV and Phase IV+, released in the early 1980s (Digital Equipment Corporation 1982); DECnet Phases V and V+ maintained compatibility with the proprietary DECnet protocols but moved more in the direction of support for the ISO-defined OSI protocol stack.

Given that DECnet was designed at roughly the same time as the internet protocol suite, and given that it connected many of the same computer system types as the internet protocols, it is again a useful point of comparison. DECnet was based on much the same *layered* protocol model that was the contemporary state of the art, and its basic architecture—a point-to-point connection layer, a routing layer, a layer for reliable sequenced delivery, and so on—is similar to that of systems like Pup, XNS, and TCP/IP. However, some key differences reveal the distinct character of the contexts within which DECnet was expected to operate.

One difference is that DECnet incorporated a sophisticated management interface, and indeed, that facilities for network management were designed into the protocol stack from an early stage. That is, DECnet was absolutely imagined to be deployed in a managed environment. TCP/IP has to be managed too, of course, but the management of TCP/IP networks is not a network function in itself. (The internet protocol suite includes a protocol, SNMP, the Simple Network Management Protocol, that is often used to create network management facilities, but network-wide, management is not a key consideration.)

A second suggestive distinction lies within the sets of services standardized within DECnet. These included services similar to TCP/IP, like network terminal access, but also some that the internet protocol suite did not natively attempt to support, such as seamless remote file system access, in which disks attached to one computer would appear to be virtually available to users of other, connected computers. Remote file access of this sort (which was also a feature that had been part of the Xerox network system) goes beyond simply file transfer by providing users with the illusion of seamless access to both local and remote files. (E-mail, on the other hand, was *not* one of the standardized protocols, although networked e-mail services were available through operating system applications.)

A third—although relatively trivial—distinction was that DECnet addresses were just sixteen bits long. Since each computer on a network needs to have a different address, the size of the address is a limit on the size of the network. With sixteen-bit addresses, DECnet implementations were limited to 64,449 hosts—a burdensome limitation in a world of desktop workstations, or PCs, but a more conscionable choice for a manufacturer of departmental minicomputers.

These three features of the DECnet design speak to a particular context of use. They highlight the expectation that DECnet deployments would be uniform, well regulated, and actively managed. This makes perfect sense in the context of DEC's sales in corporate settings, where network implementation can be phased, planned, and centrally directed. Effective use of the shared file facilities, for instance, require a coordinated approach to the layout and conventions of file systems across machines, while the network management infrastructure suggests that this was a key consideration in the settings for which DECnet was designed. An odd little implementation quirk in DECnet Phase IV similarly supports this. To make routing and discovery easier, the network software running on a DECnet computer operating over an Ethernet network would actually reset the hardware network address of the computer to an address that conformed to the DECnet host address. This would cause considerable difficulty when DECnet was running in the same environment as other protocols, but in a highly managed environment, where uniformity of access and technology could be guaranteed, it was less troublesome.

In sum, although DECnet was based on the same decentralized, peer-to-peer approach to network connectivity that characterizes the internet protocol suite, its specific configuration of that approach is one that was in practice designed for the highly managed, highly controlled setting of corporate IT.

CSNET

We saw some of the history of CSNET in the discussion of backbones in chapter 6, but here it is useful to examine it in more detail.

The conventional historical account of the emergence of today's internet traces its beginnings to the ARPANET. ARPANET was both a research project and a facility; that is, the ARPANET project developed the networking technologies that are the underpinnings of the contemporary internet, and it also operated a facility—a network—based on those underpinnings. So this was not simply a research project funded by ARPA; it was also a facility that supported ARPA research. ARPA is the research arm of the US Department of Defense (DOD), and so in order to qualify as a site to be connected to ARPANET, one had to be a DOD site or a DOD contractor. At the time, this included many prominent research universities and computer science departments, but by no means all, and not even most.[6]

Recognizing the value that DOD-contracting universities were deriving from their participation in the ARPANET effort, wanting to expand beyond the smaller-scale network arrangements on which they were already depending (Comer 1983), and concerned that "the ARPANET experiment had produced a split between the 'haves' of the ARPANET and the 'have-nots' of the rest of the computer science community" (Denning et al. 1983, 138), a consortium of US computer science departments partnered with the National Science Foundation (NSF) and other groups to put together a proposal for the Computer Science Research Network, or CSNET. CSNET integrated multiple different network technologies, with a store-and-forward e-mail system over regular phone lines as the base level of participation, with leased line and X.25 networking available for higher performance connections.

Although the development of CSNET produced many important technical contributions, CSNET's most significant legacies might be historical and institutional in that, first, CSNET represented a significant expansion in the spread of TCP/IP in the academic research community, and second, it was designed in collaboration with and in order to support the mission of the National Science Foundation (rather than, say, the military backers of ARPA and ARPANET). The CSNET effort laid the foundation for a later NSF-funded network called NSFNET, and it was the NSFNET backbone that was later opened up to commercial traffic, and then in 1995 replaced entirely by private service providers. The importance of this point is the explicit link at the time between institutional participation and connectivity, and the very idea that a network is conceived around an understanding of who and what will be permitted to connect.

The more interesting technical point for us here, though, concerns the relationship between ARPANET and CSNET. In a minor sense, CSNET was "in competition with" ARPANET; it was, after all, designed as a network for those who were institutionally denied access to ARPANET. Yet, in all the

6. In 1979, when the CSNET effort began, ARPANET had around two hundred nodes, representing fewer institutions, and spread between universities, government sites, and commercial contractors.

ways that matter, it was entirely collaborative with ARPANET; key players in the ARPANET project, such as Vint Cerf at DARPA, participated in the CSNET effort, and the networks were bridged together. The basis for that bridging was CSNET's adoption of the TCP/IP protocols that had been designed within the ARPANET effort. Through this bridging, ARPANET became a *subnet* of CSNET. We normally think of subnetting and internet-working as providing seamless interconnection, but the interconnection between CSNET and ARPANET was not quite so seamless, since they adopted different protocols for delivering services at the higher levels. For instance, the MMDF (Multichannel Memorandum Distribution Facility) network messaging facility developed as part of CSNET (Denning et al. 1983) was needed to be able to bridge the *phonenet* and TCP/IP components of CSNET, and that meant that messages destined for CSNET recipients would need to be routed explicitly to CSNET rather than simply dispatched using the usual protocols used on purely TCP/IP networks (such as SMTP, the standard internet email transfer protocol). In other words, both ARPANET and CSNET implemented the core internet protocols (TCP/IP) but not all the other protocols of what we sometimes called the *internet protocol suite*; accordingly, even though they were connected through a common TCP/IP infrastructure, they remained in some other important user-facing senses distinct networks, suggesting intriguingly that there may be more to being "an internet" than running TCP/IP on interconnected networks.

Delay-Tolerant Networking
In contrast to the networks and infrastructures above, the two examples that close this section are not non-Internet internets in quite the same way, but rather are emerging network standards or architectures that networking researchers have developed as extensions and evolutions of the classical internet protocols. The first, delay-tolerant networking (Fall 2003), is neither a specific network protocol standard nor a particular network implementation. Rather, it labels a set of related extensions or functions that address questions in the creation of TCP/IP networks. The set of concerns that DTN addresses, however, highlight specificities of TCP/IP design and implementation that can illuminate our discussion here.

Any packet-switched network must be able to tolerate some amount of delay in the delivery of individual packets. All network transmissions take a certain amount of time to be transmitted across a network line, so there is always some delay between a message being sent and being received, and since a single packet might traverse many connections between source and destination, many of these small delays might add up. Further, some network connections are faster than others; the transmission delay over a short length of fiber-optic cable is likely to be higher than that over a noisy telephone line or wireless connection. Finally, a network line might become congested, or the volume of traffic through a router might become high enough that some delay is introduced as packets are queued or even dropped in the face of traffic pressure. Some networking technologies can make end-to-end transmission time estimates or even guarantees, but most contemporary networking technologies are designed without this facility; instead, delay is something that they must simply be able to tolerate. The protocols are designed to be adaptive to different degrees of delivery delay, and this adaptation has allowed TCP/IP to be deployed in a wide range of settings, including fast links and slow links, long links and short links, and in high- and low-powered processors.

Nonetheless, some settings for network transmission test the limits of TCP/IP's adaptability. For instance, using TCP/IP to communicate from Earth to a rover on Mars or a more distant spacecraft poses major challenges. Even at the speed of light, signals can incur a round-trip delay of fifteen minutes getting to Mars and back, and a round-trip delay of three hours between Earth and, say, the Cassini probe in the Saturn system. As a second example, consider a network connection implemented by mounting Wi-Fi access points on buses in rural areas. The intermittent connectivity that could be provided here is, in theory, sufficient for basic network transactions (submitting a web search request this morning when the bus goes by, and waiting for a response this afternoon when it passes this way again), but these delays go well beyond what was imagined when TCP/IP was designed.

The reason that these long delays matter is that TCP has some designed-in constraints that are adapted to expected patterns of network use. For instance, establishing a connection necessitates what is known as a three-way handshake, which requires three messages to pass back and forth. (The three-way handshake is roughly equivalent to two musicians determining if they are ready to start performing together: "Are you ready?" "Yeah, I'm ready; are you ready?" "Yep, I'm ready.") So, establishing a connection requires the real-time simultaneous availability of the computers at each end of the connection; if one or other computer gets disconnected before the three-way handshake has been completed, then the connection cannot be established. As a second example, TCP is designed with an understanding that a packet might be lost in transmission (through corruption, or because it was dropped by a congested router, for instance). So, it must make a decision about how long to wait for a response before it decides that a packet has been lost and should be sent again. The absence of a response is used as a signal of packet loss. But in these long-delay networks, that is not necessarily an appropriate interpretation of network conditions.

Fall's work on "interplanetary networking" led to the design of an internet architecture for what he termed *delay-tolerant networking*. The key insight here is that new architectural principles were needed that could adapt to the much higher degree of delay that might characterize a network that spanned enormous distances, as well as be tolerant of intermittent connection—say, that associated with a mobile device that moves in and out of range of a network provider, or one that can only operate at particular times of day, or one that is otherwise constrained by resources of access, power, or bandwidth. This approach is particularly suited to networks that operate opportunistically or on an ad hoc basis rather than by relying on fixed infrastructure. So, for example, one might want to create a network from mobile devices (e.g., tablet computers) that never "connect" to a fixed network but simply encounter one another as they move around in space. This form of *ad hoc networking* requires new approaches to application design and to data management (see, e.g., Scott et al. 2006) as well as to network architecture in just the ways that delay-tolerant networking allows. Significantly, though, these are networks that can be deployed with radically different degrees of commitment to centralized operation or infrastructure provision, including supporting considerable interest in local, neighborhood, and DIY network arrangements (cf. Antoniadis et al. 2008; Gaved and Mulholland 2008; Jungnickel 2014; Powell 2011).

Multipath TCP

Like DTN, our final case is a response to problems or difficulties in emerging internet arrangements, although in this case, it takes the form of a network standard.

The early ARPANET was a single network, not an internet. Network transmissions were managed by the NCP, the Network Control Program. In 1974, Vint Cerf and Robert Kahn proposed a new mechanism that would allow traffic to travel over multiple different kinds of networks, which they dubbed TCP, the Transmission Control Program (Cerf and Kahn 1974). In their original design, TCP was a monolithic program that took care of both the problems of navigating different network types and those of establishing reliable communication between endpoints. Subsequently, as outlined in chapter 6, network researchers chose to break TCP into two pieces, each with responsibility for one of these functions. Reliable communication would be the responsibility of TCP (now the Transmission Control Protocol), while network navigation was delegated to a new subprotocol, the Internet Protocol (IP), with the two protocols generally operating in concert as TCP/IP. IP essentially establishes a way of transmitting data between different hosts across different network substrates; TCP manages that connection in order to achieve a smooth and reliable communication stream.

The problem that TCP/IP addressed was data transmission when different hosts might be connected to different sorts of networks (e.g., local area Ethernets, long-distance Frame Relay networks, or wireless packet radio). In our contemporary communication infrastructure, though, a new situation has arisen. We still have multiple coexisting network types, but often now a single host might be connected to multiple networks at the same time. A laptop computer, for instance, can communicate over a wireline Ethernet connection, a wireless Wi-Fi connection, and a Bluetooth connection simultaneously. TCP connections, however, are generally unable to take advantage of the multiple forms of connection between hosts; TCP connections are associated with a single IP address, and in consequence, with a single network interface. In 2013, the Internet Engineering Task Force (IETF)[7] released a standard for *Multipath TCP*, which addresses this problem (Ford et al. 2013). Multipath TCP allows a single TCP connection to take advantage of multiple network interfaces and multiple network paths, so that, for example, when a mobile phone moves from a Wi-Fi network to a cellular connection, the network connections can be maintained.

Multipath TCP introduces some interesting changes into the operation of the network, and its design reveals other changes that had already taken place, if not explicitly. One change that it introduces is to further decouple TCP and IP. Whereas traditional TCP flows are directly implemented over sequences of packets sent from one IP address to another, there may be multiple IP addresses involved in multipath flows at each end of the connection. A second related change is that Multipath TCP starts to operate in terms of hosts rather than network interfaces (since it now provides a form of coordinated transmission across multiple interfaces); while it does not introduce a new network entity, one can start to conceptualize its operation in those terms, which may have interesting consequences in the future.

With respect to the other changes already in place, one issue that proved a stumbling block in the development of Multipath TCP was the presence of *middleboxes*. Middleboxes are network nodes that, rather than simply

7. The IETF is the technical body that develops and certifies new internet protocol standards.

forwarding network data, transform it in some way. The most common example are residential gateways that perform network address translation (NAT) so that multiple computers—such as the multiple devices in most American homes—can share a single IP address (which is all that is offered as part of most residential internet service contracts). NAT devices and other middleboxes actively rewrite data as they flow through them; NAT, for instance, requires revising the source address of packets sent onto the public network (and the destination address of packets transmitted in the other direction). Some middleboxes also actively track the network state that is more commonly associated with endpoints, such as sequence numbers. In general, middleboxes violate the so-called end-to-end principle, which states that only network endpoints need understand the details of specific transmissions. The designers of Multipath TCP found that they needed to go to some lengths to ensure that their modifications would operate correctly even in the presence of middleboxes (Wischik et al. 2011; Bonaventure et al. 2012).

Learning from Othernets

This brief survey of alternative internetworking provides a basis for thinking more expansively about the network design space. Before taking up some specific details in that area, though, I should draw out some general points.

The first is that many of these networks operated (or continue to operate) simultaneously, and not just in parallel but even in coordination. At an appropriate time and in an appropriate place, one might (as I did) use a national X.25 network to connect to a host on which one might read Usenet newsgroup discussions about the relative merits of TCP/IP and XNS networking. Some networks were more densely interconnected than others, some operated over longer or shorter lifespans, and different networks operated within different institutional regimes. But seeing them as alternative realities or paths is misleading; although there might be more consensus now around TCP/IP as a universal networking standard than there was several decades ago, multiple networking technologies persist as part of our daily experience.

Similarly, some aspects of this survey also draw our attention toward the continuing evolution even within particular networking regimes. The emergence of Multipath TCP, for example, points to the fact that even core internet protocols are something of a moving target (and Multipath TCP expresses too the ongoing importance of different lower-level network substrates). The co-presence of IPv4 and IPv6, with their different commitments to addressing and to security, is also demonstration of the ongoing shift in networking arrangements.

Finally, as we saw in chapter 6, protocols are representational systems whose materialities are inextricably bound up with the materialities of transmission and the possibilities of institutional forms. Accordingly, as we think about alternative internets, it is with an eye toward uncovering the ways in which institutional and organizational commitments and political possibilities find both expression and limits within the encodings of packets, the role of different network actors, and the shape of representations. The discussion to follow demonstrates this in more detail.

Aspects of the Network Design Space

Briefly examining some of these "othernets" lets us place our contemporary experience of the internet—in its multiple capacities as a configuration of technologies, a constellation of services, and an object of cultural attention—in context. Some of that context is a *design space*—that is, a space of possibilities that are available as outcomes of specific design decisions. Some lies more in the nature of *historical circumstance*—that is, how different configurations arose, reflecting their own historical trajectories. To reflect on these in a little more detail, we can take a different cut at the same question—of the nature of the internet within a space of alternatives—by approaching it in terms of the kinds of facilities that works can offer.

Naming

Consider even this simple question: does a computer "know" or have access to its own name?

In the naming arrangement of traditional TCP/IP, the answer is no. A computer knows its address but not necessarily the name by which it might be addressed by others, and in fact it can operate in the TCP/IP environment quite effectively without one, as signaled by the fact that both TCP and IP use addresses, not names, internally. So, facilities are built into the Domain Name Service (DNS) protocols (Mockapetris 1987) that allow a computer, on booting, to ask a network server, "What's my name?" Naming is entirely delegated to the name service; that is, the network authority that answers the query "what is the address at which I can reach www.cnn.com?" is also the authority that tells a computer that it is www.cnn.com in the first place.

By contrast, other networking protocols—like AppleTalk, for example—delegate to individual computers the right to assign themselves names. This can be implemented in different ways—by having each computer register a name with a naming facility, for example, or by entirely distributing the name lookup process rather than electing particular computers to implement a name or directory service—and these different mechanisms have their own differences in terms of both technological capacities and organizational expectations. The abilities for a computer to assign itself a name and to advertise that name to others are facilities that the designers of the IETF Zeroconf protocol suite felt it important to add, in order to support the server-free "plug-and-play networking" approach of AppleTalk (Steinberg and Cheshire 2005).

The issue of naming raises a series of questions that highlight the relationship between specific technical facilities and the social organization of technological practice. Who gets to name a computer? Who is responsible for the names that network nodes use or call themselves? How is naming authority distributed? How visible are names? How centralized is control, and what temporalities shape it? Even such a simple issue as naming presents a microcosm of my larger argument that questions of online experience need to be examined in their technical and historical specificities.

Identity
If the question of host identity is a variable factor in network design, what about the identity of the network's users?

A TCP/IP internet makes no commitments to user identity, and indeed, user identity plays no role in most internet protocols. Humans appear only by proxy—in the names of network mailboxes, for example—but there is no consistency of user identity across different services, protocols, or applications (e.g., across both e-mail and website authentication). By contrast, an enterprise service like XNS requires users to be consistently identified throughout the network, while a commercial service like Minitel, which must provide a billing infrastructure for distributed services, similarly demands universal identification of end-users, or subscribers.

The absence of consistent user identification is a persistent feature of our experience online. Anonymity, for example, is key to the use of some services, and difficult or impossible to achieve in a world in which user identification is "baked in" to the protocols. Meantime, user identification at the edges of the network has become a business opportunity; social media services such as Facebook and Twitter also offer other developers authentication services, so that, when using a third-party service, we can log in using Facebook or Twitter credentials (while allowing Facebook and Twitter to track our actions at other websites). At the time of writing (early 2016), there has been considerable public debate concerning law enforcement efforts to access the data on an iPhone belonging to perpetrators of a terrorist attack; arguably, the significance of access to a device (to trace actions online) reflects the absence of consistent and thoroughgoing user identification online.

Transport and Services

How should we think about what a network provides? A key distinction is between transport (or connectivity) and services (or applications). All networks offer both, of course; services require connections, and connections are meaningless without services. But networks vary in terms of the extent to which services—and in particular, predefined services—are the key elements of the user experience. TCP/IP internets, for example, are transit-based networks in this regard; they provide connectivity between endpoints that can be exploited by any number of different applications, and though several applications are common and widely deployed (like electronic mail and web browsing), the network is not itself defined in terms of the availability of those services. Minitel, Fidonet, Usenet, BITNET, and X.25 networks like JANET, on the other hand, are (or were) service-oriented networks; they were networks that one could experience primarily through a relatively fixed set of applications (such as file transfer or discussion groups).

The transit-oriented approach is clearly more flexible; for TCP/IP networks, it reflects the end-to-end principle and the idea that new services might arise at the edges of the network. Given that the service-oriented networks tend to be older networks that have been largely displaced by TCP/IP, it might seem at first glance that the service-oriented approach has dwindled away. Two phenomena might make us think about this differently, though.

The first is that certain services now so dominate people's experience online that the distinction between "being online" and using a service begins to disappear. For instance, communication scholar Katy Pearce and her colleagues, studying network use in post-Soviet Eastern Europe, noted that many people would describe themselves as users of "Facebook" but not of "the internet" suggesting that these have become different categories for people (Pearce et al. 2012). More broadly, Kevin Driscoll (2015) has suggested that the period of general public consensus about what "the internet" is lasted only for roughly the decade 1995–2005; since then, "the internet" has essentially fragmented into a series of encounters with dominant online presences like Amazon, Facebook, or Google, or with smaller niche sites or forums, such that no unitary or consistent "internet" manifests itself as a collective user experience.

A second and related phenomenon is the development of specifically service-based forms of internet access, particularly in developing regions. A consortium led by Mark Zuckerberg of Facebook, for example, has controversially proposed that the company might provide, at very low tariffs or even free of charge, a service called internet.org (later Free Basics) in developing regions in order to bring affordable network access to large populations. *Basics* in this case means access specifically to the network services offered by participants such as Facebook; so users of Free Basics might be able to get online, but only to use a limited set of web-based services and sites, with Facebook and other consortium members as gatekeepers (Donner 2015).

A related form of service is that offered by United Villages, a nonprofit that delivers asynchronous access to network services to rural markets in India via network-connected buses, which collect "queries" to network services (including crop prices, Wikipedia searches, and e-commerce orders) and upload them to the network when the buses reach a networked population center. Responses to these queries are delivered back to the original site when the bus passes through the village again the next day.[8]

Although in quite different ways, these ways of packaging network access begin to question the transit-oriented model of access in TCP/IP networks.

Reliability

An important distinction between different sorts of networks is the nature of their relationship to reliability.

Clearly, all networks strive for reliable and accurate data transmission. Yet, different networks achieve this in different ways, and have varying degrees of tolerance for problems that might arise. As discussed above, reliability is key to the division between protocols in TCP/IP. IP offers only an unreliable datagram service; IP packets are routed independently and therefore might arrive out of order, and network routers are allowed to drop (i.e., stop trying to deliver) IP packets if they are overloaded or the network is congested. TCP achieves reliability in the face of a potentially unreliable IP network service by requiring acknowledgments for packets received, selectively retransmitting data that have not been delivered, and explicating the sequence of packets so that they can be reassembled in the correct order at

8. See http://unitedvillages.com.

the destination. In other words, TCP does not assume that the underlying network is robust or reliable; rather, it introduces protocol mechanisms to achieve reliability in the presence of potential failure. (On the other hand, TCP's definition of "reliable" does not include timely delivery; depending on network buffering or retransmission means that guarantees about real-time delivery cannot be made.) Pup uses the same model—unreliable datagram delivery at the network level, and then another, higher-level protocol (BSP, the Byte Stream Protocol) for reliable delivery.

Contrast this with an alternative approach, in which we turn reliability from a protocol problem into an engineering problem in the infrastructure. Here, we might ensure reliability by, for example, building redundancy into our network (running two lines or three lines instead of just one), by making heavy investments (buying especially durable transmission cables and mandating a frequent maintenance schedule), or by requiring the use of high-reliability and uniform network equipment. Traditional telecommunications companies, or those providing high-speed data services for customers like the financial services industry, often operate in this way.

The significance of the distinction between these two forms of reliability lies in the nature of the institutions that can achieve them. The TCP/IP arrangement allows networks to emerge in relatively uncontrolled ways, perhaps with low-quality or relatively slow equipment. The engineering approach, on the other hand, requires both significant financial investment and considerable institutional resources to maintain. This approach is more associated with large-scale and established organizations, which is perhaps why we associate it more with the long-term telecommunications providers. Different choices in protocol or application design about the need for, nature of, and provision for reliability in a network involve commitments to or biases toward different institutional realities in order to achieve them.

The Feudal Internet

The emergent structure of our internet—the market niches of transit carrier and ISP, the practical solution of CDNs, the fragmentation produced by middleboxes, the relationship between mobile carriers, telecommunications firms, and media content producers, and so on—draws attention to a simple but important truth of internetworking: the internet comprises a lot of wires, and every one of them is owned by someone. To the extent that those owners are capitalist enterprises competing in a marketplace, then the obvious corollary is that, since all the wires can do is carry traffic from one point to another, the carriage of traffic must become profit generating. The mechanisms by which traffic carriage over network connections becomes profitable are basically through either a volume-based or a per-byte mechanism—a toll for traffic—or through a contractual arrangement that places the facilities of one entity's network at the temporary disposal of another—a rental arrangement. This system of rents and tolls provides the basic mechanism by which different autonomous systems each provisions its own services, manages its own infrastructures, and then engages in a series of agreements of mutual aid.

If this system seems familiar, it is not so much that it encapsulates contemporary market capitalism but more that it is essentially feudal in its configuration. Marx argued for feudalism and capitalism as distinct historical periods with their links to material means of production—"The hand-mill gives you society with the feudal lord; the steam-mill society with the industrial capitalist" (Marx [1847] 1971, 109). Recent writers, though, have used the term *neofeudal* to describe the situation in late capitalism in which aspects of public life increasingly become private, gated domains—everything from toll lanes on the freeway and executive lounges at the airport, on the small end, to gated communities and tradable rights to pollute the environment issued to large corporations at the other (e.g., Shearing 2001). The essential consideration here is the erasure of public infrastructure and the erection of a system of tariffs, tolls, and rents that govern how we navigate a world made up of privatized but encompassing domains, within which market relations do not dominate.

Beyond the general use of the term *neofeudal* to refer to the privatization of public goods, let me take the metaphor of the feudal internet more seriously for a moment to point to a couple of significant considerations.

The first is that the operating mechanism of feudalism is not the market transaction but rather long-standing commitments of fealty, vassalage, and protection. These are not the instantaneous mutual engagements of market capitalism but temporally extended (indeed, indefinite) arrangements with little or nothing by way of choice or options. Indeed, the constraints upon feudal relations are geographical as much as anything else: infrastructural, if you will. One can see, arguably, some similarities to how geographical and infrastructural constraints lead to a pattern of relations between internet providers that also relies on long-term *residence*-based partnerships. The ties that bind individuals to their service providers in the semi-monopolistic conditions of the US broadband market, or perhaps even more pointedly, the links that connect large-scale data service providers such as Netflix with transit carriers like Level 3, are not simply conveniently structured as long-term arrangements, but rather can only operate that way because of the infrastructure commitments involved (such as the physical siting of data stores and server farms). Similarly, the need for physical interconnection between different networks makes high-provider-density interconnection nodes like One Wilshire in downtown Los Angeles (see chapter 6) into "obligatory passage points," in Michel Callon's language—that is, to get interconnection between networks, you need to be where all the other networks are, and they all need to be there too. For all that we typically talk about the digital domain as fast paced and ever-changing, these kinds of arrangements—not simply commitments to infrastructure but commitments to the institutions' relationships that infrastructure conditions—are not ones that can change quickly, easily, or cheaply. The relations that obtain here are more feudal than mercantile.

The second interesting point that a feudal approach draws attention to is the persistence of preexisting institutional structures—perhaps most obviously, the nation-state. Although John Perry Barlow's (1996) classic "Declaration of the Independence of Cyberspace" famously argues that the "governments of the industrial world ... [have] no sovereignty" in the realm of the digital, and notwithstanding the IETF's oft-repeated motto that "rejects kings [and] presidents" in favor of "rough consensus and running code" (Hoffman 2012), the truth is that governments and presidents continue to manifest themselves quite significantly in not just the governance but the fabric of our internet. National and regional concerns arise in a variety of ways—in the provision of specific linguistic content, in the regional caching of digital content, in the question of international distribution rights for digital content (e.g., which movies can be viewed online in which countries), in assertions of national sovereignty over information about citizens (e.g., Vladimir Putin's public musings that data about Russian citizens should be stored only on servers in Russia; Khrennikov and Ustinova [2014]), in the different regimes that govern information access (e.g., the 2014 EU directive known popularly as the "right to be forgotten"), and in local debates about internet censorship (from China's "Great Firewall" and Singapore's self-censorship regime to discussions of nationwide internet filters in Australia and the UK). The very fact that a thriving business opportunity exists for commercial Virtual Private Network (VPN) services that allow users to get online "as if" they were located in a different country signals the persistent significance of nation-states and national boundaries in the experience of our internet. Similarly, significant debate has surrounded the role of national interests in internet governance (e.g., Mueller 2010) and the International Telecommunications Union (ITU)—a

United Nations organization whose members are not technical experts or corporations but nation-states—remains a significant body in the development of network technologies and policy. Just as feudalism reinforced and made all aspects of everyday life subject to the boundaries of the manor, the shire, and the nation, so too does the internet—not necessarily any internet, but certainly our Internet—retain a significant commitment to the relevance of similar geographical, national, and institutional boundaries.

This Internet

As Powell (2014) has argued in her study of open hardware projects, patterns of historical evolution torque the design principles that often provide not only technical arrangements but also the social imaginaries that are mobilized in our discussions of technology. Taking up this question in the context of this book's examination of representational materialities means that we need not simply think about the pragmatics of undersea cables (Starosielski 2015), satellite downlinks (Parks 2012), and server farms (Varnelis 2008), but that we should also consider how specific representations of action and encodings of data are designed to be manipulated, transmitted, and moved in particular sorts of ways, with consequences for the resultant experience of the network as offering particular opportunities for individual and collective action.

In other words, the primary concern is to see networked arrangements as historically particular crystallizations of not just technical but also institutional, economic, and political potentialities. To do this, particularly with respect to the technology that we rather glibly call "the internet," I have suggested that two moves are needed.

The first move is from the idea of *"the* internet" to that of *"an* internet"—that is, to reencounter our contemporary network as not the only possible internet that could have been built, but as one of a range of possible networks. When we consider multiple possible networks, we start to pay attention to the range of expectations, institutional arrangements, policies, technical configurations, and other dimensions that might characterize the space of potentials. The second move is from *"an* internet" to *"this* internet"—that is, to narrow down once more and so grapple with the historical, geographical, political, and social specificities that constrain and condition the particular network with which we are engaged at any particular moment. *This* internet is not the one that was conceived of by those like Paul Baran or Donald Davies, designed by those like Vint Cerf or Robert

Kahn, or opened to commercial operation by the NSF—it has elements of each of those, but it is a historically specific construction that has encompassed, transformed, extended, and redirected those particular networks. This internet is something that we can grapple with empirically. We are not in much of a position to make general statements about "the internet"; but when we ask questions about "*this* internet," we may have a starting point for investigation.

The goal of an analysis of representational materialities is to do just this—to bring the specifics of technological arrangements into view as matters of social and cultural concern. Distinguishing between what an internet can be and what this internet can be, or differentiating the conditions that attend how we might encounter an internet or this internet, or seeing at work the institutional relations that make an internet or this internet feasible prove much easier when we can attend to encodings and mechanisms as well as metaphors and rhetorics because it is precisely the relationship between the domains that is of analytic importance.

8   Prospects and Conclusions

"It's all just bits," we often hear. In the realm of digital processing, "just bits" expresses a boundless technical optimism. It suggests almost limitless possibilities—of storage, of transformation, and of mediation. When everything is "just bits," the whole range of computational infrastructure is available to us for acting on those bits. "Parts is parts" ran the old commercial. Bits is bits.

Bits, though, are not just bits. Some matter more than others. Some arrangements of bits are more easily manipulable than others. Some are more amenable to one form of processing or another. Some arrangements of bits can be transmitted easily over unreliable networks while others cannot; some can be processed by the applications on our computers, and some cannot; some can fit into limited storage, and some cannot; some can be efficiently processed by parallel computers, and some cannot. Some are designed for concision, some for robustness, and some for interactivity. Like the Indo-Arabic and Roman numeral systems, different representations come with different consequences for the kinds of things that we can do with them. So the virtual objects that populate our world may all be bits, but they are not *just* bits.

As users of computer systems, we are quite familiar with these constraints, at least at a superficial level. We are familiar with the work of transforming data between formats, with the limits of expressivity of different tools, and with the struggle of keeping old data workable with new tools— all of which are examples of the problems of the materialities of digital information. More fundamentally, the capacities of different kinds of technological infrastructures are themselves hemmed in continually by material constraints—from the formatting of a spreadsheet to the distribution of database transactions in a server cluster or the limits of real-time network operations. Many cultural and social theorists are appropriately skeptical of Silicon Valley's hype and the grand claims made for the limitless potential of digital systems; many, too, are concerned with what kinds of erasures—of politics, of difference, of environmental consequences, of history, of power—are implicit in those claims. Diane Bailey and colleagues (2012) have warned us of the "lure of the virtual," which tempts us to treat virtual phenomena as if they were all the same. The rhetoric of the virtual also suggests an independence from material configurations and constraints that is equally alluring and equally misleading. As I have argued, it is not simply that "the virtual" depends crucially on large-scale material infrastructures of electrical power, air conditioning, servers, cables, and buildings; it is also that those virtual objects manifest themselves as signals, charges, and states that must be grappled with materially in digital systems and which come with their own constraints—constraints that bleed through to the human experience and to the social arrangements within which digital and virtual entities are embedded.

There are many possible accounts of the materialities of information. I have chosen to focus in particular on those associated with information representations, for a number of reasons. One is that these representations span the domains of the technical and the human. Another is that they reflect conscious decision making among alternatives that can be assessed for their consequences. A third is that they constitute forms of infrastructure that, as Geoffrey Bowker and Susan Leigh Star (1999) painstakingly detail, are embedded in organizational processes, professional practice, and institutional histories that point both backward and forward. A fourth is that they connect contemporary discussions of digitality to a longer intellectual history of inscription, action, and knowledge.

Late in the writing process, I discussed this book with a colleague who asked, "What's at stake here?" It's an urgent question, and one that I often pose to my own graduate students as they struggle to frame their dissertation research. Asking what's at stake requires that we understand not only what the significance of the work might be, but also what might need to be given up if one accepts the argument—not to mention what we might individually, as researchers and writers, need to put on the table.

So what *is* at stake here? Certainly not a pristine separation between social and material; that mirage faded from view long ago. What remains in play, though, is the commitment to compartmentalization that attends most disciplinary practice. Traditional academic training and scholarly methods all too often depend on boundaries and boundedness that may simply be unsustainable in the world of real objects and real practice. There must be limits to any investigation, of course, so boundaries of some sort will always be with us. However, the studies that have unfolded here suggest that we need to make our cuts in new ways that are more expansive and that speak to the interconnections among elements rather than to the separations between them. These cuts run orthogonally to the traditional separations between the domains of organizations and culture, institutions and infrastructure, policy and packets, networks and applications. They show instead how a focus on digital manifestations and the production of computational experiences requires that we have all of these in view at once.

Also at stake is our notion of the virtual. Although much of the discussion presented here, particularly in chapter 3, has striven to undermine casual claims of virtuality, this is not because I feel that the concept has lost all utility. Rather, I have sought to focus attention on what sustains it. If virtual objects have particular properties, in terms of their movements across networks or their availability to algorithmic processing, then what is it that makes this so? Further, if the essence of virtuality is some kind of constructed equivalence to the physical, then what does it take—materially, politically, economically, and conceptually—to maintain this correspondence? How do discursive and material practices entwine in the ongoing production and enactment of virtuality? By looking at how specific materialities are bound up in the production and sustenance of practical virtuality, to borrow Adrian Mackenzie's term, the studies presented here begin to suggest a strategy for answering these questions.

If a narrow conception of the virtual is at stake, so too is any equation of the material with the tangible. Throughout this investigation, I have sought to develop an understanding of materiality through the lens of digital representations. Representational systems are material in their manifestations; they occupy space, they constrain human action, they are coupled to practice, and they condition technological configurations. While one might reasonably balk at first at the idea of thinking materially about something as apparently abstract as a representation, closer examination reveals how representations are material in their connection to practice. Digital representations are formal; their forms are what matter, and forms are material in the ways in which they can and cannot be used. In particular, by looking at them comparatively, we have been able to see the material implications of different representational strategies. The material in this case is much more than the tangible, and yet intangibility does not inevitably mean a withdrawal into the sphere of the ineffable.

From the outset, the first overriding injunction has been to take technology seriously, not just in its uses but also in its specifics. This requires that we attempt not to fall into the traps that surround the casual slippages between ideas of digitality, virtuality, speed, binary encodings, and so forth. After all, even though "digital" often enters conversation as a synonym for "quick," there is nothing inherently speedy about the digital; electronic switching may be fast, but digitality and electronics are quite independent of each other. Similarly, while we think of digital information in terms of bits and binary encodings, computers are not by definition binary (ENIAC, the first general-purpose electronic computer, manipulated numeric data in a decimal format—Haigh et al. [2016]). Understanding actual technological capacities requires at times a tedious degree of technical detail, and yet this seems unavoidable if we want to understand the material constraints and conditions of digital experience.

This turns out to be harder—or at least more unusual—than it seems. I recently attended a symposium featuring a keynote talk given by a major figure in the digital humanities, whose acclaim derives not least from how, with a background in both engineering and English literature, this scholar's work can bridge technology and the humanities. During a part of the lecture that discussed the promiscuous and leaky nature of networked interactions, audience members were exhorted to open the terminal windows on their laptops, type an obscure command, and see the data flowing past that demonstrated how networks capture everything but throw away what is not immediately needed. It was a compelling demonstration and made an impact in the room—gasps were audible—but, technically, it was almost entirely wrong. Ethernets did *once* see everything and throw away what wasn't wanted, but they have not operated in that way for decades. Not a single one of the networked laptops in the room that day operated in that manner; on Wi-Fi networks, data are encrypted, while channel, layer, and conversation management mean that one generally sees only one's own traffic, even in so-called promiscuous mode. Maybe the confusion comes from the similarly promiscuous use of the term *Ethernet*, which these days bears little technical resemblance to Bob Metcalfe and David Boggs's original 1973 design; indeed, Metcalfe has argued that *Ethernet* names not a technical approach but a business model.[1] So the data that audience members saw streaming across their screens were in fact something quite other than they seemed. This moment at the lecture was not a demonstration that takes technology seriously, for all that it displayed the trappings of technological authenticity; certainly, the social science and humanities

---

1. See the interview of Robert Metcalfe by Len Shustek, November 29, 2006, and January 31, 2007, for the Computer History Museum, http://archive.computerhistory .org/resources/access/text/2013/05/102657995-05-01-acc.pdf.

professors in the room were impressed with the lecturer's interpretation of the letters and numbers flashing past on their laptop screens. Ironically, though, the speaker's key point about the need to engage the digital with all the critical faculties of humanistic scholarship was (or should have been) rather undermined by this failure to take the technology seriously. It was rather like going to a meeting of the Modern Language Association and offhandedly referring to Moby Dick as a goldfish.

This most certainly should not be read as a suggestion that only those who code or are trained in computer science should undertake work in this domain. Nor, as it happens, is it meant to suggest that an ability to code or a background in computer science necessarily means that one speaks with authority (or accuracy) on matters of digital technology. What I mean to suggest, though, is that specific technical arrangements are worthy of close attention, and that, if any sort of "close reading" is to be undertaken, it requires that we treat the source materials of digital culture with the same kind of seriousness, sensitivity, and attention that humanists would give to their texts or ethnographers to their field sites and participants. It is not sufficient to examine the rhetoric of digitality, the formal structure of programs, the pained lexicon of @, #, and !, or the questionable metaphors of "the cloud," if those rhetorical or structural analyses are undermined by the actual operation of digital systems. This is a lesson that science studies has most certainly learned; the point of analyses of social constructionism is not to say that scientific fact is merely a matter of popular opinion, but that the establishment of scientific facts requires that disciplinary communities and the physical world be wrestled into some kind of tentative agreement. Similarly, in domains like software studies, we need to understand both cultural practice and technological operations, because the important questions that we seek to answer are precisely about the relationship between the two. Wendy Chun (2008) cautions us against fetishizing "code" or other technological artifacts in software studies, arguing quite rightly that this risks obscuring the other elements involved in making software happen and making software act; that said, we cannot see source code or any other technological element as either metaphorical or incidental.

This book's investigation of materialities, then, has been the means to do just this, as an attempt to bridge these different domains. Moving from an account of the broad or brute materiality of digital infrastructures toward an understanding of specific materialities that may be manifest in digital representations. Among those that have been significant here are granularity, or the scale of object representation; fixedness, or the degree to which objects are amenable to transformation; convergence, or the extent to which and the timescales over which diverse representations can be brought into alignment; fragility, or the forms of distortion, transformation, and error that representations can withstand; and isolation, or the relationship between units of perception and units of encoding.

This, then, is the rejoinder (finally) to that colleague of mine who complains that the term "material" loses all meaning if everything becomes material. That's true, and it is to be guarded against, but the goal here is not simply to argue for the material nature of information but to unpick, examine, and document just *how* things are material and with what import. Tim Ingold (2007b) is quite right to warn against the academic tendency to reify and conceptualize, which manifests itself here as a move toward materiality that leaves the materials themselves behind; but in the realm of digital information, an examination of specific materialities is in fact an attempt to make the materials visible and to encounter them perhaps for the first time. In order to say something useful about digital materials, one must first get a handle on how digital materialities operate.

Finding these materialities at work in digital systems means delving deep into them. There are two related aspects to this "depth." The first is that one goes deep because one needs to push down from an application, a service, or a user experience into the bits, bytes, protocols, packages, and data structures that enliven it. The second, perhaps even more important, is that as one pushes from the high level to the low, one has to be able to develop an understanding of the interlocking of these various components. One has to undo the separation between different "layers" and "levels" that computer scientists refer to as "the stack" and recognize that the actual encounter with technology is not a serial encounter with each layer but a simultaneous encounter with a slice through the whole (Bratton [2016] explores this metaphor much further.)

Notwithstanding the requirement to take technology seriously, however, and similarly notwithstanding the insights of the vital materialists whose work was outlined in chapter 2, I have chosen in this project to retain a focus on human experience. This is more a matter of perspective than of primacy, a human-oriented rather than human-centered view. Nonetheless, retaining a (post)humanist perspective is an acknowledgment of some issues of central relevance.

One of these is slightly counterintuitive and so requires elaboration. It concerns the limits to design. Digital systems are artificial; they are the products of design, and those design processes express individual and collective intent, embed assumptions and imaginings of conditions of use, arise in particular institutional conditions, and reflect the needs and values of their sites of production. Accordingly, it is common—not to mention appropriate and indeed necessary—for scholars to draw attention to the kinds of power that are embedded with design processes and within design-oriented corporations (e.g., Winner 1980; MacKenzie and Wajcman 1999; Vaidhyanathan 2011). These scholars have pointed out the need to be able to hold design processes accountable, and to be able to see designed realities not as natural or inevitable but as social, cultural, and contingent. Much of what we have seen in cases throughout this book, such as in the discussion of internet routing and its institutional structures, is consonant with this perspective.

Yet, this examination of the materialities of information and its digital forms and the alternative cuts that we have taken through sociotechnical systems also draw attention to the limits of design. Each part of the technological assembly is designed, but the overall experience is not. The operating system on my phone is a designed product, and each of the apps installed there is a designed product, and yet the overall experience of my phone, as something that has a particular set of capacities arrayed in particular ways is not a product of design intent (unless we frame my own actions in the app store as design actions). A materialist perspective must create the space for us to talk about emergence, constraint, and accident, and we must give these an adequate place within our understanding of the shaping of digital experience. Even in an entirely artifactual space, not everything is a reflection of design intent. Social scientists studying the contexts of technology development have, appropriately, been at pains to draw attention to the problematic myths of "the heroic designer" in trying to open up a space for a process of design that acknowledges people and politics (e.g., Suchman et al. 1999). Ironically enough, however, efforts to revise or champion the alternative concerns that designers and design institutions should acknowledge might still fall into the trap of imagining the design as the singular point at which technological arrangements come into being.

Acknowledging the limits of design involves acknowledging the limits of intent in the production of digital systems. It simultaneously involves recognizing the human, social, and cultural processes by which disparate technologies are brought into alignment as coherent experiences. If design processes and design practice are not themselves the things that create a unified experience, then it must be the human encounter with their products.

This brings us to the second reason for a humanistic perspective here, which is the question of interpretation and the production of experience and meaning in the human encounter with sociomaterial systems. Notwithstanding the focus on technological capacities or limits, I am not advocating a technological determinism here; the question of how digital systems arise as cultural objects, as objects that populate our world, lies for me firmly in the realm of the human. The relevance of the materialities of information, for my own project at least, is in how they manifest themselves within the design, application, and use of information systems. They are a part of a series of interpretive and cultural processes that produce digital systems as objects in our world—as things to which we turn for particular kinds of effects; as objects that have capacities and limits; as media forms that arise as particular formations of production, transmission, and consumption; and as entities that we associate with particular kinds of tasks, institutions, and processes.

Stephanie Ricker Schulte (2013) has compellingly demonstrated the ways in which these interpretations are culturally and historically grounded narratives. What does it mean for something to be a computer? As Jennifer Light (1999) reminds us, this was originally a term that described a job, not a machine; largely women, computers performed calculations that supported scientific, technical, and military work. What does it mean for something to be information? Ronald Day (2008) instructively notes that information is an evolving concept, one that was radically transformed by the appearance of Claude Shannon's mathematical theory. Similarly, what we expect that computers can do, what information can represent, how we can have access to it or make it do something for us, are evolving ideas, shaped as much by institutional conventions and social norms as by technological arrangements. What scholars in the social construction of technology call *interpretive flexibility* is often used to capture how different social groups understand technology differently as it corresponds to their own needs and contexts, but we see this also as a flexibility over time, which provides us with something of a warrant for historicizing the digital.

So, having undertaken such an investigation, what conclusions can we draw?

One conclusion is that there are many materialities. I mean this in two distinct ways. The first is that, while accounts of the materiality of digital information might be useful as a corrective for overly casual assertions of virtuality and immateriality, they do not take us very far. The digital is material, yes, but just how, and with what significance? Digital systems have many ways of being material, and many different materialities characterize the nature of our encounters with them. They are material in diverse ways, and their materiality is deployed to different ends. We have encountered a range of material properties that differently shape both the phenomenological encounter and the cultural encounter with digital information. What is more—and this is the second reading of "multiple materialities"—digital information can be material in different ways at the same time. To the extent that materialities are properties that constrain, limit, and inspire patterns of engagement—that is, that underwrite the "reflective conversation" that Donald Schön spoke of—then digital media exhibit different materialities, just as they are enrolled in different simultaneous "conversations."

We have seen too that materialities manifest themselves and operate at multiple scales. Indeed, one of the primary dimensions along which the case studies that have anchored the argument are arrayed is one of scale, in terms of the engagement between the human and the technical—from an individual using an emulator to recapture a lost digital experience to the ways in which we find ourselves bound up in largely unseen institutional relationships as users of internet services. Scale is a crucial problem that remains underexamined in digital contexts and is all too easily confused for size or number. Scale and size, though, are not the same thing at all. If we think about simple massification, we might talk about the difference between a single cell and ten million cells, but that's not the same as talking about a human arm. Scale is a dimension along which different objects arise; the arm exists as an object at one scale, the cell at another. Similarly, different materialities manifest themselves at different scales, or manifest themselves in different ways; the fragility of network connections, the fragility of network packets, and the fragility of peering arrangements are fragilities of quite different sorts. These materialities are not scale independent, and scales most certainly interact.

One reason to pay attention to representational forms is that they are both the sites of, and objects that reflect the terms of, institutional relations. The grid of the spreadsheet kept the goals and needs of different organizational units aligned but separate; policy routes specify how network carriers will treat each other's traffic. The expressivity of these representations as well as other material properties, such as their persistence, dynamism, and patterns of distribution, are part of how institutional relations are negotiated and enacted. Similarly, then, these representations and their material constraints coevolve with social, cultural, and institutional practices and relations. Indeed, it is this observation that has motivated a historical reading of the progression of, for instance, routing algorithms as expressions of emerging institutional practices. Both representational stabilities and patterns of change reflect expectations of use, needs, and conventions that are themselves organized around the effectiveness (or ineffectiveness) of representational forms. Similarly, digital representations such as protocols, APIs, and database schemas can act as sites that make visible the institutional and organizational multiplicity of the online world—the many different actors whose actions are coordinated in the production of the digital experience.

The "many materialities" conclusion also undermines any talk of the digital as a medium in itself. This is not to say that we cannot talk of digital media, since some media are certainly digital. Let's lay to one side the undeniable but uninspiring observation that "the digital" is simply a way of talking about a world of analog phenomena—voltages, shades, and magnetic fluxes. Even if we take the digital as read, though, *digitality* is not in itself much of a descriptive. Digitality tells us nothing about fast or slow, robust or fragile, temporary or long lived, malleable or fixed, simple or complex, dynamic or static—properties that characterize aspects of our media experience. Digitality per se conveys little. Even in more specific domains, such as photographic images or audio recordings, to say that something is digital conveys little of value even in very general terms. Consequently the idea of, for instance, a *transition* from analog to digital media (for archiving, processing, or preservation) or broad comparisons between analog and digital equivalents are similarly uninformative without an elaboration of the specific digital materialities in question.

Finally, here, we have needed to attend to the ways in which digital representations are rhetorical and mechanical artifacts. Representations and inscriptions have been a focus of attention for scholars from STS for as long as that discipline has been established (e.g., Star 1983; Latour and Woolgar 1986; Coopmans et al. 2014). Digital representations do not solely represent, though; they also provide a material framework for computation. What makes the representational materialities of digital inscriptions worthy of attention is this dual nature as both rhetorical and mechanical devices, simultaneously.

Given that digital systems are representational from top to bottom, it is not a surprise that most systems spend much of their time translating between representations—turning search terms into structured queries, turning configuration files into expression trees, translating domain names into IP addresses, turning input events into commands, and on. Translation is the essence of the move from one abstraction level to another, or the shift of control from one module to a second. These objects in translation are mechanical too, however, being structurally reconfigured, expanded, contracted, augmented, and divided. The language of "translation" neglects this more material aspect of transformation. Stefan Helmreich (2007) offers a different way of gaining a handhold on these issues. Drawing on a metaphor offered by Mackenzie (2002), he suggests the need for what he calls "transductive ethnography," which would attend to the processes of mediation, transformation, and recoding that attend much or all of our sensory lives. Helmreich's particular concern is with the auditory environment, and the role of technologies, media, and material objects in both the production of soundscapes and the experience of immersion. Yet, his thinking goes beyond sound:

Transduction can be used as a device for recognizing the hidden conditions of immersion. The metaphor of transduction can tune one in to textures of disjuncture, to the corporeal character of transferring signals, particularly in cyborgian settings. If the information sciences have it that information is an abstract property that can be transferred across boundaries and substrates—the transcoding dream of the cyborg—the concept of "transduction" recalls the physical, material dimension of such transfers and summons up questions of resistance and distortion, complicating a rhetoric of flow with one of turbulence. (Helmreich 2007, 631)

Of course, Helmreich is absolutely right in noting the claims on abstraction and virtuality staked by information science, although these claims are what this volume and other writings cited here attempt to reconsider. An account of digital information that is alive to the roles of "resistance and distortion" is at the heart of this investigation, and indeed one might tie those two phenomena directly to Schön's idea of the "reflective conversation with materials" that provided its initial impetus. Transduction, though, has more to offer us. Transduction is more than translation; it is not simply a reencoding, but a reproduction. When human speech at a telephone handset is transformed into electrical signals of many different kinds and then reassembled as sound at the other end, the end product is not simply a movement of the original speech but a new sonic production based on it—an analog but not a copy. Similarly, when we think about the mediating roles that digital representations play in taking objects in the world, encoding them in digital systems, and producing them for us again—people as database records, organizational processes as spreadsheets, institutional relations as routing policies, or whatever—they are transduced. We are forced to attend to turbulence rather than flow, in Helmreich's terms. Transduction turns our attention to active mediation and to the question of what these processes add and take away as representations are filtered through the "stack" of protocols, applications, and software services making up contemporary information systems.

Reconfigurations

The mathematical computer scientist Edsger Dijkstra is reputed to have remarked that "computer science is no more about computers than astronomy is about telescopes."[2] We may read this as a comment that computation should be seen as independent of its material manifestations. By contrast, recent approaches to the study of information infrastructures have demonstrated the importance of paying close attention to the processes and conditions under which information and information systems are produced, maintained, and put to work (Bowker et al. 2010). In turn, this investigation here, while it is certainly not computer science in any of the usual meanings of that term, has itself accorded far more attention to computers and computational devices than Dijkstra might have allowed for in computer science. He might have argued that computation should be seen as independent of its material manifestations, but computing in the world cannot be. As I stressed a few pages ago, though, I am certainly not attempting to argue that only computer scientists can undertake this work. In fact, I might argue in the other direction that thinking through materialities offers the opposite—a means of reconfiguring and reconceptualizing the computer science enterprise in a way that places the digital back in its historical, geographical, political, and cultural locations.

   For instance, many people in computer science research have become interested in what is termed *computational thinking*, originally articulated by Jeanette Wing (2006). The computational thinking manifesto argues that computational processes and representations are now so central to everyday life that a literacy in algorithmics and computational mechanics is as important in contemporary education as an understanding of the fundamentals of mathematics, logic, and symbolic reasoning. We can distinguish this program from earlier calls for "computer literacy" in education, which frequently revolved around basic competencies with digital tools (like word processors and search engines), in that it shifts attention from such mechanics toward how computational systems work and act in the world. Leaving to one side the question of educational priorities, the argument being made is that grappling with computational media requires a new way of thinking, and that new kinds of thinking can be engendered by the encounter.

2. It is at best questionable whether Dijkstra himself ever said this. Though rarely at a loss for a pithy comment, as his impressively snotty archives (http://www.cs.utexas .edu/users/EWD) attest, Dijkstra is to computer science as Mark Twain is to the United States and Winston Churchill to the UK: one of those quotable characters to whom all manner of comments are often attributed.

Yet, this view of computational thinking is one that is largely dehistoricized and dematerialized. The computational thinking with which we are familiar is one particular computational thinking, one that has arisen in parallel with particular kinds of computer systems, particular kinds of software systems, and thus particular kinds of representational and modeling practices. It is one among a possible range of computational thinkings. It is important to recognize and to challenge the dominance of specific modes of knowledge practice embedded in computational thinking, while recognizing that there might be other ways of thinking computationally than those espoused by current computer science or information science research (Dourish 2010). In opening up a discussion about the materialities of information, my goal is to avoid the key flaws in this idea—a decontextualized account of the technological encounter, the casual technological determinism, and a prejudging of what is and isn't inherently computational.

One area where these ideas might have particular significance is in contemporary discussions of algorithms and algorithmic accountability (e.g., Gillespie 2014; Ziewitz 2016). Only a few years ago, the term *algorithm* was a technical term, but not one that had entered the popular discourse. People want to know whether a search engine is biased in the way that it selects the top-ranked results, or whether the face-detection mechanisms inside digital cameras might be better attuned to some skin tones than others (e.g., Roth 2009; Hankerson et al. 2016). Algorithms have come to popular prominence as people debate the mediating effects they can have on our lives and the associated questions of accountability and regulation (e.g., Gillespie 2014; Pasquale 2015; Introna 2016). What issues might come into view if we look at these questions through the lens of representational materialities?

One is the recognition that our understanding of what algorithms can and might do is always relative to the computer systems that can embody and represent them. Recall, for example, the case of nuclear weapon simulation, outlined in the opening pages of chapter 1. I drew a distinction there between what an algorithm made possible and what an implementation makes feasible. The same algorithm, implemented on different computers or supported by different technical infrastructures, has quite different capacities. Mathematically, what it can achieve is the same, but practically, a new architecture or implementation of an algorithm can bring new possibilities into view and new achievements into the realm of the possible. To be able to process data streams in real time, for example—perhaps to do advanced facial recognition on real-time high-definition video signals, or to recognize words in continuous speech, or to model and respond to traffic flows on highways—depends not simply on an algorithm but on the capacity to execute that algorithm within appropriate timing constraints. To be able to carry out these tasks "offline" (i.e., not in real time but operating over stored data) is a technical achievement, of course, but being able to process the data in real time creates radically new possibilities for surveillance, for speech-based user interfaces, or for urban management. To describe these achievements as consequences of "algorithms," then, is somewhat misleading, because what it takes to apply these technologies does not lie solely within the domain of the algorithm but rather depends crucially on how that algorithm is manifest in a larger technical infrastructure.

A second issue to which a materialist account would draw our attention is what it takes, in software, to manifest an algorithm. Algorithms are abstract descriptions of computational procedures, but the realization of an algorithm as a program requires the programmer to incorporate not just the algorithmic procedure itself but also the ancillary mechanisms needed to make it operate—checking for errors, testing bounds, establishing network connections, managing memory, handling exceptions, giving user feedback, encoding information, storing files, loading data, specifying modules, initializing variables, discarding old results, and myriad other "housekeeping" tasks. The result is that, while algorithms are at the heart of programs, much of what our computer programs do is not actually specified by algorithms. Programs are mechanistic and procedural but not entirely "algorithmic" in the sense of being specified by an algorithm (or something that is called an algorithm).

Both of these observations suggest that current discussions of algorithms, governance, and accountability need, if they are to be effective, to be placed in the context of a materialist account of how algorithms have effects in the world. We can be conscious of Chun's (2008) injunction to avoid the fetish of the algorithm while still recognizing that, as a term of art, it has limits and boundaries that should be attended to. Indeed, any effective intervention into the domain of algorithmic processing must, as a matter of political practicality, be grounded in some ethnographic responsibility about members' terms.

Thinking about algorithms in terms of their materialities also provides a route by which we can return to some of the discussions in chapter 2 that spoke to the different disciplinary conversations within which this exploration has been situated. It demonstrates, for example, an alternative conception of the topics and responsibilities of human–computer interaction as a discipline, for example, which requires that an attention to materialities in user experience reach well beyond the materials from which an interface is constructed. To the extent that a materialist account requires us to engage with the materials from which digital experiences are constructed, and that might themselves be distributed in the world (technically, geographically, and institutionally), it signals or at least points the way toward what a broader approach to the constitution of interaction might be. It also attempts to carve a space within software studies for a form of analysis that is committed to a serious engagement with technological arrangements without becoming dazzled by superficial strangeness of code as text nor overly inclined toward its metaphorical resonances.

The observations about algorithms, then, exemplify a complicated (perhaps overly complicated) interdisciplinary perspective that this volume has tried to maintain. From computer science, it draws a concern with the production of technical systems, but it focuses too on how these are cultural objects. From science studies, it draws an attentiveness to the lived work of technoscience, but it recognizes that it is also a vehicle for intervention and change. From software studies, it draws a concern with the rhetorics of digital representations, but hews closely to an understanding of technical mechanism. From media studies, it draws a historical perspective on information infrastructures, but with a focus on encodings and representational practice. The challenge, of course, is to find whether such an intersectional blend can be produced effectively without either dissolving into incoherence or so narrowly defining its project that it disappears altogether. Readers will, I am certain, have their own assessments. Nevertheless, as more and more of our engagements with institutions, with corporations, and with each other are mediated by material representations with both rhetorical and mechanical impact, such an approach seems urgently needed.

References

Adorno, T. 1991. *The Culture Industry*. London: Routledge.

Alač, M. 2011. *Handling Digital Brains: A Laboratory Study of Multimodal Semiotic Interaction in the Age of Computers*. Cambridge, MA: MIT Press.

Al-Fares, M., A. Loukissas, and A. Vahdat. 2008. A Scalable, Commodity Data Center Network Architecture. *Computer Communication Review* 38 (4): 63–74.

Alsubaiee, S., Y. Altowim, H. Altwaijry, V. Borkar, Y. Bu, et al. 2014. AsterixDB: A Scalable, Open Source BDMS. *Proceedings of the VLDB Endowment* 7 (14): 1905–1916.

Angus, I. 2016. *Facing the Anthropocene: Fossil Capitalism and the Crisis of the Earth System*. New York: Monthly Review Press.

Antoniadis, P., B. Le Grand, A. Satsiou, L. Tassiulas, R. Aguiar, J. P. Barraca, and S. Sargento. 2008. Community Building over Neighborhood Wireless Mesh Networks. *IEEE Society & Technology* 27 (1): 48–56.

Apperley, T., and J. Parikka. 2016. Platform Studies' Epistemic Threshold. *Games and Culture*. DOI: 10.1177/1555412015616509. Published online February 2016.

Ashcraft, K., T. Kuhn, and F. Cooren. 2009. Constitutional Amendments: "Materializing" Organizational Communication. *Academy of Management Annals* 3 (1): 1–64.

Aspray, W. 1990. *John von Neumann and the Origins of Modern Computing*. Cambridge, MA: MIT Press.

Astrahan, M., M. Blasgen, D. Chamberlin, K. Eswaran, J. Gray, P. Griffiths, W. King, et al. 1976. System R: Relational Approach to Database Management. *ACM Transactions on Database Systems* 1 (2): 97–137.

Bailey, D., P. Leonardi, and S. R. Barley. 2012. The Lure of the Virtual. *Organization Science* 23 (5): 1485–1504.

Bannon, L., and S. Bødker. 1997. Constructing Common Information Spaces. In *Proceedings of the Fifth European Conference Computer- Supported Cooperative Work ECSCW'97 (Lancaster, UK)*, J. Hughes (ed.), 81–96. Dordrecht: Kluwer.

Barad, K. 2003. Posthumanist Performativity: Toward an Understanding of How Matter Comes to Matter. *Signs* 28 (3): 801–831.

Barad, K. 2007. *Meeting the Universe Halfway: Quantum Physics and the Entanglements of Matter and Meaning.* Durham, NC: Duke University Press.

Baran, P. 1964. *On Distributed Communications* . RAND Memorandum RM-4320-PR. Santa Monica, CA: Rand.

Barlow, J. P. 1996. A Declaration of the Independence of Cyberspace. Davos, Switzerland. Accessed June 4, 2014, https://projects.eff.org/~barlow/Declaration-Final.html.

Bennett, J. 2010. *Vibrant Matter: A Political Ecology of Things.* Durham, NC: Duke University Press.

Bergström, J., B. Clark, A. Frigo, R. Mazé, J. Redström, and A. Vallgårda. 2010. Becoming Materials: Material Forms and Forms of Practice. *Digital Creativity* 21 (3): 155–172.

Berry, D. 2011. *The Philosophy of Software: Code and Mediation in the Digital Age.* Basingstoke, UK: Palgrave Macmillan.

Birrell, A., R. Levin, R. Needham, and M. Schroeder. 1982. Grapevine: An Exercise in Distributed Computing. *Communications of the ACM* 25 (4): 260–274.

Blanchette, J.-F. 2011. A Material History of Bits. *Journal of the American Society for Information Science and Technology* 62 (6): 1024–1057.

Blum, A. 2012. *Tubes: A Journey to the Center of the Internet.* New York: HarperCollins.

Boellstorff, T., G. Bell, M. Gregg, B. Maurer, and N. Seaver. 2015. *Data: Now Bigger and Better!* Chicago, IL: Prickly Paradigms Press.

Boggs, D., J. Shoch, E. Taft, and R. Metcalfe. 1980. Pup: An Internetwork Architecture. *IEEE Transactions on Communications* 28 (4): 612–624.

Bolter, J., and R. Grusin. 1999. *Remediation: Understanding New Media.* Cambridge, MA: MIT Press.

Bonaventure, O., M. Handley, and C. Raiciu. 2012. An Overview of Multipath TCP. *;login: The Usenix Magazine* 37 (5): 17–23.

Borkar, V., M. Carey, and C. Li. 2012. Big Data Platforms: What's Next? *ACM Crossroads* 19 (1): 44–49.

Bowers, J., G. Button, and W. Sharrock. 1995. Workflow from Within and Without: Technology and Cooperative Work on the Print Industry Shopfloor. In *Proceedings of the Fourth European Conference on Computer-Supported Cooperative Work ECSCW '95 (Stockholm, Sweden)*, H. Marmolin, Y. Sundblad, and K. Schmidt (eds.), 51–66. Dordrecht: Kluwer.

Bowker, G., K. Baker, F. Millerand, and D. Ribes. 2010. Toward Information Infrastructure Studies: Ways of Knowing in a Networked Environment. In *International Handbook of Internet Research*, J. Hunsinger, L. Klastrup, and M. Allen (eds.), 97–117. New York: Springer.

Bowker, G., and S. L. Star. 1999. *Sorting Things Out: Classification and Its Consequences.* Cambridge, MA: MIT Press.

Bratton, B. 2016. *The Stack: On Software and Sovereignty.* Cambridge, MA: MIT Press.

Breslau, L., and D. Estrin. 1990. Design of Inter-administrative Domain Routing Protocols. *Computer Communication Review* 20 (4): 231–241.

Brubaker, J., and G. Hayes. 2011. SELECT * FROM USER: Infrastructure and Sociotechnical Representation. Proc. ACM Conf. Computer-Supported Cooperative Work CSCW 2011 (Hangzhou, China), 369–378.

Brubaker, J., G. Hayes, and P. Dourish. 2013. Beyond the Grave: Facebook as a Site for the Expansion of Death and Mourning. *Information Society* 29 (3): 152–163.

Buechley, L., M. Eisenberg, J. Catchen, and A. Crockett. 2008. The LilyPad Arduino: Using Computational Textiles to Investigate Engagement, Aesthetics, and Diversity in Computer Science Education. Proc. ACM Conf. Human Factors in Computing Systems CHI 2008 (Florence, Italy), 423–432.

Cacciatori, E. 2008. Memory Objects in Project Environments: Storing, Retrieving and Adapting Learning in Project-Based Firms. *Research Policy* 37 (9): 1591–1601.

Cacciatori, E. 2012. Resolving Conflict in Problem-Solving: Systems of Artefacts in the Development of New Routines. *Journal of Management Studies* 49 (8): 1559–1585.

Carlile, P., D. Nicolini, A. Langley, and H. Tsoukas. 2013. *How Matter Matters: Objects, Artifacts, and Materiality in Organization Studies.* Oxford: Oxford University Press.

Castelle, M. 2013. Relational and Non-Relational Models in the Entextualization of Bureaucracy. *Computational Culture*, no. 3. http://computationalculture.net/article/relational-and-non-relational-models-in-the-entextualization-of-bureaucracy.

Castells, M. 1996. *The Rise of the Network Society.* Oxford: Blackwell.

Castells, M. 2009. *Communication Power.* Oxford: Oxford University Press.

Cattell, R. 2010. Scalable SQL and NoSQL Data Stores. *SIGMOD Record* 39 (4): 12–27.

Cerf, V., and R. Kahn. 1974. A Protocol for Packet Network Intercommunication. *IEEE Transactions on Communications* 22 (5): 637–648.

Chang, F., J. Dean, S. Ghemawat, W. Hsieh, D. Wallach, M. Burrows, T. Chandra, A. Fikes, and R. Gruber. 2008. Bigtable: A Distributed Storage System for Structured Data. *ACM Transactions on Computer Systems* 26 (2), 4:1-4:26.

Chen, A. 2014. The Laborers Who Keep Dick Pics and Beheadings Out of Your Facebook Feed. *Wired*, October. http://www.wired.com/2014/10/content-moderation.

Chun, W. 2008. On "Sourcery," or Code as Fetish. *Configurations* 16 (3): 299–324.

Chun, W. 2011a. The Enduring Ephemeral, or The Future Is a Memory. In *Media Archaeology: Approaches, Applications, Implications*, E. Huhtami and J. Parikka (eds.), 184–203. Berkeley: University of California Press.

Chun, W. 2011b. *Programmed Visions: Software and Memory*. Cambridge, MA: MIT Press.

Chun, W. 2016. *Updating to Remain the Same: Habitual New Media*. Cambridge, MA: MIT Press.

Clark, D., and D. Tennenhouse. 1990. Architectural Considerations for a New Generation of Protocols. *ACM SIGCOMM Communications Review* 20 (4): 200–208.

Coase, R. 1937. The Nature of the Firm. *Economica* 4 (16): 386–405.

Codd, E. 1970. A Relational Model of Data for Large Shared Data Banks. *Communications of the ACM* 13 (6): 377–387.

Collins, H. M. 1974. The TEA Set: Tacit Knowledge and Scientific Networks. *Science Studies* 4 (2): 165–185.

Collins, H. M. 1985. *Changing Order: Replication and Induction in Scientific Practice*. Chicago: University of Chicago Press.

Comer, D. 1983. The Computer Science Research Network CSNET: A History and Status Report. *Communications of the ACM* 26 (10): 747–753.

Coole, D., and S. Frost, eds. 2010. *Materialisms: Ontology, Agency, and Politics*. Durham, NC: Duke University Press.

Coopmans, C., J. Vertesi, M. Lynch, and S. Woolgar. 2014. *Representation in Scientific Practice Revisited*. Cambridge, MA: MIT Press.

Corbett, J., J. Dean, M. Epstein, A. Fikes, C. Frost, J. Furman, S. Ghemawat, et al. 2012. Spanner: Google's Globally-Distributed Database. Proc. USENIX Conf. Operating System Design and Implementation OSDI 2012 (Hollywood, CA), 251–264.

Curry, M. 1998. *Digital Places: Living with Geographical Information Systems*. London: Routledge.

Dahlberg, L. 2001. Democracy via Cyberspace: Examining the Rhetorics and Practices of Three Prominent Camps. *New Media & Society* 3:187–207.

Day, R. 2008. *The Modern Invention of Information: Discourse, History, Power*. Carbondale: Southern Illinois University Press.

Dean, J., and S. Ghemawat. 2004. MapReduce: Simplified Data Processing on Large Clusters. Proc. USENIX Conf. Operating Systems Design and Implementation OSDI'04 (Broomfield, CO), 137–149.

DeCandia, G., D. Hastorun, M. Jampani, G. Kakulapati, A. Lakshman, A. Pilchin, S. Sivasubramanian, P. Vosshall, and W. Vogels. 2007. Dynamo: Amazon's Highly-Available Key-Value Store. Proc. ACM Symp. Operating System Principles SOSP 2007 (Stevenson, WA), 205–220.

DeLanda, M. 2006. *A New Philosophy of Society: Assemblage Theory and Social Complexity*. London: Continuum.

Demers, A., D. Greene, C. Houser, W. Irish, J. Larson, S. Shenker, H. Sturgis, D. Swinehart, and D. Terry. 1988. Epidemic Algorithms for Replicated Database Maintenance. *SIGOPS Operating System Review* 22 (1): 8–32.

DeNardis, L. 2012. Governance at the Internet's Core: The Geopolitics of Interconnection and Internet Exchange Points (IXPs) in Emerging Markets. Available at SSRN: http://ssrn.com/abstract=2029715 or http://dx.doi.org/ 10.2139/ssrn.2029715.

Denning, P., A. Hearn, and W. Kern. 1983. History and Overview of CSNET. *Computer Communication Review* 13 (2): 138–145.

Digital Equipment Corporation. 1982. *DECnet DIGITAL Network Architecture (Phase IV): General Description*. Order number AA-N149A-TC. Maynard, MA: Digital Equipment Corporation.

DiSalvo, C. 2012. *Adversarial Design*. Cambridge, MA: MIT Press.

Dolphijn, R., and I. van der Tuin. 2012. *New Materialism: Interviews & Cartographies*. Ann Arbor, MI: Open Humanities Press.

Donner, J. 2015. *After Access: Inclusion, Development, and a More Mobile Internet*. Cambridge, MA: MIT Press.

Doornbusch, P. 2015. *The Music of CSIRAC: Australia's First Computer Music*. Champaign, IL: Common Ground.

Douglas, M., and B. Isherwood. 1979. *The World of Goods: Towards an Anthropology of Consumption*. New York: Basic Books.

Dourish, P. 2006. Implications for Design. Proc. ACM Conf. Human Factors in Computing Systems CHI 2006 (Montreal, QC), 541–550.

Dourish, P. 2010. The View from Arnhem Land in Australia's Remote North: "Computational Thinking" and the Postcolonial in the Teaching from Country Program. *Learning Communities: The International Journal of Learning in Social Contexts* 2: 91–101.

Dourish, P., and G. Bell. 2011. *Divining a Digital Future: Mess and Mythology in Ubiquitous Computing*. Cambridge, MA: MIT Press.

Dourish, P., and M. Mazmanian. 2013. Media as Material: Information Representations as Material Foundations for Organizational Practice. In *How Matter Matters: Objects, Artifacts, and Materiality in Organization Studies*, P. Carlile, D. Nicolini, A. Langley, and H. Tsoukas (eds.), 92–118. Oxford: Oxford University Press.

Driscoll, K. 2015. Beyond End-to-End: Lessons from Store-and-Forward Internetworking. Presentation at the Annual Meeting of the Society of Cinema and Media Studies Conference (Montreal, Canada), March.

Dumitrescu, D., H. Landin, and A. Vallgårda. 2011. An Interactive Textile Hanging: Textile, Context, and Interaction. *Studies in Material Thinking* 7:1–13.

Edwards, P. 2011. *A Vast Machine: Computer Models, Climate Data, and the Politics of Global Warming*. Cambridge, MA: MIT Press.

Elmer-Dewitt, P. 1993. First Nation in Cyberspace. *Time* 49 (Dec.): 6.

Ernst, W. 2012. *Digital Memory and the Archive*. Minneapolis: University of Minnesota Press.

Ernst, W. 2015. Kittler-Time: Getting to Know Other Temporal Relationships with the Assistance of Technological Media. In *Media After Kittler*, E. Ikoiadou and S. Wilson (eds.). London: Rowman and Littlefield.

Escriva, R., B. Wong, and E. Sirer. 2012. Hyperdex: A Distributed, Searchable Key-Value Store. *Computer Communication Review* 42 (4): 25–36.

Estrin, D., and M. Steenstrup. 1991. Inter Domain Policy Routing: Overview of Architecture and Protocols. *Computer Communication Review* 21 (1): 71–78.

Fall, K. 2003. A Delay-Tolerant Network Architecture for Challenged Internets. *Computer Communication Review* 33 (4): 27–34.

Farman, J. 2013. The Materiality of Locative Media: On the Invisible Infrastructure of Mobile Networks. In *The Routledge Handbook of Mobilities*, P. Adey, D. Bissell, K. Hannam, P. Merriman, and M. Sheller (eds.), 233–242. New York: Routledge.

Faulkner, W. 1951. *Requiem for a Nun*. New York: Random House.

Ford, A., C. Raiciu, M. Handley, and O. Bonaventure. 2013. TCP Extensions for Multipath Operation with Multiple Addresses. Request for Comments RFC 6824. Internet Engineering Task Force. http://www.rfc-editor.org/info/rfc6824.

Fuller, M. 2005. *Media Ecologies: Materialist Energies in Art and Technoculture*. Cambridge, MA: MIT Press.

Fuller, M. 2008. *Software Studies: A Lexicon*. Cambridge, MA: MIT Press.

Fuller, V., T. Li, J. Yu, and K. Varadhan. 1993. Classless Inter-Domain Routing (CIDR): An Address Assignment and Aggregation Strategy, Request for Comments RFC 1519. Internet Engineering Task Force. http://www.rfc-editor.org/info/rfc1519.

Galison, P., and B. Hevly. 1992. *Big Science: The Growth of Large-Scale Research.* Stanford, CA: Stanford University Press.

Galloway, A. 2004. *Protocol: How Control Exists after Decentralization.* Cambridge, MA: MIT Press.

Garfinkel, H. 1967. *Studies in Ethnomethodology.* Cambridge, UK: Polity.

Gaved, M., and P. Mulholland. 2008. Pioneers, Subcultures, and Cooperatives: The Grassroots Augmentation of Urban Places. In *Augmented Urban Spaces: Articulating the Physical and Electronic City*, A. Aurigi and F. De Cindio (eds.), 171–184. Aldershot, UK: Ashgate.

Gaver, W. W. 1991. Technology Affordances. Proc. ACM Conf. Human Factors in Computing Systems (CHI '91) (New Orleans, LA), 79–84.

Gazzard, A. 2016. *Now the Chips Are Down: The BBC Micro.* Cambridge, MA: MIT Press.

Geertz, C. 1973. *The Interpretation of Cultures.* New York: Basic Books.

Ghamari-Tabrizi, S. 2005. *The World of Herman Kahn: The Intuitive Science of Thermonuclear War.* Cambridge, MA: Harvard University Press.

Ghemawat, S., H. Gobioff, and S.-T. Leung. 2003. The Google File System. Proc. ACM Symposium on Operating System Principles (Bolton Landing, NY).

Gibson, J. J. 1979. *The Ecological Approach to Visual Perception.* New York: Houghton-Mifflin.

Gillespie, T. 2006. Engineering a Principle: "End-to-End" in the Design of the Internet. *Social Studies of Science* 36 (3): 427–457.

Gillespie, T. 2014. The Relevance of Algorithms. In *Media Technologies: Essays on Communication, Materiality, and Society*, T. Gillespie, P. Boczkowski, and K. Foot (eds.), 167–193. Cambridge, MA: MIT Press.

Gitelman, L., ed. 2013. *"Raw Data" Is an Oxymoron.* Cambridge, MA: MIT Press.

Goggin, G. 2012. Global Internets. In *The Handbook of Global Media Research*, I. Volkmer (ed.), 352–364. Oxford: Wiley-Blackwell.

Goldberg, A., and D. Robson. 1983. *Smalltalk-80: The Language and its Implementation.* Boston, MA: Addison-Wesley.

Goodwin, C. 1994. Professional Vision. *American Anthropologist* 96 (3): 606–633.

Goody, J. 1977. *The Domestication of the Savage Mind.* Cambridge, UK: Cambridge University Press.

Goody, J. 1986. *The Logic of Writing and the Organization of Society.* Cambridge, UK: Cambridge University Press.

Goody, J. 1987. *The Interface Between the Written and the Oral*. Cambridge, UK: Cambridge University Press.

Goody, J., and I. Watt. 1963. The Consequences of Literacy. *Comparative Studies in Society and History* 5 (3): 304–345.

Gorman, S. P., and E. J. Malecki. 2000. The Networks of the Internet: An Analysis of Provider Networks in the USA. *Telecommunications Policy* 24:113–134.

Graham, S., and S. Marvin. 2001. *Splintering Urbanism: Networked Infrastructures, Technological Mobilities, and the Urban Condition*. London: Routledge.

Gray, J. 1978. Notes on Data Base Operating Systems. In *Lecture Notes on Computer Science*, vol. 60, R. Bayer, R. N. Graham, and G. Seegmueller (eds.), 393–481. New York: Springer-Verlag.

Gray, J. 1981. The Transaction Concept: Virtues and Limitations. Proceedings of the 7th International Conference on Very Large Database Systems (Cannes, France, Sept. 9–11), ACM, New York, 144–154.

Green, T. R. G., and M. Petre. 1996. Usability Analysis of Visual Programming Environments: A "Cognitive Dimensions" Framework. *Journal of Visual Languages and Computing* 7:131–174.

Greenberg, A., J. Hamilton, D. Maltz, and P. Patel. 2008. The Cost of a Cloud: Research Problems in Data Center Networks. *Computer Communication Review* 39 (1): 68–73.

Greenfield, A. 2014. *Against the Smart City*. The City Is Here for You to Use 1. New York: Do Projects.

Grier, D., and M. Campbell. 2000. A Social History of Bitnet and Listserv, 1985–1991. *IEEE Annals of the History of Computing* 22 (2): 32–41.

Grinter, R. 2005. Words About Images: Coordinating Community in Amateur Photography. *Computer Supported Cooperative Work* 14:161–188.

Grusin, R., ed. 2015. *The Nonhuman Turn*. Minneapolis: University of Minnesota Press.

Gusterson, H. 1996. *Nuclear Rites: A Weapons Laboratory at the End of the Cold War*. Berkeley: University of California Press.

Gusterson, H. 2001. The Virtual Nuclear Weapons Laboratory in the New World Order. *American Ethnologist* 28 (2): 417–437.

Haigh, T. 2014. Actually, Turing Did Not Invent the Computer. *Communications of the ACM* 57 (1): 36–41.

Haigh, T., T. Priestley, and C. Rope. 2016. *ENIAC in Action: Making and Remaking the Modern Computer*. Cambridge, MA: MIT Press.

Haimson, N., J. Brubaker, L. Dombrowski, and G. Hayes. 2016. Digital Footprints and Changing Networks During Online Identity Transitions. Proc. ACM Conf. Human Factors in Computing Systems CHI 2016 (San Jose, CA).

Hall, S. 1980. Encoding/Decoding. In *Culture, Media, Language: Working Papers in Cultural Studies, 1972–79*, S. Hall, D. Hobson, A. Lowe, and P. Willis (eds.), 128–138. London: Hutchinson.

Hall, S., G. Hall, and J. McCall. 2000. *High-Speed Digital System Design: A Handbook of Interconnect Theory and Design Practices*. New York: John Wylie.

Halverson, J. 1992. Goody and the Implosion of the Literacy Thesis. *Man* 27 (2): 301–317.

Hankerson, D., A. Marshall, J. Booker, H. El Mimouni, I. Walker, and J. Rode. 2016. Does Technology Have Race? In *Extended Abstracts of the ACM Conf. Human Factors in Computing Systems CHI 2016 (San Jose, CA)*, 473–486. New York: ACM.

Haraway, D. 2007. *Where Species Meet*. Minneapolis: University of Minnesota Press.

Harris, R. 1986. *The Origin of Writing*. Chicago: Open Court Publishing.

Harris, R. 1996. *Signs of Writing*. London: Routledge.

Harris, R. 2000. *Rethinking Writing*. Bloomington: Indiana University Press.

Harvey, D. 2006. *Spaces of Global Capitalism: A Theory of Uneven Geographical Development*. New York: Verso.

Hauben, M., and R. Hauben. 1997. *Netizens: On the History and Impact of Usenet and the Internet*. Los Alamitos, CA: IEEE Computer Society Press.

Havelock, E. 1963. *Preface to Plato*. Cambridge, MA: Harvard University Press.

Havelock, E. 1982. *The Literate Revolution in Greece and Its Cultural Consequences*. Princeton, NJ: Princeton University Press.

Havelock, E. 1986. *The Muse Learns to Write: Reflections on Orality and Literacy from Antiquity to the Present*. New Haven, CT: Yale University Press.

Hayles, K. 1999. *How We Became Posthuman: Virtual Bodies in Cybernetics, Literature, and Informatics*. Chicago, IL: University of Chicago Press.

Hecht, G. 2002. Rupture-Talk in the Nuclear Age: Conjugating Colonial Power in Africa. *Social Studies of Science* 32 (5–6): 691–727.

Heddaya, M. 2014. Warhol Computer Art Discovered on 1985 Floppy Discs. April 24. http://hyperallergic.com/122381/warhol-computer-art-discovered-on-1985 -floppy-discs.

Heft, H. 2001. *Ecological Psychology in Context: James Gibson, Roger Barker, and the Legacy of William James' Radical Empiricism*. Hove, UK: Psychology Press.

Helmreich, S. 2007. An Anthropologist Underwater: Immersive Soundscapes, Cybmarine Cyborgs, and Transductive Ethnography. *American Ethnologist* 34 (4): 621–641.

Herndon, T., M. Ash, and R. Pollin. 2014. Does High Public Debt Consistently Stifle Economic Growth? A Critique of Reinhart and Rogoff. *Cambridge Journal of Economics* 38 (2): 257–279.

Hiltzik, M. 1999. *Dealers of Lightning: Xerox PARC and the Dawn of the Computer Age.* New York: HarperCollins.

Hindman, M. 2008. *The Myth of Digital Democracy.* Princeton, NJ: Princeton University Press.

Hoffman, P. 2012. The Tao of IETF. Accessed June 4, 2014,http://www.ietf.org/tao .html.

Hogan, M. 2015. Data Flows and Water Woes: The Utah Data Center. *Big Data & Society* 2 (2): 1–12.

Hopper, A., and R. Needham. 1988. The Cambridge Fast Ring Networking System. *IEEE Transactions on Computers* 37 (10): 1214–1223.

Horst, H., and D. Miller. 2012. *Digital Anthropology.* London: Bloomsbury.

Hu, T.-H. 2015. *A Prehistory of the Cloud.* Cambridge, MA: MIT Press.

Huhtamo, E., and J. Parikka. 2011. Introduction: An Archaeology of Media Archeology. In *Media Archaeology: Approaches, Applications, Implications,* E. Huhtamo and J. Parikka (eds.), 1–21. Berkeley: University of California Press.

Ingold, T. 2000. *The Perception of the Environment: Essays on Livelihood, Dwelling and Skill.* London: Routledge.

Ingold, T. 2007a. *Lines: A Brief History.* London: Routledge.

Ingold, T. 2007b. Materials against Materiality. *Archaeological Dialogues* 14 (1): 1–16.

Ingold, T. 2011. *Being Alive: Essays on Movement, Knowledge and Description.* London: Routledge.

Ingold, T. 2013. *Making: Anthropology, Archeology, Art and Architecture.* London: Routledge.

Introna, L. D. 2016. Algorithms, Governance, and Governmentality: On Governing Academic Writing. *Science, Technology & Human Values* 41 (1): 17–49.

Irani, L. 2015. The Cultural Work of Microwork. *New Media & Society* 17 (5): 720–739.

Isaacson, W. 2014. *The Innovators: How A Group of Hackers, Geniuses, and Geeks Created the Digital Revolution.* New York: Simon and Schuster.

Ishii, H., and B. Ullmer. 1997. Tangible Bits: Towards Seamless Interfaces between People, Bits, and Atoms. Proc. ACM Conf. Computer-Human Interaction CHI'97 (Atlanta, GA).

Jacobson, V. 1990. Compressing TCP/IP Headers for Low-Speed Serial Links. Request for Comments RFC 1144 (February). Network Working Group. http://www.rfc-editor.org/info/rfc1144.

Johnson, C. 2013. Thanks to an Online Archive, Here's a *Karateka* Review in 2013. *Ars Technica*, October 28. http://arstechnica.com/gaming/2013/10/playing-apple-iic-games-30-years-late-through-an-online-emulator-museum.

Jungnickel, K. 2014. *DIY WIFI: Re-imagining Connectivity.* Basingstoke, UK: Palgrave Pivot.

Kaplan, S. 2011. Strategy and PowerPoint: An Inquiry into the Epistemic Culture and Machinery of Strategy Making. *Organization Science* 22 (2): 320–346.

Karat, J., C.-M. Karat, and J. Ukelson. 2000. Affordances, Motivation, and the Design of User Interfaces. *Communications of the ACM* 43 (8): 49–51.

Khrennikov, I., and A. Ustinova. 2014. Putin's Next Invasion: The Russian Web. *Business Week*, May 1. http://www.businessweek.com/articles/2014-05-01/russia-moves-toward-china-style-internet-censorship.

Kirschenbaum, M. 2008. *Mechanisms: New Media and the Forensic Imagination.* Cambridge, MA: MIT Press.

Kirschenbaum, M. 2016. *Track Changes: A Literary History of Word Processing.* Cambridge, MA: MIT Press.

Kitchin, R. 2014. *The Data Revolution: Big Data, Open Data, Data Infrastructures and Their Consequences.* London: Sage.

Kitchin, R., and M. Dodge. 2011. *Code/Space: Software and Everyday Life.* Cambridge, MA: MIT Press.

Kittler, F. 1990. *Discourse Networks 1800/1900.* Trans. M. Metteer and C. Cullens. Stanford, CA: Stanford University Press.

Kittler, F. 1999. *Gramophone, Film, Typewriter.* Trans. G. Winthrop-Young and M. Wurz. Stanford, CA: Stanford University Press.

Kline, R. 2015. *The Cybernetics Moment, or Why We Call Our Age the Information Age.* Baltimore, MD: Johns Hopkins University Press.

Knoblauch, H. 2013. *PowerPoint, Communication, and the Knowledge Society.* Cambridge, UK: Cambridge University Press.

Kohn, E. 2013. *How Forests Think: Toward an Anthropology Beyond the Human.* Berkeley: University of California Press.

Laffont, J.-L., S. Marcus, P. Rey, and J. Tirole. 2001. Internet Peering. *Annual Economic Review* 91 (2): 287–291.

Landin, P. 1964. The Mechanical Evaluation of Expressions. *Computer Journal* 6 (4): 308–320.

Latour, B. 1999. On Recalling ANT. In *Actor-Network Theory and After*, J. Law and J. Hassard (eds.), 15–25. Oxford: Blackwell.

Latour, B. 2004a. *The Politics of Nature: How to Bring the Sciences into Democracy*. Cambridge, MA: Harvard University Press.

Latour, B. 2004b. Why Has Critique Run Out of Steam? From Matters of Fact to Matters of Concern. *Critical Inquiry* 30:225–248.

Latour, B., and S. Woolgar. 1986. *Laboratory Life: The Construction of Scientific Facts*. Princeton, NJ: Princeton University Press.

Leavitt, N. 2010. Will NoSQL Databases Live Up to Their Promise? *IEEE Computer* 43 (2): 12–14.

Lemonnier, P. 2012. *Mundane Objects: Materiality and Non-Verbal Communication*. Walnut Creek, CA: Left Coast Press.

Leonardi, P. 2012. *Car Crashes Without Cars: Lessons About Simulation Technology and Organizational Change from Automotive Design*. Cambridge, MA: MIT Press.

Leonardi, P., and S. Barley. 2008. Materiality and Change: Challenges to Building Better Theory about Technology and Organizing. *Information and Organization* 18:159–176.

Leonardi, P., and S. Barley. 2010. What's Under Construction Here? Social Action, Materiality, and Power in Constructivist Studies of Technology and Organizing. *Academy of Management Annals* 4 (1): 1–51.

Leonardi, P., B. Nardi, and J. Kallinikos. 2013. *Materiality and Organizing: Social Interaction in a Technological World*. Oxford: Oxford University Press.

Levi-Strauss, C. 1955. The Structural Analysis of Myth. *Journal of American Folklore* 68 (270): 428–444.

Levy, D. 1994. Fixed or Fluid? Document Stability and New Media. Proc. ACM European Conf. Hypertext (Edinburgh, UK), 24–31.

Liboiron, M. 2013. Plasticizers: A Twenty-first Century Miasma. In *Accumulation: The Material Politics of Plastics*, J. Gabrys, G. Hawkins, and M. Michael (eds.), 134–149. London: Routledge.

Light, J. S. 1999. When Computers Were Women. *Technology and Culture* 40 (3): 455–483.

Lim, H., B. Fan, D. Andersen, and M. Kaminsky. 2011. Silt: A Memory-Efficient, High-Performance Key-Value Store. Proc. ACM Symp. Operating Systems Principles SOSP '11 (Cascais, Portugal), 1–13.

Lindholm, T., and F. Yellin. 1996. *The Java Virtual Machine Specification*. Reading, MA: Addison-Wesley.

Lovink, G. 2014. Reflections on the MP3 Format: Interview with Jonathan Sterne. *Computational Culture*, no. 4. http://computationalculture.net/article/reflections-on-the-mp3-format.

Lynch, M. 1997. *Scientific Practice and Ordinary Action: Ethnomethodology and Social Studies of Science*. Cambridge, UK: Cambridge University Press.

Mackenzie, A. 2002. *Transductions: Bodies and Machines at Speed*. London: Continuum.

Mackenzie, A. 2003. These Things Called Systems: Collective Imaginings and Infrastructural Software. *Social Studies of Science* 33 (3): 365–387.

Mackenzie, A. 2005a. The Performativity of Code: Software and Cultures of Circulation. *Theory, Culture & Society* 22 (1): 71–92.

Mackenzie, A. 2005b. Protocols and the Irreducible Traces of Embodiment: The Viterbi Algorithm and the Mosaic of Machine Time. In *24/7: Time and Temporality in the Network Society*, R. Hassan and R. Purser (eds), 89–108. Stanford, CA: Stanford University Press.

Mackenzie, A. 2006a. *Cutting Code: Software and Sociality*. Oxford: Peter Lang International Academic Publishers.

Mackenzie, A. 2006b. Java: The Practical Virtuality of Internet Programming. *New Media & Society* 8 (3): 441–465.

Mackenzie, A. 2012. More Parts than Elements: How Databases Multiply. *Environment and Planning D: Society & Space* 30:335–350.

Mackenzie, A., and T. Vurdubakis. 2011. Codes and Codings in Crisis: Signification, Performativity and Excess. *Theory, Culture & Society* 28 (6): 3–23.

MacKenzie, D. 2009. *Material Markets: How Economic Agents Are Constructed*. Oxford: Oxford University Press.

MacKenzie, D., and J. Wajcman. 1999. *The Social Shaping of Technology*. Buckingham, UK: Open University Press.

Maher, J. 2012. *The Future Was Here: The Commodore Amiga*. Cambridge, MA: MIT Press.

Mailland, J. 2016. 101 Online: American Minitel Network and Lessons from Its Failure. *IEEE Annals of the History of Computing* 38 (1): 6–22.

Mailland, J., and K. Driscoll. Forthcoming. *Minitel: Welcome to the Internet*. Cambridge, MA: MIT Press.

Malecki, E. 2002. The Economic Geography of the Internet's Infrastructure. *Economic Geography* 78 (4): 399–424.

Manovich, L. 2001. *The Language of New Media*. Cambridge, MA: MIT Press.

Manovich, L. 2013. *Software Takes Command*. London: Bloomsbury.

Mansell, R. 2012. *Imagining the Internet: Communication, Innovation, and Governance*. Oxford: Oxford University Press.

Marino, M. 2006. Critical Code Studies. *Electronic Book Review*. December 4. http://www.electronicbookreview.com/thread/electropoetics/codology.

Marino, M. 2014. Field Report for Critical Code Studies 2014. *Computational Culture*, no. 4. http://computationalculture.net/article/field-report-for-critical-code-studies-2014.

Marx, K. (1847) 1971. *The Poverty of Philosophy*. Reprint, New York: International. Citations refer to the International edition.

Mathison, S., L. Roberts, and P. Walker. 2012. The History of Telenet and the Commercialization of Packet Switching in the I.S. *IEEE Communications Magazine* (May): 28–45.

Mazmanian, M., M. Cohn, and P. Dourish. 2013. Dynamic Reconfiguration in Planetary Exploration: A Sociomaterial Ethnography. *Management Information Systems Quarterly* 38 (3): 831–848.

McCray, W. P. 2000. Large Telescopes and the Moral Economy of Recent Astronomy. *Social Studies of Science* 30 (5): 685–711.

McGrenere, J., and W. Ho. 2000. Affordance: Clarifying and Evolving a Concept. *Proc. Conf. on Graphical Interfaces* (Montreal, QC), 179–186.

McVeigh-Schultz, J., and N. K. Baym. 2015. Thinking of You: Vernacular Affordance in the Context of the Microsocial Relationship App, Couple. *Social Media + Society* 1 (2): 1–13.

Medina, E. 2001. *Cybernetic Revolutionaries: Technology and Politics in Allende's Chile*. Cambridge, MA: MIT Press.

Miller, D. 1988. Appropriating the State on the Council Estate. *Man* 23 (2): 353–372.

Miller, D., ed. 1998. *Material Culture: Why Some Things Matter*. Chicago, IL: Chicago University Press.

Miller, D. 2003. The Virtual Moment. *Journal of the Royal Anthropological Institute* 9:57–75.

Miller, D., ed. 2005. *Materiality*. Durham, NC: Duke University Press.

Miller, D. 2008. *The Comfort of Things*. Cambridge, UK: Polity.

Miller, D., E. Costa, N. Haynes, T. McDonald, R. Nicolescu, J. Sinanan, J. Spyer, S. Venkatraman, and X. Wang. 2016. *How the World Changed Social Media*. London: UCL Press.

Miller, D., and S. Woodward. 2007. Manifesto for the Study of Denim. *Social Anthropology* 15 (3): 335–351.

Miller, D., and S. Woodward, eds. 2010. *Global Denim*. London: Bloomsbury.

Mills, D. 1984. Exterior Gateway Protocol Formal Specification. Request for Comments RFC 904. Network Working Group. https://www.rfc-editor.org/info/rfc904.

Mockapetris, P. 1987. Domain Names—Concepts and Facilities. Request for Comments RFC 1034. Network Working Group. https://www.rfc-editor.org/info/rfc1034.

Mol, A. 2002. *The Body Multiple: Ontology in Medical Practice*. Durham, NC: Duke University Press.

Montfort, N., P. Baudoin, J. Bell, I. Bogost, J. Douglass, M. Marino, M. Mateas, C. Reas, M. Sample, and N. Vawter. 2012. *10 PRINT CHR$(205.5+RND(1));: GOTO 10*. Cambridge, MA: MIT Press.

Montfort, N., and I. Bogost. 2009. *Racing the Beam: The Atari Video Computer System*. Cambridge, MA: MIT Press.

Mosco, V. 2014. *To the Cloud: Big Data in a Turbulent World*. Abingdon, UK: Routledge.

Mueller, M. 2010. *Networks and States: The Global Politics of Internet Governance*. Cambridge, MA: MIT Press.

Nagy, P., and G. Neff. 2015. Imagined Affordance: Reconstructing a Keyword for Communication Theory. *Social Media + Society* 1 (2): 1–9.

Nardi, B. 1993. *A Small Matter of Programming: Perspectives on End-User Computing*. Cambridge, MA: MIT Press.

Nardi, B., and J. Miller. 1991. Twinkling Lights and Nested Loops: Distributed Problem Solving and Spreadsheet Development. *International Journal of Man-Machine Interaction* 34 (2): 161–184.

Negroponte, N. 1995. *Being Digital*. New York: Knopf.

Norman, D. 1988. *The Psychology of Everyday Things*. New York: Basic Books.

Norman, D. 2008. Signifiers, Not Affordances. *ACM Interactions* (November–December): 18–19.

O'Dwyer, R., and L. Doyle. 2012. This Is Not a Bit-Pipe: A Political Economy of the Substrate Network. *Fiberculture Journal* 20:10–32.

Ong, W. 1988. *Orality and Literacy: The Technologizing of the Word*. London: Routledge.

Oppen, D., and Y. Dalal. 1981. *The Clearinghouse: A Decentralized Agent for Locating Named Objects in a Distributed Environment*. Office Systems Division Tech Report OSD-T8103. Palo Alto, CA: Xerox.

Orlikowski, W. 1993. Learning from Notes: Organizational Issues in Groupware Implementation. *Information Society* 9 (3): 237–250.

Orlikowski, W. 2007. Sociomaterial Practices: Exploring Technology at Work. *Organization Studies* 28:1435–1448.

Orlikowski, W. J. 2010. The Sociomateriality of Organisational Life: Considering Technology in Management Research. *Cambridge Journal of Economics* 34 (1): 125–141.

Orlikowski, W., and S. Scott. 2008. Sociomateriality: Challenging the Separation of Technology, Work and Organization. *Academy of Management Annals* 2 (1): 433–474.

Orlikowski, W. J., and S. V. Scott. 2014. What Happens When Evaluation Goes Online? Exploring Apparatuses of Valuation in the Travel Sector. *Organization Science* 25 (3): 868–891.

Overgaard, M. 1980. UCSD Pascal: A Portable Software Environment for Small Computers. Proc. National Computer Conference AFIPS'80 (Anaheim, CA), 747–754.

Panko, R., and R. Halverson. 1996. Spreadsheets on Trial: A Survey of Research on Spreadsheet Risks. Proc. 29th Annual Hawaii International Conference on Systems Science HICSS (Wailea, HI), 326–335.

Parks, L. 2005. *Cultures in Orbit: Satellites and the Televisual*. Durham, NC: Duke University Press.

Parks, L. 2012. Satellites, Oils, and Footprints: Eutelsat, Kazsat, and Post-Communist Territories in Central Asia. In *Down to Earth: Satellite Technologies, Industries, and Cultures*, L. Parks and J. Schwoch (eds.), 122–142. New Brunswick, NJ: Rutgers University Press.

Partridge, C. 1994. *Gigabit Networking*. Boston, MA: Addison-Wesley.

Pasquale, F. 2015. *The Black Box Society: The Secret Algorithms that Control Money and Information*. Cambridge, MA: Harvard University Press.

Pearce, K. E., J. S. Slaker, and N. Ahmad. 2012. Is Your Web Everyone's Web? Theorizing the Web through the Lens of the Device Divide. Paper presented at the Theorizing the Web Conference (College Park, MD).

Pellow, D., and L. Park. 2002. *The Silicon Valley of Dreams: Environmental Injustice, Immigrant Workers, and the High-Tech Global Economy.* New York: NYU Press.

Peters, B. 2016. *How Not to Network a Nation: The Uneasy History of the Soviet Internet.* Cambridge, MA: MIT Press.

Pickering, A. 2010. *The Cybernetic Brain: Sketches of Another Future.* Chicago, IL: University of Chicago Press.

Pink, S., E. Ardèvol, and D. Lanzeni. 2016. *Digital Materialities: Design and Anthropology.* London: Bloomsbury.

Poster, M. 1990. *The Mode of Information: Poststructuralism and Social Context.* Chicago, IL: University of Chicago Press.

Pouzin, L. 1975. The CYCLADES Network—Present State and Development Trends. Symposium on Computer Networks (Gaithersburg, MD, IEEE Computer Society), 8–13.

Powell, A. 2011. Metaphors, Models and Communicative Spaces: Designing Local Wireless Infrastructure. *Canadian Journal of Communication* 36 (1): 91–114.

Powell, A. 2014. The History and Future of Internet Openness: From "Wired" to "Mobile." In *Materialities and Imaginaries of the Open Internet,* A. Herman, J. Hadlaw, and T. Swiss (eds.), 25–44. London: Routledge.

Purdy, J. 2015. *After Nature: A Politics for the Anthropocene.* Cambridge, MA: Harvard University Press.

Rayburn, D. 2014. Here's How the Comcast & Netflix Deal is Structured, With Data and Numbers. *Streaming Media Blog,* February 27. http://blog.streamingmedia.com/2014/02/heres-comcast-netflix-deal-structured-numbers.html.

Reinhart, C., and K. Rogoff. 2010. Growth in a Time of Debt. *American Economic Review* 100 (2): 573–578.

Richter, P., M. Allman, R. Bush, and V. Paxson. 2015. A Primer on IPv4 Address Scarcity. *ACM SIGCOMM Communication Review* 45 (2): 21–31.

Riles, A. 2006. *Documents: Artifacts of Modern Knowledge.* Ann Arbor: University of Michigan Press.

Robles-Anderson, E., and P. Svensson. 2016. One Damn Slide After Another: PowerPoint at Every Occasion for Speech. *Computational Culture,* no. 5. http://computationalculture.net/article/one-damn-slide-after-another-powerpoint-at-every-occasion-for-speech.

Rosner, D. K., M. Ikemiya, and T. Regan. 2015. Resisting Alignment: Code and Clay. Proc. ACM Conference on Tangible, Embedded, and Embodied Interaction TEI'15 (Stanford, CA), 181–188.

Rosner, D. K., and K. Ryokai. 2008. Spyn: Augmenting Knitting to Support Storytelling and Reflection. Proc. Intl. Conference on Ubiquitous Computing Ubicomp'08 (Seoul, South Korea), 340–349.

Rosner, D. K., and K. Ryokai. 2009. Reflections on Craft: Probing the Creative Process of Everyday Knitters. Proc. ACM Conference on Creativity and Cognition (Berkeley, CA), 195–204.

Roth, L. 2009. Looking at Shirley, the Ultimate Norm: Colour Balance, Image Technologies, and Cognitive Equity. *Canadian Journal of Communication* 34:111–136.

Sale, S., and L. Salisbury. 2015. *Kittler Now: Current Perspectives in Kittler Studies*. Cambridge, UK: Polity.

Saltzer, J., D. Reed, and D. Clark. 1984. End-to-End Arguments in System Design. *ACM Transactions on Computer Systems* 2 (4): 277–288.

Satyanarayanan, M., G. St Clair, B. Gilbert, Y. Abe, J. Harkes, D. Ryan, E. Linke, and K. Wester. 2015. *One-Click Time Travel*. Technical Report CMU-CS-15-115, School of Computer Science, Carnegie Mellon University (Pittsburgh, PA).

Schiller, H. 1986. *Information and the Crisis Economy*. Oxford: Oxford University Press.

Schiller, H. 1989. *Culture, Inc.: The Corporate Takeover of Public Expression*. Oxford: Oxford University Press.

Schön, D. 1984. *The Reflective Practitioner: How Professionals Think in Action*. New York: Basic Books.

Schön, D. 1990. *Educating the Reflective Practitioner: Towards a New Design for Teaching and Learning in the Professions*. San Francisco, CA: Jossey-Bass.

Schroeder, M., A. Birrell, and R. Needham. 1984. Experiences with Grapevine: The Growth of a Distributed System. *ACM Transactions on Computer Systems* 2 (1): 3–23.

Schulte, S. R. 2013. *Cached: Decoding the Internet in Popular Culture*. New York: NYU Press.

Scott, J., J. Crowcroft, P. Hui, and C. Diot. 2006. Haggle: A Networking Architecture Designed around Mobile Users. Proc. Third Annual Conference on Wireless On-Demand Network Systems and Services WONS 2006 (Les Ménuires, France), 78–86.

Scott, S. V., and W. J. Orlikowski. 2012. Reconfiguring Relations of Accountability: Materialization of Social Media in the Travel Sector. *Accounting, Organizations and Society* 37 (1): 26–40.

Shannon, C., and W. Weaver. 1949. *The Mathematical Theory of Communication*. Urbana: University of Illinois Press.

Shapin, S., and S. Schaffer. 1986. *Leviathan and the Air-Pump: Hobbes, Boyle, and the Experimental Life*. Princeton, NJ: Princeton University Press.

Shearing, C. 2001. Punishment and the Changing Face of Governance. *Punishment and Society* 3 (2): 203–220.

Shirky, C. 2008. *Here Comes Everyone: The Power of Organizing Without Organizations*. New York: Penguin.

Smith, B. C. 1994. Coming Apart at the Seams: The Role of Computation in a Successor Metaphysics. Position paper for workshop on Biology, Computers, and Society: At the Intersection of the "Real" and the "Virtual"—Cultural Perspectives on Coding Life and Vitalizing Code, June 2–4, 1994, Stanford University (Stanford, CA).

Smith, R. 1986. Experiences with the Shared Reality Kit: An Example of the Tension Between Literalism and Magic. *IEEE Computer Graphics and Applications* 7 (9): 42–50.

Srinivasan, R. 2013. Bridges Between Cultural and Digital Worlds in Revolutionary Egypt. *Information Society* 29 (1): 49–60.

Star, S. L. 1983. Simplification in Scientific Work: An Example from Neuroscience Research. *Social Studies of Science* 13 (2): 205–228.

Starosielski, N. 2015. *The Undersea Network*. Durham, NC: Duke University Press.

Steele, G., and R. Gabriel. 1993. The Evolution of Lisp. Proc. ACM Conf. History of Programming Languages HOPL-II (Cambridge, MA), 231–270.

Steenson, M. 2011. Interfacing with the Subterranean. *Cabinet* 41:82–86.

Steinberg, D., and S. Cheshire. 2005. *Zero Configuration Networking: The Definitive Guide*. Sebastopol, CA: O'Reilly Media.

Sterne, J. 2012. *MP3: The Meaning of a Format*. Durham, NC: Duke University Press.

Sterne, J. 2014. "What Do We Want?" "Materiality!" "When Do We Want It?" "Now!" In *Media Technologies: Essays on Communication, Materiality, and Society*, T. Gillespie, P. Boczkowski, and K. Foot (eds.), 119–128. Cambridge, MA: MIT Press.

Stonebraker, M. 1986. The Case for Shared Nothing. *Database Engineering* 9:4–9.

Stonebraker, M. 2010. SQL Databases vs. NoSQL Databases. *Communications of the ACM* 53 (4): 10–11.

Strathern, M. 2000. *Audit Cultures: Anthropological Studies in Accountability, Ethics and the Academy*. London: Routledge.

Suchman, L. 2007. *Human-Machine Reconfigurations: Plans and Situated Actions*. 2nd ed. New York: Cambridge University Press.

Suchman, L., J. Blomberg, J. Orr, and R. Trigg. 1999. Reconstructing Technologies as Social Practice. *American Behavioral Scientist* 43 (3): 392–408.

Tangmunarunkit, H., R. Govindan, S. Shenker, and D. Estrin. 2001. The Impact of Routing Policy on Internet Paths. *Proceedings—IEEE INFOCOM* 2:736–742.

Thacker, C., E. McCreight, B. Lampson, R. Sproull, and D. Boggs. 1979. *Alto: A Personal Computer*. Technical Report CSL-79-11. Palo Alto, CA: Xerox Palo Alto Research Center.

Tomlinson, B. 2010. *Greening through IT: Information Technology for Environmental Sustainability*. Cambridge, MA: MIT Press.

Traweek, S. 1988. *Beamtimes and Lifetimes: The World of High-Energy Physics*. Cambridge, MA: Harvard University Press.

Trigg, R., J. Blomberg, and L. Suchman. 1999. Moving Document Collections Online: The Evolution of a Shared Repository. In *Proceedings of the Sixth European Conference on Computer-Supported Cooperative Work ECSCW'99 (Copenhagen, Denmark)*, S. Bodker, M. Kyng, and K. Schmidt (eds.), 331–350. Dordrecht: Kluwer.

Tsing, A. 2015. *The Mushroom at the End of the World: On the Possibility of Life in Capitalist Ruins*. Princeton, NJ: Princeton University Press.

Tufte, E. 2006. *The Cognitive Style of PowerPoint: Pitching Out Corrupts Within*. 2nd ed. Chesire, CT: Graphics Press.

Turing, A. 1936. On Computable Numbers, with an Application to the Entscheidungsproblem. *Proceedings of the London Mathematical Society* 42 (2): 230–265.

Turner, F. 2006. *From Counterculture to Cyberculture: Stewart Brand, the Whole Earth Network, and the Rise of Digital Utopianism*. Chicago, IL: University of Chicago Press.

Vaidhyanathan, S. 2011. *The Googlization of Everything (And Why We Should Worry)*. Berkeley: University of California Press.

Vallgårda, A. 2008. PLANKS: A Computational Composite. Proc. Nordi CHI'08 (Lund, Sweden).

Vallgårda, A., and J. Redström. 2007. Computational Composites. Proc. ACM Conf. Human Factors in Computing Systems CHI'07 (San Jose, CA), 513–522.

Vallgårda, A., and T. Sokoler. 2010. A Material Strategy: Exploring Material Properties of Computers. *International Journal of Design* 4 (3): 1–14.

Varnelis, K. 2008. *The Infrastructural City: Networked Ecologies in Los Angeles*. Barcelona: Actar.

Vaughan, D. 1996. *The Challenger Launch Decision: Risky Technology, Culture and Deviance at NASA*. Chicago, IL: University of Chicago Press.

Vertesi, J. 2014a. Drawing as: Distinctions and Disambiguation in Digital Images of Mars. In *Representation in Scientific Practice Revisited*, C. Coopmans, J. Vertesi, M. Lynch, and S. Woolgar (eds.), 15–35. Cambridge, MA: MIT Press.

Vertesi, J. 2014b. Seamful Spaces: Heterogeneous Infrastructures in Interaction. *Science, Technology & Human Values* 39 (2): 264–284.

Vertesi, J. 2015. *Seeing Like a Rover: How Robots, Teams, and Images Craft Knowledge of Mars.* Chicago, IL: University of Chicago Press.

Vertesi, J., and P. Dourish. 2011. The Value of Data: Considering the Context of Production in Data Economies. Proc. ACM Conf. Computer-Supported Cooperative Work CSCW 2011 (Hangzou, China), 533–542.

Voida, A., R. Grinter, N. Duchenaut, K. Edwards, and M. Newman. 2005. Listening In: Practices Surrounding iTunes Music Sharing. Proc. ACM Conf. Human Factors in Computing Systems CHI 2005 (Portland, OR), 191–200.

Wang, Z., and J. Crowcroft. 1992. A Two-Tier Address Structure for the Internet: A Solution to the Problem of Address Space Exhaustion. Request for Comments RFC 1335. Internet Engineering Task Force. http://www.rfc-editor.org/info/rfc1335.

Watts, L. 2014. Liminal Futures: Poem for Islands at the Edge. In *Subversion, Conversion, Development: Cross-Cultural Knowledge Exchange and the Politics of Design,* J. Leach and L. Wilson (eds.), 19–38. Cambridge, MA: MIT Press.

Webster, F. 2006. *Theories of the Information Society.* 3rd ed. London: Routledge.

Webster, F., and K. Robins. 1986. *Information Technology: A Luddite Analysis.* Norwood, NJ: Ablex.

Weiser, M. 1991. The Computer for the Twenty-First Century. *Scientific American* 265 (3): 94–104.

Wiberg, M. Forthcoming. *The Materiality of Interaction: From Metaphors to Materials.* Cambridge, MA: MIT Press.

Wiberg, M., and E. Robles. 2010. Computational Compositions: Aesthetics, Materials, and Interaction Design. *International Journal of Design* 4 (2): 65–76.

Williams, R. 1974. *Television: Technology and Cultural Form.* London: Fontana.

Willow, A., and S. Wylie. 2014. Politics, Ecology, and the New Anthropology of Energy: Exploring the Emerging Frontiers of Hydraulic Fracking. *Journal of Political Ecology* 21 (12): 222–236.

Wing, J. 2006. Computational Thinking. *Communications of the ACM* 49 (3): 33–35.

Winner, L. 1980. Do Artifacts Have Politics? *Daedalus* 109 (1): 121–136.

Winsberg, E. 2010. *Science in the Age of Computer Simulation.* Chicago, IL: University of Chicago Press.

Winther, M., and A. Vallgårda. 2016. A Basic Form-Language for Shape-Changing Interfaces. Proc. ACM Symp. Tangible, Embedded, and Embodied Interfaces TEI'16 (Eindhoven, Netherlands).

Winthrop-Young, G. 2011. *Kittler and the Media*. Cambridge, UK: Polity.

Wischik, D., C. Raiciu, A. Greenhalgh, and M. Handley. 2011. Design, Implementation and Evaluation of Congestion Control for Multipath TCP. Proc. USENIX Conference on Network Systems Design and Implementation (Boston, MA), 99–112.

Wood, D. 1992. *The Power of Maps*. New York: Guilford Press.

Yates, J. 1993. *Control through Communication: The Rise of System in American Management*. Baltimore, MD: Johns Hopkins University Press.

Yates, J., and W. Orlikowski. 2007. The PowerPoint Presentation and Its Corollaries: How Genres Shape Communicative Action in Organizations. In *Communicative Practices in Workplaces and the Professions: Cultural Perspectives on the Regulation of Discourse and Organizations*, M. Zachry and C. Thralls (eds.), 67–92. Amityville, NY: Baywood.

Zielinski, S. 2006. *Deep Time of the Media: Toward an Archaeology of Hearing and Seeing by Technical Means*. Trans. G. Custance. Cambridge, MA: MIT Press.

Ziewitz, M. 2016. Governing Algorithms: Myth, Mess, and Methods. *Science, Technology & Human Values* 41 (1): 3–16.

Index

Printed in the United States
by Baker & Taylor Publisher Services